A Region among States

A Region among States

Law and Non-sovereignty in the Caribbean

LEE CABATINGAN

The University of Chicago Press
Chicago and London

The University of Chicago Press, Chicago 60637
The University of Chicago Press, Ltd., London
© 2023 by The University of Chicago
All rights reserved. No part of this book may be used or reproduced in any manner whatsoever without written permission, except in the case of brief quotations in critical articles and reviews. For more information, contact the University of Chicago Press, 1427 E. 60th St., Chicago, IL 60637.
Published 2023
Printed in the United States of America

32 31 30 29 28 27 26 25 24 23   1 2 3 4 5

ISBN-13: 978-0-226-82559-5 (cloth)
ISBN-13: 978-0-226-82561-8 (paper)
ISBN-13: 978-0-226-82560-1 (e-book)
DOI: https://doi.org/10.7208/chicago/9780226825601.001.0001

Library of Congress Cataloging-in-Publication Data

Names: Cabatingan, Lee, author.
Title: A region among states : law and non-sovereignty in the Caribbean / Lee Cabatingan, The University of Chicago Press.
Description: Chicago : The University of Chicago, 2023. | Includes bibliographical references and index.
Identifiers: LCCN 2022045944 | ISBN 9780226825595 (cloth) | ISBN 9780226825618 (paperback) | ISBN 9780226825601 (ebook)
Subjects: LCSH: Caribbean Court of Justice. | Courts—Caribbean Area. | Justice, Administration of—Caribbean Area.
Classification: LCC KGL5502.C3 C33 2023 | DDC 347.729/035—dc23/eng/20221201
LC record available at https://lccn.loc.gov/2022045944

♾ This paper meets the requirements of ANSI/NISO Z39.48-1992 (Permanence of Paper).

*For my children
Leif and Hesper*

The Court is the realisation of a vision of our ancestors, an expression of independence and a signal of the region's coming of age.
　　CARIBBEAN COURT OF JUSTICE, October 4, 2021

Contents

Orientation: The Caribbean Court of Justice   1

1	**Introduction**	8
2	**A Myth**	34
3	**A Territory**	59
4	**A People**	82
5	**A Language**	102
6	**A Brand**	119
7	**A Region**	144

Acknowledgments 151
Appendix: Methods and Positionality 155
Notes 161
References 179
Index 189

Plates follow page 144.

ORIENTATION

The Caribbean Court of Justice

At the heart of this book rests the Caribbean Court of Justice (CCJ or Court). It is the institution that served as the focus of my research and where I spent more than a year volunteering and observing, as a lawyer and an anthropologist. Although a more detailed discussion of the CCJ and how it came to be constitutes the substance of a later chapter, I thought it helpful to begin with an orientation to this still relatively new institution.

The Caribbean Court of Justice exists, in part, to address a chronological anomaly within the Caribbean; specifically, a great swath of independent, English-speaking Caribbean states continues to appeal its cases to the Judicial Committee of the Privy Council in England. What this means more straightforwardly is that states celebrating thirty, forty, fifty, and, now, even sixty years of independence continue to accept the judicial oversight of their former colonizer. While many of those living in the Caribbean find great solace in this, believing British justice to be superior for one reason or another, others find it deeply troubling, questioning the possibility of state sovereignty in the face of ongoing legal entanglements. It is this puzzle that drew me to the Court in the first place. How could such a situation—wherein independent states appeal their cases to the court of their former colonizer—continue to persist? Was this an example of a "declaration of dependence," like those that James Ferguson has reflected on in southern Africa? Or, was there movement in the Caribbean, with the advent of an institution such as the CCJ, to break this bond and "cast off . . . [this] relation of hierarchical subordination" that is so "discomfiting to the emancipatory liberal mind"?[1]

In only its seventh year of existence at the time I began my fieldwork, the CCJ is a regional court headquartered in Trinidad and Tobago. It has two jurisdictions—an appellate jurisdiction and an original jurisdiction. For those states that so desire, the appellate jurisdiction offers a means to end the region's dependence on the Privy Council by replacing it as a final court of appeal, while the original jurisdiction offers a tribunal that could further the ambitions of the Caribbean Community and Common Market (CARICOM) to deepen the economic integration of the region. It is, therefore, as the Court likes to tell it, "two courts in one." It is a unique jurisdictional division of labor bundled into one novel institution, bringing together, under one roof and within one vision, a goal of enhanced state independence, a dream of regional togetherness, a hope for a (re)newed Caribbean pride, and a recognition of the region's colonial legal heritage. It is these complexities, viewed in the context of lingering colonial influence, that shape the inquiries of this book.

The CCJ was a long time in the making. It is the product of decades of deliberation and negotiation within the Anglophone Caribbean. More pointedly, it is the result of two regional documents: the Revised Treaty of Chaguaramas Establishing the Caribbean Community and the Agreement Establishing the Caribbean Court of Justice, both signed in 2001. The Revised Treaty outlines the aims and objectives of CARICOM, a regional economic integration effort much like many others around the world. The Agreement Establishing the CCJ fleshes out what the Revised Treaty includes in skeleton form: the creation of a new regional court with an appellate and an original jurisdiction. While there are fifteen full member states and territories of CARICOM, only twelve of these are signatory states of the CCJ:

- Antigua and Barbuda
- Barbados
- Belize
- Dominica
- Grenada
- Guyana
- Jamaica
- Saint Lucia
- Saint Kitts and Nevis
- Saint Vincent and the Grenadines
- Suriname
- Trinidad and Tobago

The Bahamas, Haiti, and Montserrat are the three CARICOM states and territories that did not sign the Agreement. Following the signing of the founding documents and the necessary logistical work in building a new institution, the CCJ opened its doors for business in 2005 at its headquarters in Trinidad and Tobago, a twin island country located in the far south of the Caribbean Sea only seven miles, at its closest point, off the coast of Venezuela.[2] As host country, Trinidad and Tobago provides a courthouse for the CCJ in downtown Port of Spain, the most populous city—with a metro population of over 250,000—on Trinidad, the bigger of the two islands.[3]

The CCJ has a novel organizational structure designed, in many ways, to thwart and appease ongoing anxieties over the advisability of even having a regional court. One of the most frequently voiced concerns is the possibility of political influence within a local court. In the structuring of the CCJ, then, protecting against such manipulation and, just as important, creating an image of such uprightness was a primary concern, and to this end, the Agreement calls for the creation of the Regional Judicial and Legal Services Commission (the RJLSC or Commission), consisting of eleven individuals—the majority of whom are nominated by the private regional legal bar. Among its responsibilities, the Commission appoints and disciplines the judges of the CCJ, other than the president. The president, on the recommendation of the RJLSC, is appointed or removed from office by a three-quarters majority vote by the signatory states to the Agreement. As both the CCJ website and tours of the CCJ make clear, the signatory states cannot select the president without that person first being nominated by the RJLSC. This, as one tour guide regularly points out, ensures that there can be no political influence, since the signatory parties can only consider a candidate nominated by the Commission. The Commission is also responsible for the hiring and discipline as well as determining the terms and conditions of the staff of the CCJ, of which there were about sixty, not including the judges, at the time I was there. Most of the staff was and continues to be Trinidadian, but the RJLSC makes an effort to employ a regional workforce, and, as a result, there were also Jamaicans, Barbadians, and Guyanese court employees while I was conducting research. By all accounts, the Court offers a prestigious job that pays well, and many staff members have remained at the CCJ for many years. While the RJLSC has certainly gone a long way toward quelling suspicions of political tampering, the Court continues to weather accusations of political manipulation or at least the possibility of it.[4] For good reason, therefore, this remains a sensitive topic for those working at the CCJ.

Because it appoints the judges, the RJLSC is also responsible for addressing another of the chief concerns regarding the Court: the caliber of legal minds working for it, something I take up in chapter 6. To attract such talent and to calm any fears that the Caribbean may be too small to house such talent, any vacant seats on the bench are advertised broadly, even beyond the

Caribbean. Interested job seekers must submit an application, and the most promising candidates are invited to an interview with the Commission. The application process has attracted a varied group of judges in terms of legal background, judicial experience, and geography. Whereas the Agreement allows for no fewer than five and as many as nine judges, in addition to the president, the RJLSC has determined that seven judges are sufficient to handle the Court's caseload thus far. When I was in residence at the Court, the seven judges were as follows:

- The Right Honourable Sir Charles Michael Dennis Byron, president (Saint Kitts and Nevis), sworn into office in 2011
- The Honourable Mr. Justice Rolston Nelson (Trinidad and Tobago), sworn into office in 2005
- The Honourable Mr. Justice Adrian Saunders (Saint Vincent and the Grenadines), sworn into office in 2005
- The Honourable Mr. Justice Jacob Wit (Netherlands), sworn into office in 2005
- The Honourable Mr. Justice David Hayton (United Kingdom), sworn into office in 2005
- The Honourable Mme. Justice Désirée Bernard (Guyana), sworn into office in 2005
- The Honourable Mr. Justice Winston Anderson (Jamaica), sworn into office in 2010

Since December 2013, when I completed the bulk of my fieldwork, there have been several retirements (President Byron, Justice Nelson, Justice Hayton, and Justice Bernard), and replacements—Justice Maureen Rajnauth-Lee (Trinidad and Tobago), Justice Denys Barrow (Belize), Justice Andrew Burgess (Barbados), and Justice Peter Jamadar (Trinidad and Tobago), some of whom I had met before they were appointed to the CCJ bench and others whom I had the opportunity to meet during later visits to the Court. Although I have included the judges' real names here as a matter of public record, in the remainder of the book they appear through pseudonyms, as do all other persons. As in most ethnographic work, pseudonyms are imperfect; with some labor, the reader can often identify the speaker. However, I have decided to use pseudonyms throughout this text—even for public figures like the CCJ judges—because certainly in some instances, the promise of (at least attempted) anonymity allowed the judges and others to speak more frankly with me. Therefore, in the interest of respecting their positions, their wishes, my tempered assurances to them, and the consistency of this book, I use pseudonyms for all figures that appear in these pages.

The individual biography of each of the seven judges I worked with most closely is fascinating and impressive, but I want to draw attention to several notable characteristics of the CCJ bench as it existed during my fieldwork.[5] Perhaps the most surprising is that of the seven sitting judges, five were from the Caribbean region, one from the United Kingdom, and one from the Netherlands, though he had spent the previous two decades as a judge in Curaçao, a dependent territory of the Kingdom of the Netherlands. Despite the fact that the Court is promoted as an indigenous tribunal capable of developing a Caribbean jurisprudence, few people I interviewed took issue with the fact that were non-Caribbean jurists sitting on the bench. "No problem," said one Jamaican judge in response to my question on this issue. "I think it's probably a good thing to keep the balance being more Caribbean than not, but I think it's a good idea [to have judges from outside the Caribbean]." This judge had, incidentally, just finished making a point about the more limited pool of expertise in the Caribbean regarding commercial law, suggesting an underlying belief that non-Caribbean judges could supplement any deficits in expertise. Offering another perspective, a Jamaican attorney said that the process in which judges were selected has a "level of insulation that is kind of ridiculous, but probably necessary given our tendencies to doubt ourselves," and for the same reason believed that they (the CCJ) "do and they should . . . have judges who are not from the region. . . . It's for the public consumption." Whereas this attorney did not consider this problematic, a Trinidadian attorney did: "I don't think we need to exclude anybody on the basis of nationality, but you do want to make sure that you are not struggling to lend legitimacy to the Court by bringing in external people because that would sort of undermine the entire—what you are going for in terms of a Caribbean Court. I hope that that was not the reason they would have sought those people." The Trinidadian attorney, however, was only one of two interviewees for whom the decision to hire non-Caribbean judges gave pause.

It is similarly notable that of the five judges who were from the Caribbean region, all but one received some part of their education in the United Kingdom. In fact, the link to the UK goes even deeper for some. The president at the time I was there, Sir Dennis Byron, was knighted by Queen Elizabeth II in 2000, and both Sir Dennis, as he is called by those familiar to him, and his predecessor in the president's seat, Michael de la Bastide, were sworn in as members of the Privy Council in 2004, earning them the formidable title of "The Right Honourable." The fact that the two earliest presidents of the CCJ are also members of the Privy Council is regularly held up by the Court and its supporters as illustrative of the quality of judicial minds that serve the CCJ, and, generally, this is accepted as fairly convincing proof. However, much like the aforementioned Trinidadian attorney, who worried that the Court was seeking legitimacy through questionable avenues, some observers have expressed concerns regarding the seeming contradiction between having a Right Honourable president of the CCJ, on the one hand, and celebrating the Court as something that is thoroughly Caribbean, on the other. Clearly, in trying to address one concern (lack of confidence in Caribbean judges), the Court inevitably exposes itself to new criticism (self-contradiction in the Court's stance toward the UK) and, unfortunately, provides refreshed fodder for arguments against it. Indeed, the debate over the wisdom of having a regional court has not subsided.

The CCJ Trust Fund is another feature of the Court that the aforementioned Jamaican attorney also felt was "a little overboard" but necessary to calm public fears. Established by a separate agreement, the Revised Agreement Establishing the Caribbean Court of Justice Trust Fund, the Trust Fund is also intended to temper the concern over political influence; the CCJ website describes how, because of the Trust Fund, "the expenditures of the Court, including the remuneration of the Judges, is not dependent on the disposition of governments." Indeed, the website continues, the Court's innovative funding structure makes the CCJ "the only integration court of its kind financially independent of the largesse of governments and free from their administrative control."[6] It does this by introducing a layer of separation between the Court and the politics of individual states by way of the Caribbean Development Bank (CDB). As part of the initial structuring of the Court, the CDB raised US$100 million in international capital markets to be placed in the Trust Fund and used for financing the daily operations of the Court "in perpetuity."[7] The Contracting Parties, pursuant to previously executed loan agreements, must repay the $100 million to the CDB. Nine Trustees from the private sector and civil society, whose identities are determined by the Revised Agreement Establishing the Trust Fund, oversee distribution of the fund, and a professional manager selected by the CDB manages it. For those who have heard of it and understand it, the Trust Fund has garnered praise for the level of stability it offers to the CCJ. It "is a model for the world," said the same Jamaican attorney who had said that it might be a little "extreme." More commonly, though, the Trust Fund is little known and less understood.

Although both the RJLSC and the Trust Fund have helped minimize the recurring questions about the soundness of a regional court, they have not made this Court a simple study. As much as they are "unique and innovative" solutions to troublesome problems, they are also complicated and cumbersome structures appended to the CCJ and necessitate fairly elaborate description and close attention in order to fully understand.[8] Indeed, the snapshot I offer here has, at times, inevitably introduced some of the much larger issues that undergird this book: the profound doubt harbored by many of those in the region; the complicated relationship of the CCJ to the Privy Council; and the ongoing dance between the nation-state and the region.

1

Introduction

It was pouring. The type of rain that accumulates quickly, cascades down the narrow, hilly streets, overwhelms the gutters, and rises to reach your ankles in a matter of minutes, making umbrellas a farce and shoes a lost cause. I knew because I had been caught in not just one but two such storms within my first few days in Port of Spain, Trinidad and Tobago. And I had the tattered umbrella and rain-stretched shoes to show for the unfortunate timing of my first trip to the Caribbean Court of Justice (CCJ) during the rainy season of 2012. This court, a relatively newly established regional tribunal, was the intended focus of my research, not Trinidad and Tobago. As a result, I had read nearly everything—and there was not much—available about the Court but had done little to prepare for life in Trinidad. Trinidadian thunderstorms, as a case in point, had not made it onto my radar prior to my arrival.

To her credit, my guesthouse host had warned me about the "fast-rising water" on the night that I arrived, but her warning did not solve for me the underlying problem: walking was the only form of transportation I had. I had arrived fully unaware of Trinidadian transportation options. Private cars and taxis must be booked ahead of time, the minibuses were still a mystery (and little help in avoiding the rain), and driving was not a possibility, as I had yet to acquire a car, not to mention learn to navigate the traffic-clogged streets of the city. So, when I awoke at 5:00 a.m. to the sound of torrential rain—that went on and on, hammering, deafening—I wondered how I would be able to make it to the CCJ for my first visit later that morning. The Court was not far from where I was staying in the Belmont neighborhood, not even a mile, but as I suspected and fellow guests later confirmed, the street was a veritable river. The whole neighborhood, they reported, was bustling to protect their houses from the flooding, and the red, white, and black decorations that had

INTRODUCTION 9

been hung in advance of Trinidad's Independence Day celebrations clung precipitously to the homes to which they had been attached, heavy with rain and whipped by the wind.

I was incredibly grateful, therefore, for the call I received later that morning from Justice Robert Matthews, one of seven judges at the Court, inquiring whether "the weather wasn't too much" for me.[1] "Oh, no, of course not," I said eagerly, hoping to head off any suggestion that we postpone my visit. "Good," he replied, telling me that the Court was sending a driver to pick me up. After a couple of coordinating phone calls from Matthews's secretary intended to minimize my wait in the rain, I moved as quickly as possible into the back seat of a waiting dark blue Lexus SUV. Wet, but not drenched, I thanked the driver profusely and asked whether he had had any trouble finding the guesthouse. He chuckled and admitted that Justice Matthews had asked him to conduct some "reconnaissance" the day before to make sure that I was staying in a safe place. The Belmont neighborhood, I learned once I arrived, did not have the most salubrious reputation, nor did much of Port of Spain or even all of Trinidad, which regularly reports high levels of crime.[2] It seemed that as much as I wanted to arrive at the CCJ dry and presentable, the CCJ also wanted to put its best foot forward by keeping me safe, dry, and welcome. It was not lost on me that this regional court worked hard to overcome the challenges posed by life in Trinidad and Tobago, a tension between region and state that resurfaced in my conversation with Justice Matthews later that day and remains at the center of this book.

My meeting with Justice Matthews, though, was the final event on my schedule for that morning at the Court. First, I had scheduled a tour, making contact with the CCJ through a difficult-to-find link on its website a month earlier. Sara, the sole member of the CCJ's Public Education and Communication Unit, who had responded to my tour request, was the first person to greet me at the courthouse after I had passed through the metal detector and received my visitor's badge. She was the picture of legal professionalism wearing a black suit and a welcoming smile. Over the next hour, she offered a thorough introduction to this regional tribunal as she guided me through its four floors, from the library and registry on the ground floor to the courtroom on the first floor, the administrative offices on the second, and, at last, the judges' chambers on the third. Sara did not point out, but I certainly noticed, that the CCJ, with its Registry Office and the way its floors were ordered—beginning with the "ground floor," not the "first floor"—clearly drew from British custom. This quiet adoption of the region's British heritage, however, changed when we reached the judges' chambers, where the Caribbean was intentionally introduced into the Court's physical structure. On the third floor, Sara drew my attention to the "very pink walls," which were part of the Court's "Caribbean" color scheme, she told me. They were, indeed, a bubblegum pink and contrasted with the subdued attire of the all-female secretarial staff to whom I was next introduced. Marianne, who served as Justice Matthews's longtime secretary and whose desk was located just outside of his office, laughed when she saw me. "We spoke several times earlier," she exclaimed, and remarked that she was glad to see that I had arrived dry and safe. She gently knocked on Matthews's open door and ushered me in to my meeting.

Like everyone else at the Court, Justice Matthews greeted me with a smile. He invited me into his capacious corner office—not pink but a far more somber white, with cherrywood furniture—and offered me a seat at his desk, which was covered in neat stacks of files and books. He was disarmingly friendly and immediately likable. He was also, I soon realized, deeply curious and intellectually introspective about the work of the CCJ, its place in history, and its potential to shape the future. He was, in this same spirit of intellectual curiosity, open to the prospect of having an anthropologist working in the Court for the next year or so, believing that he, the other judges, the Court in general, and even the public at large could benefit from a fresh perspective on the Court's work as it continued to navigate the early years of its existence (an expectation of my yet-to-begin fieldwork that induced mild anxiety). The Court, at that time, had only been in operation for seven years.

In part because of its newness and certainly owing to its explicitly regional focus, the CCJ, I suggested to Justice Matthews as our conversation turned to my interest in the Court, presented a fascinating opportunity to explore any number of research questions. One such question, I proposed, might be to better understand how the Court combined the values and traditions of the individual nation-states that made up its membership with the forward-moving, standard-creating, and regionalizing goals of the CCJ, a query that came to me through my perusal of the Court's website, my reading about the Court, and my just completed tour of the courthouse, in which state sovereignty and Caribbean regionality seemed to be equally touted as goals of the CCJ. Justice Matthews explained that as he saw it, there was not much "combining" that the CCJ needed to do. "The states and their values, traditions, and culture can take care of themselves," he told me. "They are overexpressed," as it is, he continued. He explained that there has long been a shared regional identity among Caribbean nations, particularly as former British colonies or, more generally, European colonies. They have struggled together in many ways, and they have formed a strong regional force. That is, until independence. According to Matthews, as soon as independence reached the horizon of thinkability in the Caribbean, sometime in the first half of the twentieth century, each country wanted nothing more than to be fully (even stubbornly) independent, with its own nationalism, cultural pride, and unique history. And so, he believed, "it is the job of the Court, as a regional institution, to help move the pendulum back"—not to "combine" sovereignty with regionhood, as I had put it, but to shift attention back toward the regionality that has always been there but that had, as he saw it, been somewhat recently overshadowed by aspirations to state sovereignty.

The seemingly intractable tension between region building and state sovereignty that I alluded to in my conversation with Matthews was something he had become well accustomed to hearing and defending against. It is a tension throughout the globe that has been well covered in academic literature and the media alike, as regional integration projects continue to forge ahead, despite the turmoil of Britain's departure from the European Union, an event widely known as "Brexit."[3] And it is a tension that resurfaced many times over in the debates leading to the formation of the CCJ, an institution established through the efforts of the Caribbean Community and Common Market (CARICOM), the Caribbean's (primarily) Anglophone regional integration endeavor. Processes such as globalization and regionalization are often held up as the means by which sovereign statehood will meet its end—not just in the Caribbean but in the North, South, East, and West alike. Indeed, the threat of the region to the sovereignty of the state has been both blamed for Brexit and exploited by state leaders the world over, such as the United States' President Donald Trump, who extolled the virtues of sovereign self-reliance at the expense of global and regional agreements.[4] In the CARICOM region, too, large swaths of the public are enormously wary that the CCJ, one of the more recent incarnations of regionalization there, will further encroach on their still relatively newly gained independence. But Matthews refused this narrative. According to him, it is not the region that should cause concern at all, but sovereignty itself, which washed over the shores of the Caribbean in an all-consuming wave just as the tide of colonialism rolled out. It is this idea of state sovereignty—even the idea of the modern nation-state itself—as a problem and the region as a possible solution that guides my inquiry.[5]

The Aim and the Argument

The region as a possible solution is my primary object of analysis, and it is through an ethnographic exploration of how a relatively new court with lofty ambitions pursues the project of region making that I also seek to say something about sovereignty. This is not, however, a completed story that has reached a successful ending, in that the "problem" of sovereignty has not yet been solved and a region has not yet materialized. Instead, this book explores the *possibility* of constituting a region on a geopolitical and ideological terrain dominated by the nation-state. It explores, from the perspective of an institution explicitly devoted to regional integration, what the pursuit of this possibility actually looks like, what it entails when there is no functional blueprint available. Even more specifically, it explores how this pursuit and that possibility take shape within a world very much structured by colonial legacies.

What the work of the CCJ shows us is that whereas there is no blueprint for building a successful region, there is an array of tools, techniques, and approaches that have been long employed in world-making projects not unsimilar but certainly not identical to the one pursued by the Court.[6] As the CCJ pursues its project of region building, therefore, it selects, experiments, and adjusts these tools and techniques, rather than create a wheel wholly anew. And, as this book will show, many of these tools and techniques are those that have been and are continuously employed in ongoing projects of sovereign nation-state making. In other words, for the CCJ, sovereignty does not serve as an aspirational model but serves as a valuable tool kit that can be used for a different end. To be clear, while the CCJ adopts and adapts a number of techniques that have become closely associated with the making of modern nation-states, I do *not* suggest that the CCJ is "mimicking" the processes and goals associated with the making of modern nation-states.[7] There are several reasons why this cannot be so. First, there is no tried-and-true master plan to making a sovereign nation-state. Instead, the modern nation-state is very much an ongoing project forced to adjust to the ever-changing geopolitics of the world. The model, in other words, is not static; the nation-state is never a fait accompli such that a blueprint could not be said to exist. Second, the tools and techniques that have been employed in the ongoing construction of the sovereign nation-state are not associated exclusively with the sovereign nation-state. Whereas some, such as the creation of a territory, have become closely wed to the idea of the state, others, such as branding, are techniques that are used by a wide variety of institutions. It is hard to say, then, that the CCJ is mimicking nation-state branding any more than it is copying the branding success of Disneyland (as we will see in chapter 6). Third, the CCJ looks to the region as a solution to the problem of sovereignty, as Justice Matthews made clear. Mimicking the sovereign nation-state—that is, modeling the region after the sovereign state—would merely return it to the very problem it hoped to solve.

I suggest, therefore, that the CCJ's use of so many of the same tools of sovereign nation-state building serves a critical *indexical* purpose. That is, by taking up these familiar tools, the Court points to familiar processes of nation-state making, thereby suggesting that the region shares common ground with the nation-state. There is precedent, in other words, to the CCJ's labor. But just as precedent works in the law—when one legal judgment cites another from the past—this provides a foundation for innovation, not stagnation or repetition. The Court's citation of the nation-state is characterized by a productive simultaneity of sameness and difference, as Constantine Nakassis has observed in other instances; "citation," he writes, "is based on an irreducible sameness," allowing the CCJ, for example, to claim some level of relatedness to the sovereign nation-state, and it is also, Nakassis continues, "based on an irreducible difference, or gap, between the indexical source and its intended target, the citing [the region, in this discussion] and cited events [the sovereign nation-state]," giving the CCJ space to deviate and innovate.[8]

To understand something as citation, as I do the CCJ's region-making efforts, is to call out the irreducible distance between the nation-state and the region at the same time I acknowledge their necessary similarities.[9] Indeed, the CCJ indexes the sovereign nation-state to create something new—a nonsovereign region—that can address the circumstances of the Caribbean in a way that is not so strange, so out of context, or so unrecognizable that it will be immediately and outright rejected. As much as it needs the nation-state to make the region legible, it relies on the distance of citation to find the freedom to diverge from it. The Westphalian sovereign nation-state, after all, belongs to what Michel-Rolph Trouillot has called "North Atlantic universals":

> words that project the North Atlantic experience on a universal scale that they themselves helped to create . . . particulars that gained a degree of universality, chunks of human history that have become historical standards. They do not describe the world; they offer visions of the world . . . they are rooted in a particular history, they evoke multiple layers of sensibilities, persuasions, cultural assumptions, and ideological choices tied to that localized history. . . . And yet, since they are projected as universals, they deny their localization, the sensibilities and the history from which they spring.[10]

The idea of the sovereign nation-state, in short, was not created by or for the Caribbean.[11] Thus, though the CCJ cites it, through its adoption of recognizable tools, it pursues a distinctly Caribbean innovation. This is, as I show throughout book, the work to which the CCJ devotes a great deal of time, resources, and thought. It takes instruments associated with sovereignty, which have become closely linked to the making of modern nation-states, and uses them to construct a region.

Sovereignty, in this way, is acknowledged, as it must be—for the CCJ is charged with fulfilling the sovereignty of its member states through its appellate jurisdiction—but is also cleverly deconstructed and reconstructed, as the Court repurposes some of the same tools used in the project of sovereign nation-state making to pursue a region. This is a careful and critical indexical practice that helps the CCJ balance the demands of a deeply skeptical public with the pressing problems associated with sovereignty. It is also a careful and critical indexical practice that suggests the wider impact the CCJ's work can have; the hopeful possibility of constructing a region by drawing on and citing the stuff of sovereignty is something that the Court offers not just to the Caribbean but to a much broader audience. The fetishization of the sovereign nation-state— its placement on a pedestal of global governance and its gatekeeping role to the doors of global acceptance—has led to a good deal of grief, disappointment, and sedimented inequality around the world.[12] The "inability" of so many states to attain the ideal form of state sovereignty has led scholars to revisit it as a concept and reconfigure it in a way that better reflects the ethnographic reality.[13] The CCJ, however, is engaged in a project of another kind. Rather than revisiting and reconfiguring sovereignty, the Court refuses it and reuses it. It disassembles sovereignty and inspects its component parts to determine how each might be put to a new use. It takes the "ruins" of empire—here, the largely unachievable model of the sovereign nation-state—to create something else, all the while acknowledging, through its indexical practice, sovereignty's presence and stature in the world.[14] Indeed, why cling to something that has not worked for so many for so long? Why not look to the Caribbean, which once served as a "crucible of European modernity,"[15] for the possibility of something new, of a distinctly non-sovereign form of governance of value to the world?

The Problem of the Sovereign Nation-State

Residing uncomfortably alongside the possibility of the region is the problem of the sovereign nation-state—a problem that is difficult to understate as far as its impact on the CCJ's endeavors is concerned. As I came to learn over the course of my fieldwork, from the Court's perspective, the problem with state sovereignty is multiplex and pernicious. To begin, the state is "overexpressed," as Justice Matthews said, and this overexpression of the state vis-à-vis the near invisibility of the region is deeply problematic for a regional court. Even in Trinidad, the Court's own backyard, so to speak, there is widespread celebration of the state and frequent denigration—or, also frustrating, total ignorance—of regional projects like the CCJ's. But there is more to it than this. The sovereign state also poses a problem in that it is the quintessential form of modern governance worldwide, a veritable requirement for global recognition.[16] The CCJ, though, while avidly asserting its modernity, remains ambivalent about the state form—in one jurisdiction sustaining it and in the other refusing it—forcing the question of whether other forms of governance can be similarly modern and sit authoritatively at the proverbial global table. Lastly, there is the issue of non-sovereignty, a concept introduced by anthropologist Yarimar Bonilla, who draws from the work of Trouillot.[17] Non-sovereignty captures the predicament of much of the Global South, in which state sovereignty is held up as the equally available and ideal standard of governance—a "North Atlantic universal," as noted previously—but is, at the same time, a form of governance that was never meant to be achieved by much of the world, which remains, therefore, non-sovereign when measured against this ideal. I discuss each of these problems in turn.

OVEREXPRESSION

Justice Matthews never elaborated on what he meant when he argued that the state was "overexpressed," but after my extended time in Trinidad and shorter visits to a handful of the Court's member states, I came to appreciate what his comment likely referred to. Relatively newly independent from Great Britain, the independent English-speaking Caribbean proudly displays its national colors, histories, and heroes. Indeed, I arrived in Trinidad not only to pouring rain, but also to a landscape adorned in the colors of Trinidad's flag, artfully draped over doorways, woven through balconies, and displayed on bodies in celebration of Trinidad and Tobago's fiftieth year of independence (see figure 1). I celebrated, not too long later—during an impromptu national holiday—the success of Trinidadian javelin thrower Keshorn Walcott, who had triumphantly won the gold medal at the 2012 Summer Olympic Games. I participated as well in Trinidad's largest cultural claim, Carnival, and I relished Trinidad's delicious cuisine, which combines Indian, African, Asian, and Caribbean flavors and textures. I followed Trinidadian news, abided by Trinidadian laws, and benefited from Trinidadian subsidized gasoline prices once I had acquired a car and learned to drive it. The point is that I was *in* Trinidad and Tobago, and that state's presence was by far the most significant, the most clearly expressed, and the most, I tend to agree, *over*expressed presence that I experienced. What this means is that regional pursuits such as CARICOM and the CCJ have almost no felt presence at all.[18]

A senior staff member at the CCJ completed a study several years before I had arrived.[19] In his search for answers to why the CCJ's member states have been so slow in accepting the jurisdiction of the Court, he concluded, "Most significantly, the data revealed that the prevailing element affecting public opinion of the CCJ is ignorance. People simply *do not know* the court or its

FIGURE 1. One of many homes in the Belmont neighborhood of Port of Spain, Trinidad and Tobago, festively decorated in red, white, and black for the nation's fiftieth anniversary of independence, 2012. Photograph by author.

nature of mission sufficiently."[20] My experience in Trinidad, four years after his study, echoed his findings exactly. Almost no one, even in the Court's hometown, knows about the Court's very existence, and it took very little time for me to realize this; a confused "what?" was by far the most common reaction I received whenever I explained to Trinidadians why I was living there. People do, however, know about CARICOM, the umbrella regional endeavor, but even CARICOM has little relevance to their everyday lives; it does not subsidize their gasoline, win gold medals, enforce the law, or have an Independence Day to celebrate. It does host a smattering of regional events, such as the Caribbean Festival of Arts (CARIFESTA), but after reading a short article about the opening ceremony of CARIFESTA XI in Suriname, I asked Lynette, a young and in-the-know CCJ employee, about it. Her telling reply: "What's CARIFESTA?" Her response, I think, is broadly representative of the widespread problem that many, if not most, regional endeavors do not register in the consciousness of the people of the region, even of those who work for it, like Lynette.

While this lack of knowledge is damaging and deflating to the Court's regional ambitions, the emotions expressed by those who *do* know about the

CCJ are often far more bruising. They often see the Court and its work as nothing short of inadvisable or, worse, farcical. Their sharp criticisms, which surface throughout this book in the form of offhand comments, newspaper editorials, and even jokes and laughter, are not without historical foundation. As I detail in chapter 2, the Court's regional project is frequently viewed as merely the latest in a long line of regional projects within the Caribbean that have fallen short—over and over again—of expectations, a now-familiar pattern that has produced a profoundly skeptical public who see the Court as nothing more than an ill-advised last-ditch effort to resuscitate a regionalist vision of Caribbean modernity.[21] Such skepticism has played out in one of the most damaging ways for the CCJ: the failure of many of its member states (including its host country, Trinidad and Tobago) to accede to its appellate jurisdiction, hoping to heed, it might seem, the Marxian warning that history often repeats itself, "the first time as tragedy, the second time as farce."[22]

In sum, the state's overexpression—as well as its knowability and relative historical stability—poses a problem to the Court and its pursuit of possibility. The signs and symbols of the sovereign nation-state dominate the landscape; its politics and news take over the airwaves; and its history and celebrations bring pride and joy to its people, who identify first and sometimes exclusively as citizens of a particular state. The state leaves little physical space, airspace, or emotional space for something like a region to gain any traction. Indeed, the hegemony of the sovereign nation-state as an aspirational model, an ideological goal, and a political form make it impossible for the CCJ, or any other regional endeavor, to make a clean break toward a new regional future.

MODERNITY

What I could not appreciate on that very rainy day of my first visit was the CCJ's mirrored facade. In the sunshine, it positively glimmered, standing apart from the cinder block and stucco buildings surrounding it (see figure 2). The four-story structure at 134 Henry Street in downtown Port of Spain had been remodeled prior to the Court's opening. Its interior, like its exterior, was notably modern, showcasing clean lines, bright lights, fresh paint, and well-maintained surfaces. Being modern, I learned, is highly valued by the Court. An instructional video produced by the CCJ for attorneys preparing to appear before it announces, "We are a modern court begun in the twenty-first century to take the Caribbean region forward. . . . It is therefore integral to this that we are forward-looking and forward-thinking." And it is in the name of such forward movement and modernization that the Court proudly upholds the rule of law, prioritizes access to justice, operates under

FIGURE 2. The Caribbean Court of Justice, 134 Henry Street, Port of Spain, Trinidad and Tobago, 2012. Photograph by author.

a contemporary code of judicial conduct, exists pursuant to a cutting-edge funding structure, and utilizes trailblazing courtroom technology. It is actively "going green," striving to reduce its use of paper and encouraging its users to do the same. It hosts conferences in which panels and keynote speakers address topics such as women's and gay rights in the Caribbean, choices that have raised at least one eyebrow; in an anonymous survey administered after a 2013 conference, for which I was part of the organizing committee, one attendee questioned whether the CCJ had an "agenda," given its proclivity to highlight gender and sexual identity issues. During the debrief session on this conference, this comment caused one CCJ judge to exclaim upon reading it, "You're darn right we have an agenda!" This agenda, as the Court is unashamed to admit, is to be modern. In other words, its allegiance to the issues, processes, and priorities of what might be described as a globally northern and geographically western culture of legality, is closely aligned with its desire to be perceived as modern.[23]

Having an updated exterior, a remodeled interior, and an operating program that supports equal rights, environmental awareness, and the rule of law does not, however, pose an obvious problem. In other words, showcasing the hallmarks of liberal modernity, on its own, is not the issue. Rather, the issue is what has become sutured to the idea of modernity. As numerous scholars have shown, modernity has come to be linked almost inseparably to the sovereign nation-state, such that for a polity to be considered modern, it must necessarily also be a sovereign nation-state.[24] It is this definitional relationship between modernity and the nation-state that creates an obstacle for the Court, which seeks to create not a modern state but a modern *region*.

The relationship between sovereignty, the nation, and the state deserves comment here, as they are frequently used interchangeably in a way that underscores their now-naturalized connection. It is at least in part because they share modernity as a defining characteristic that it has become difficult to parse the nation from the state—the hyphen linking the two having become increasingly standardized—and it has become similarly challenging to discuss the nation-state as distinct from sovereignty, as the nation-state has, at least since the 1648 Treaty of Westphalia, long-served as the ultimate vehicle for sovereign power.[25] In fact, Justice Matthews and many others at the CCJ regularly meld the three concepts together, often referring to the state in a way that presumes a nation of people is always-already attached to it and that this nation-state is ever aspiring toward sovereignty. It is not only in the ethnographic context that this happens; those writing about the state, the nation, and sovereignty also often consider them as a unitary concept, referring to "the sovereign state," in which the nation is a presumed part.[26] Such is certainly true in the Caribbean context, where Linden Lewis has noted that "the idea of sovereignty in the Caribbean is rooted in the received wisdom of European articulation of the Westphalian understandings of the same," wherein state, nation, and sovereignty come together.[27] Because the sovereign nation-state is considered as such in both ethnographic and analytic frameworks, this is how I, too, engage with these concepts throughout this book: as a not indistinguishable but complexly intertwined triad that is held out as the ideal form of modern governance in which a unified and uniform people live within a clearly bounded territory under an exclusive jurisdictional authority, creating a tidy "isomorphism of people, territory, and legitimate sovereignty."[28]

It is to achieving this isomorphic ideal of quintessential modern governance, then, that so many efforts have been devoted and a tool kit of techniques and building blocks has been developed, leading to a wealth of scholarship exploring the ways in which these instruments have been employed in projects of modern nation-state making. *Myths of origin*, which emphasize shared ethnocultural identities and shape "memories" of heroic events, for example, continue to do much in the making and sustaining of the nation-state.[29] So too, and relatedly, does the introduction and imposition of a shared "national" *language*, which seeks to erase problematic differences between the various ethnicities and cultures that have been gathered under the auspices of a nation-state.[30] If everyone speaks the same language, the rough logic suggests, then everyone must share the same culture, and everyone, thus, naturally belongs together. And any state, even one with a supposedly homogeneous population all speaking the same language, can hardly be said to exist without a border that defines it and protects it against others. Defining the *territory* of the state is also, therefore, a foundational step in claiming sovereign nation-statehood.[31] Equally important is joining the nation to the state in a way that transgresses a mere physical connection and containment. The process of *interpellating* a people into the state's ideological apparatus—that is, making people understand that they are subjects of the state in which they live—therefore finds a notable place in the tool kit of sovereignty.[32] More recent literature has identified *branding* as a means for a nation-state to establish and promote its unique and marketable contribution to the world.[33] Quite often, the branding campaign relies on the heroic and historical figures and events and the cultural characteristics of the nation that had been constructed through earlier efforts of nation-state making. And, finally, there is the need for *law*.[34] Not just any law, but a law unique to that nation-state, made by and for it, and exercised through its legitimate authority. These various building blocks—myths of origin, language, territory, interpellation, branding, and law—have all become closely associated with the idealized model of the modern nation-state and also, not coincidentally, constitute the topics explored in the chapters of this book. Thus, it is no longer just the nation-state that is understood to be modern; the techniques and tools of state crafting, nation making, and sovereignty building have also become signposts of modernity, progress, and civilization.

All of this, then—the expansive nature of the relationship between the sovereign nation-state and modernity—causes a problem for the CCJ because it is *not* in the nation-state-making business, but it *does* aspire to be modern.

NON-SOVEREIGNTY

Closely related to the problem of modernity for the Court is the problem of non-sovereignty. Not only does the sovereign nation-state stand at the pinnacle of modern governance—leaving little space for other forms, but the very idea of a sovereign nation-state is "a concept, a norm, an ideal . . . that has been thoroughly shaped by the institutional, epistemic, and ontological orders of empire."[35] It is, as Bonilla and others have persuasively argued, a globally northern, notably white, and enduringly imperialistic invention that benignly offers itself as an unmarked and equally available possibility

INTRODUCTION

for successful governance when, in fact, it is hardly that.[36] Instead, it has been used as a powerful and effective tool throughout the colonial project; it provided the legal technologies through which to accomplish and justify the often violent process of colonization[37] and thereby found its place in what has been described as the "cutting edge of colonialism."[38] It was in the name of efficient and effective governance, for example, that colonial administrators wielded their legal authority to carve up much of Africa into administrative territories, without regard (or with grossly misplaced regard) for preexisting native boundaries.[39] These territories later became states, and these states now often find themselves struggling to prove their sovereign status. In other words, the seemingly neutral techniques of sovereignty I have described have been historically employed (or deployed) as effective tools in transforming and subjectifying populations, carving out new territories, and asserting legal regimes.[40] Sovereignty was for the benefit of the colonizer, not the colonized.

Despite the waning (though surely not the end) of the age of imperialism, this construct of colonial modernity has not only remained but has solidified its hegemony.[41] It has become the mostly unchallenged model for participation on the world's politicoeconomic stage. To be recognizable, to be uninvadable, to be tradeworthy and creditworthy, and to be protected is to be a sovereign nation-state.[42] And many nations without states, states without stable nations, and nation-states without "completed" sovereignty continue to strive to achieve this ideal, as it has calcified into the sine qua non of international existence. And this is the crux of the problem. The sovereign nation-state, as much as it stands for modernity, as much as it serves as a gatekeeper for global participation, and as much as every polity is expected to continually strive for it, was never meant for everyone, something that Justice Matthews recognized all too well.

In the months that followed my initial visit to the Court, and as I settled into my dual roles as anthropological researcher and legal intern, Justice Matthews and I continued our conversations about the state and the region—specifically, Caribbean states and the Caribbean region. During one such conversation, we discussed a case before the CCJ that he found particularly vexing because of the international laws that technically applied but awkwardly fit the regional context. Our discussion of the case and the challenges it posed quickly pivoted to a broader reflection on the state of the Caribbean more generally. "As a judge from a third world country," he said, as he pushed the case file aside, he was highly conscious of the terms on which the region was supposed to enter "the globalized world." Specifically, the Caribbean must come in on the terms of "the big boys," as he dubbed them. The problem, he told me, is that these so-called international standards were not necessarily put in place by or good for the Caribbean, such that any pretense of "a level playing field" was patently false. For him, this meant that in his role as a judge at a regional court serving Caribbean states, he would not "blindly embrace" them, though he realized he could not ignore them. Matthews was clearly aggravated by this state of affairs and determined not to let the Caribbean dissolve into "international standards" without a fight. At the same time, he was contemplatively resigned: "But that is how the world is," he sighed. What is so frustrating, he explained, is that the Caribbean is entering a world stage that is fraught with inequalities, and many of these are "the same inequalities as colonialism."

Justice Matthews's lamentations identify with remarkable clarity the core of the problem of sovereignty for the Court, the Caribbean, and much of the Global South more generally. The Court, as he indicated, is painfully aware of the trap set by "North Atlantic universals" such as sovereignty,[43] which promise entry into and equal treatment by "this world" but are, in fact, nothing more than impossible, inappropriate, and, at best, aspirational models that have never worked in the Caribbean (or elsewhere, for that matter).[44] In her work on Jamaica, for example, Deborah A. Thomas shows exactly how the particularities and pressures of (post)colonial state formation can lead to devasting consequences—namely, the pervasive violence and political cronyism that have become part of the fabric of life in Kingston today.[45] So, while the sovereign nation-state remains *the* model for political organization and international participation, it is not a model readily available to or advisable for all—and not one equally attainable by the Caribbean.[46]

The impossibility of sovereignty, however, has not led to its diminution in stature. Rather, the model of the sovereign nation-state has become a measuring stick of development, security, and creditworthiness. Alternate forms of governance are largely unrecognizable on their own terms and only become visible as distortions and mutations of the dominant model; "failed" states, "rogue" nations, and "incomplete" sovereignties—whose failures, rogueness, and incompletion are often tied to breakdowns in law and order of one sort or another—are then viewed suspiciously by those predominantly globally northern entities that hold the world's purse strings, a situation that inevitably leads to the protracted "failure," "rogueness," and "incompletion" of these nations and states.

But is this a fair depiction of the Global South, for which the sovereign nation-state was never meant to be achieved? As Bonilla has argued, large swaths of the Caribbean, for instance, have purposefully pursued *non-sovereign futures*.[47] They have eschewed sovereignty for something else—namely, "a positive project and a negative place-holder for an anticipated future characterized

INTRODUCTION

by something *other than* the search for sovereignty."[48] The result is a long and varied list of non-sovereign political formations in the Caribbean, from still dependent territories of the United Kingdom, the Kingdom of the Netherlands, and the United States to states that have achieved "flag independence" but retain some fundamental link to their former colonizer—such as the continued use of its court system. What these non-sovereign entities have in common is an ongoing struggle "with how to forge a more robust project of self-determination, how to reconcile the unresolved legacies of colonialism and slavery, how to assert control over their entanglements with foreign powers, and how to stem their disappointment with the unfilled promise of political and economic modernity."[49] Justice Matthews's reflection on "big boy" standards that echo "the same inequalities as colonialism" captures just this notion and highlights not only the problem posed by the aspirational yet unattainable model of sovereignty but also the untenability of this type of (neo/post)colonial non-sovereignty as well.

The Region as a Non-sovereign Solution

Enter the region. Unable to address the problem of its member states' non-sovereignty with sovereignty, the CCJ, I argue in this book, pursues something else: a *non-sovereign region*, the contours of which begin to take shape through the Court's concerted efforts, vast resources, strategic planning, and a good deal of creative thinking. At the same time the CCJ indexes various marks of sovereignty, it strategically sidesteps ongoing British legacies and logics, asserting instead Caribbean culture and values; it refuses to adopt the legal practices associated with North Atlantic conceptions of sovereignty, such as an authoritative legal sovereign;[50] and it strives as well to remain untethered to one or another nation-state or superstate. It is, as I noted earlier, a careful balance between respecting the sovereign aspirations of its member states and pushing for something new and better suited to the Caribbean context. The region thus offers "an alternative non-sovereign future" for the non-sovereign states still wrestling with their dependence on Britain.[51] It allows for the possibility "to break free from the epistemic binds of political modernity, even while still being compelled to think through its normative categories."[52] The "big boy" standards that Justice Matthews spoke of, in other words, do not go away, but the CCJ endeavors, through its indexical labor, to acknowledge them yet move past them, without giving in to them.

Done right, this regional non-sovereignty, as the Court shapes it, also holds out a promise to address the other issues associated with the nation-state—namely, its overexpression and its hegemonic claim to modern governance.

The Court works to raise the flag (quite literally, as it turns out) of the region and promote the Caribbean above the stifling presence of the state. It does this, ingeniously and tirelessly, with tools and techniques often associated with sovereignty building, nation making, statecraft, and modernity. This is citational work through which the CCJ proffers an argument: that a non-sovereign region shares common ground with the sovereign state; it can be modern and, with this modernity, should be regarded and respected by the international community.

It also makes the argument that this region can be modern in a particularly Caribbean way. International standards, as Justice Matthews noted, do not always suit the Caribbean reality; nor do the chilly strictures of modernity, classically conceived. And, so, being a modern *Caribbean* court is very much at the core of the CCJ's objectives and further defines what it means to be a non-sovereign region. The Court's founding vision statement, for example, proclaimed that Caribbean "history, values and traditions" would be at the center of the Court's work.[53] My experience visiting the CCJ for the first time underscores the Court's commitment to this vision. While modernity is often associated with a cool indifference and distanced authority, I, a virtual stranger, had received a personal phone call from a sitting judge at the highest court in the region who was concerned that the rain would dampen my visit. His concern, too, over my safety had led him to check up on my housing arrangement, a thoughtful gesture that does not square with modernity's iron cage of cold rationality and efficiency.[54] Justice Matthews's own personality certainly had something to do with these considerate gestures, but so, too, I think, did the Court's conscious effort to establish itself as "Caribbean," with all the warmth, welcoming, and person-to-person contact that that suggests. Caribbean people, as Justice Gupta, then a judge for Trinidad and Tobago and now a judge for the CCJ, told me when we were discussing the video conferencing technology used by the Court, are "touchy-feely." "How does an indigenous court find acceptance if you are deploying a European technology, which is more suited to their normative behavior? Maybe this works in Europe, where their norms are different, but what about here where we are touchy-feely?" he ruminated. "My own view," he added, "is that the CCJ would have more impact . . . if they traveled and met people. People will measure the way he looked at me, and he smiled. . . . This is who we are. We have to be careful that it is not another imperial imposition. And technology can create this experience that it is imposed, distant, and far away." Modernity, in other words, can be softened, even indigenized, with a Caribbean touch, something that the CCJ certainly tried to do, with its pink Caribbean walls and its personal phone calls. This is a cultural turn, moreover, that helps the

Court assert a shared ground on which a region might be built among members states and national publics that are quite often sharply divided.

To be sure, the region pursued by the CCJ is neither a one-size-fits-all solution to the varied challenges that (post)colonial states and territories may face nor the only form that non-sovereignty might take. Instead, in this book, I present the non-sovereign Caribbean region as a somewhat hopeful alternative to the only-ever aspirational model of the sovereign nation-state. It is an alternative that has not materialized out of thin air but that cites tools of sovereignty and builds on a localized history and ontology of regional thinking within the Caribbean.[55] But it is not the only alternative, as other non-sovereign models of governance—many of which can also be found in the Caribbean—illustrate. Distinct strategic balances between an ongoing aspiration to sovereignty and a persistent recognition of impossibility can and have been achieved. Bonilla, for instance, describes the efforts of trade unionists and grassroots activists in the still-dependent territory of Guadeloupe, who pursue non-sovereign futures that are markedly different from the Court's region.[56] While Bonilla's working-class interlocutors craft a non-sovereign future that allows them to claim rights, goods, and livelihoods in the absence of formal state sovereignty, the elite class of legal actors with whom I conducted my research actively shape a non-sovereign future from "above," hoping to shore up a long-deferred regional dream. This makes the CCJ into an institution in which the possibility of a non-sovereign region clashes with ordinary desires for sovereignty. It requires the CCJ to wrestle with a long-lasting structure of feeling within the Caribbean that, despite decades of arrested postcolonial development, is yet to wane. That is, the sovereign nation-state remains for many people the only palatable future. And these fault lines, which cleave between sovereign aspirations and non-sovereign imaginaries, run deep, complexifying the Court's work at every step.

The Region as a Project

As should be apparent from the foregoing discussion and will become more obvious in the chapters that follow, the Caribbean Court of Justice approaches the task of constructing a modern, Caribbean, non-sovereign region with admirable and inexhaustible gusto. For the CCJ, region making is a fundamentally important *project*. This viewpoint is in contrast to the region as *process*, though the Caribbean is that, too. This distinction, which I take from the work of Naor Ben-Yehoyada, between "region-making projects" and "region-formation processes," is a useful one when understanding what it is that the CCJ is attempting to accomplish and in what context it is attempting to accomplish it.[57] I call what the CCJ is doing "a project" because it is an explicit, conscious, and institutionally organized effort to bring together a group of states into an identifiable region. Such region-making projects are hardly new to the Anglophone Caribbean, which has seen its share of proactive regionalization attempts dating at least back to the colonial era. Britain, for example, undertook its own region-making projects when it grouped together various Caribbean territories to form administratively convenient groupings known as the "Leeward Islands" and the "Windward Islands." The West Indies Federation, too, represented a short-lived (1958–1962) region-making project intended to ease the way to independence for a handful of British colonies in the Caribbean. And the autochthonous creation known as CARICOM aims to establish a region of now-independent economically integrated Anglophone states. It is this most recent iteration of region making that locates the Caribbean's efforts within the global trend of regional economic integration projects such as the Mercado Común del Sur (MERCOSUR) in South America, the Common Market for Eastern and Southern Africa (COMESA), the Economic Community of West African States (ECOWAS), the Association of Southeast Asian Nations (ASEAN), and, of course, the European Union (EU). As an institution associated with CARICOM, the CCJ falls within the ambit of these region-making projects.

These projects often find their origins in and justify their continued existence with reference to the international community and the global market. The guiding idea behind CARICOM and its 2001 restructuring as the CARICOM Single Market and Economy (CSME), for example, is that regional integration will provide an economic life preserver and, even better, an economic accelerator for each of its mostly small, mostly island member states, which, without the CSME, would struggle for air in the certain and certainly overwhelming tide of globalization.[58] Globalization, in other words, undergirds CARICOM's and other regional integration projects' very being, while regional betterment in the context of this new world market serves as their motivation. In many ways, then, we can see regional integration endeavors, of which CARICOM is only one, as phenomena comprehensible only through globalization and the spaces, economies, polities, subjectivities, and temporalities they create as likewise related to globalization.

Indeed, even though these projects regularly posit themselves and are commonly understood as economic endeavors, they often actively pursue wider-reaching goals. Cris Shore, for example, has provided a fascinating glimpse into the cultural ambitions of the European Union.[59] A great deal of work, as Shore points out, goes into the "Europeanisation" of the people living within the EU in an effort to build a border-crossing identity and a newly realized subjectivity that could assist, ultimately, with the creation of a politically integrated Europe.[60] CARICOM, similarly, aims to accomplish more than economic integration, as is evidenced by the wide-ranging topics and programs included under the "Our Work" category on its website: from gender to health to sports and youth development.[61] What this all means is that region-making projects present an opportunity to explore far more than transnational economics (though that in itself is a mighty topic). Culture, art, health, sports, education, and law, for example, are all rolled into such wide-ranging region-making projects as that represented by CARICOM. As one of its key institutions, the CCJ, too, necessarily encompasses far more than legal regional integration.

Region-formation *processes* differ from the projects described earlier in this section in that the "shift in scale [from state to region] overflows any single project . . . regions form, but no one person or institution *forms* them."[62] Instead, persons and institutions might themselves be rolled up into the process. In the Caribbean, colonialism can be considered a region-formation process, with its swirling movements of people and products, that is not attributable to a single institution or particular person, though institutions such as the British Crown are certainly implicated in the process and people, like millions of enslaved Africans, are clearly at the heart of the region.[63] In fact, it is the shared colonial history and the region formed through this process that shape many of my interlocutors' understandings of "the Caribbean," and it is this Caribbean that provides the backdrop against which any region-making *project* takes shape.

Thus, while I am primarily interested in the region as a project as it is pursued anew by the CCJ, this book recognizes—as do those who work at the Court—that this project does not take place on a tabula rasa. The Caribbean, as both a project and process, is already in existence in a multitude of shifting "transnational constellations," which compete with and contribute to the project undertaken by the Court.[64] The Court's work, therefore, must be understood as responding to both the hegemony of the modern sovereign nation-state (and the impossible promise that it holds out) and the complicated terrain of preexisting regional projects and processes.

Law, Process, and the Non-sovereign Region

It is significant that this book, which seeks to explore possibilities outside of sovereignty, focuses on the labor of those who work in a court of law. After all, law has come to occupy a sacred place in the modern conceptualization of state sovereignty, such that state sovereignty is regularly understood to be constituted by, and no less than, supreme authority over the law within a given territory.[65] Building on this understanding, some scholars have argued—helpfully providing a foothold for the ethnographic study of law's role in the constitution of sovereignty—that it is through the speaking of law, or "jurisdiction," that the bounds of sovereign power are established, such that sovereignty cannot be said to exist without law's speech.[66] The point to be drawn is that law has become linked to the ideal definition of the sovereign nation-state, which, as discussed earlier, is closely associated with modernity. Law, in short, has become a necessary condition of modernity. And not just any law, but law that belongs to the same conceptual universe as the nation-state—that is, law in its recognizably North Atlantic instantiation.

Classic texts in political and legal anthropology make just this point across wide-ranging contexts. Sally Engle Merry has shown, for example, how Anglo-American law and legal systems were, initially, eagerly adopted by Indigenous Hawaiians who sought to "civilize" and "modernize" the image of their islands in an effort to ward off relentless incursions and demands.[67] And more relevant to the CCJ, Mindie Lazarus-Black traced the passage and implementation of the Domestic Violence Act in Trinidad and Tobago, arguing that the passage of such a law, which was inspired in part by international women's movements, was "an important symbol of the 'modern' state."[68] What these and other similar examples illustrate is what legal historian Lauren Benton has argued: that across the wide geographic and temporal expanse of colonial endeavors and through the competing and complex motivations of various local, global, and imperial actors, "state law" (as opposed to "nonstate legal authorities") has come to be associated with "modern" (as opposed to "traditional").[69]

Significantly, however, what these texts also show is that despite the association of law with modernity and modernity with state sovereignty, the connection between law and sovereignty is not as definitionally certain as reigning theories suggest. To be sure, Hawaii's adoption of an Anglo-American legal system resulted *not* in its sovereignty but in its complete colonization. And Trinidad and Tobago's pursuit of "modern" laws has not changed the fact that it continues to appeal its cases to the Privy Council in London, throwing its claim to state sovereignty into question. Benton, too, points out that the development of modern state law occurred "even before the colonial state articulated claims to sovereignty."[70] In other words, although the development and acquisition of "modern" laws and legal regimes may be a necessary component of state sovereignty, these particular laws and legal regimes can—and do—lead to the development of something other than state sovereignty. It is this possibility that has offered the CCJ a window of opportunity. Specifically, this book shows how law—its making, its administration, its actors, its institutions, and its speech—can further a project of modernity at the same time it avoids a pursuit of sovereignty. In other words, and as the Court's work illustrates, something *other than* sovereignty might take shape within a place of and through the workings of "modern" law. It is this possibility, of being modern and non-sovereign, that invites an imagined future much brighter than the unattainable future of sovereignty.

Clearly, the CCJ's efforts to present itself as a modern court with modern laws for a modern region complicates its simultaneous objective of presenting itself as a Caribbean court representing "traditional" Caribbean values. As later chapters address, the Court holds itself out as a court for the people, informed by the history of the region, and representative of Caribbean customs. While the Court is less concerned with "customary law," it is fundamentally concerned with defining and depicting Caribbean culture in a way that can lend legitimacy to its efforts. Indeed, such citations to Caribbean "customs" operate similarly to continued references to "customary laws," as described by Sally Falk Moore. Moore has described how "customary laws"—as fabricated as they are through political deliberations and decisions and as altered as their operation might be through changed political and economic circumstances—are continually cited throughout the entire colonial and postcolonial process in Africa in ways that can lend legitimacy to the endeavor at hand, the case at issue, or the authority in charge.[71] The CCJ's work shows how the Court also turns to "customary" Caribbean culture as a means to garner support for its region-making efforts, in which "customs" are, much as Moore described, reworked and referenced thoughtfully and strategically. It is a turn to custom and tradition, in other words, that assists the Court in sidestepping or, at least, distracting from, sticky, divisory interstate politics and preferences. It is a turn to culture and cultural practices that does not threaten the modernity of the law the CCJ pursues.

Finally, it bears noting that this ethnography of the Court's region-making work can be read as a contemporary example of "law as process."[72] As I hope this introductory chapter established, the CCJ conducts its work on an almost impossibly complex terrain. It pursues a regional project in the face of unrelenting public doubt and unflagging support of the nation-state form; it seeks to establish a non-sovereign polity when the world seems to require sovereignty; it hopes to harness the modernity of law without the stateness that has come to be associated with it; and it endeavors to move the region forward, while still planting its roots in traditional Caribbeanness. To be sure, there is no possible way in which law, legal actors, a legal institution, or a legal system more broadly could single-handedly—no matter how determinedly—craft a Caribbean region to its own specifications. Instead, as can be seen through the CCJ's region-making endeavor, the Caribbean shapes the Court as much as the Court seeks to shape it.

Organization of Chapters

This book explores the CCJ's pursuit of a non-sovereign future by highlighting how the Court takes up various techniques of nation-state building in its efforts to craft a Caribbean region. Each of the remaining chapters, then, focuses on one technique of statecraft or nation building and interrogates how the Court indexes and adjusts it to meet its own regional objectives. Always motivated by the goal of constituting a modern non-sovereign Caribbean region, the CCJ, as will be evident, is not always intentional, knowing, or certain of outcome when it cites these techniques and tools of nation-state making. Those who work at the Court do not necessarily, in other words, realize that they are indexing tools of statecraft to build a region; rather, this is how I have analyzed what I heard, saw, read, participated in, and researched over the course of my relationship with the CCJ. What I also came to learn—and what is reflected in each chapter—is that the CCJ's efforts are imperfect at best. They might best be characterized as experimental.[73] There are failures, setbacks, fizzled-out plans, questionable decisions, unconvincing arguments, and bad ideas amid the Court's significant successes. In the period covered in this book, the region, therefore, never becomes more than a possibility, egged on by trials (literally), errors, and the Court's unrelenting pursuit of a regional future better than what sovereignty could (never) offer.

The chapter following this introduction, chapter 2, "A Myth," offers the first opportunity to see the Caribbean Court of Justice at work. It also presents a history of the Court, as recorded in textbooks and treaties, and provides a tour of the courthouse, an activity I participated in dozens of times following my initial visit. The tour takes visitors through the four floors of the courthouse and is accompanied by the narration of several staff members, who tell visitors about the genesis of this regional court and its truly Caribbean characteristics. It is a presentation of the region that highlights a spirit of regionalism, a "myth of origin," I call it, rather than a more textbook postcolonial history. Through this myth, the CCJ places itself at the teleological end point of a distinctly Caribbean timeline, one that transcends the year-by-year, historically recorded development of the Court. The chapter ends, though, with a hard reentry to earthly time; simply, the Court's myth of creation has not yet persuaded many people, who continue to place the CCJ within a postcolonial chronology replete with postcolonial disappointments.

INTRODUCTION 31

In addition to narratively constructing a transcendent Caribbean, the Court also endeavors to create a more grounded one. Chapter 3, "A Territory," takes up the state-making technique of carving out a landmass. The CCJ cites this process in its effort to etch a region from a space already claimed by numerous states. To show how the Court works to accomplish this, chapter 3 centers on a landmark case that moved through the CCJ during my time there. *Shanique Myrie and the State of Jamaica v. the State of Barbados* is a case in which a Jamaican woman had been denied entry to the State of Barbados, leading her to sue Barbados pursuant to her rights as a citizen of a CARICOM member state. In its handling of this case, which the Court knew from the moment it arrived would be newsworthy, the CCJ emphasized the interconnectivity of the region through its use of technology and its embrace of travel. Though thousands of miles separated the parties, attorneys, and judges, the region, I argue, was temporarily and repeatedly condensed and bound into a discernible territory through the technological possibilities afforded by videoconferencing. The CCJ also endeavored to draw the region together in a more physical way. The *Myrie* trial, in a first for the Court, was an itinerant event, which moved the CCJ, its full panel of seven judges, numerous staff members, and a mound of material items across the Caribbean to hear testimony in Jamaica and Barbados. These movements, I show, worked to emplace the region, ephemerally, in space and time. This ephemerality is where a regional territory deviates from the state model, offering a glimpse of an alternative to the rigidity of state territoriality.

Chapter 4 turns to the CCJ's work in gathering together "A People" who might understand this regional territory as their home, this regional myth as their story, and this regional court as their own. Indeed, despite having states as its membership, the Court very much sees itself as serving what it calls the "ordinary" people of the Caribbean. The problem, however, is that many ordinary people in the Caribbean do not share the Court's sentiments about the region. To some of them, in fact, the region does not even exist. In this chapter, then, I show how the CCJ interpellates a Caribbean public. Coined by philosopher Louis Althusser, "interpellation" gives a name to the way in which a person becomes a subject of state ideology.[74] Using Althusser as a starting point, I explore how the Court, as an agent of the region, works to interpellate a public as subjects of *regional* ideology through a variety of the CCJ's written materials and public activities. I ask whom, exactly, the Court intends to interpellate, how it goes about this work, and to what effect. Ultimately, I argue that the Court has not yet been able to interpellate the Caribbean public it desires, but it has whittled out an arena in which it has found success: the courtroom. Here, it holds the attention of a much more circumscribed audience that has already, to some extent, willingly subjectified itself to the region, having willingly brought itself into the courtroom. It is in this setting that the CCJ is able to stoke a fleeting regional affinity, which provides an ember for the development of a broader regional public.

Yet there is more to the Court's speech than interpellative hails, and in chapter 5, "A Language," I turn to other ways that the CCJ employs language in pursuit of its regional project. Those who work at the Court seem to intuitively understand language's constitutive potential, which has been used, both productively and destructively, to build nations, states, and sovereignties. Using many of the same linguistic techniques, the CCJ looks to language to build communities across national differences, to distinguish the Caribbean region from its British colonizer, and to provide an audible delineation between those who belong to the Court and those who do not. Significantly, what chapter 5 also shows is that amid this linguistic labor, which resembles the work that language does in the constitution of sovereign nation-states, the CCJ manages to assert the *non-sovereignty* of the region. It does so, again, through language. Instead of jealously guarding its authority over legal speech—or "juris-diction"—the Court devolves it, announcing to its (still incompletely formed) public a new relationship between the law, those who administer it, and the people.[75]

Chapter 5, then, contributes to this book's assertion that the Court is not interested in establishing a sovereign region, despite the seeming similarities between the CCJ's approach to region making and historical projects of sovereign nation-state building. The chapter also works to unsettle the presumed relationship between law and sovereignty because it is through the speaking of law that the CCJ manages to undermine the constitution of sovereignty rather than, as has been traditionally conceived, constitute sovereignty itself. Thus, while chapters 2, 3, and 4 provide examples of how the CCJ cites standard state-making tools to rough-cut the Caribbean region, chapter 5 offers a closer look at the way in which the Court works to deviate from the impossible model of sovereignty at the same time it pursues a region.

The final substantive chapter, chapter 6, "A Brand," interrogates how the CCJ has undertaken a marketing strategy that attempts to revalue the Caribbean of colonial creation (one marred by a reputation of incompetence and corruption) into the Caribbean of the Court's construction (one that is notable for being modern and professional). Branding, like the techniques central to earlier chapters, has become an increasingly prevalent tool in nation-state making. Much like in the sale of consumer goods, states, as several scholars have pointed out, also seek a market for their own wares, whether these be history, ethnicity, democracy, or a tax-free business environment.[76] By creating a brand that can represent its added value, a state aims to attract more consumers, so to speak. It can build the loyalty of a nation and even, or especially, the patronage of the global community. This, I show in chapter 6, is what the CCJ hopes to accomplish through its own branding efforts. The Court's brand, which marries high quality, modernity, and Caribbeanness, intends to persuade the region's public of the Court's legitimacy, but it is also, more significantly, an effort to rebrand the Caribbean region to the global market as one that is fully capable of producing high-quality jurisprudence of its own; the Caribbean, this brand suggests, should be taken seriously. Through this rebranding of the Caribbean, the CCJ works to locate the region alongside the modern nation-state, despite its non-sovereign status.

The book's concluding chapter, chapter 7, "A Region," addresses the ongoing nature of the CCJ's region-making work. The same arguments for and arguments against the CCJ continue to plague the Court some seventeen years after its opening. The caseload remains slim, and states remain reticent to join its appellate jurisdiction. Yet, the Court continues to display a somewhat baffling optimism. I suggest in the closing pages that this is because the region, like the nation-state, will never be a finished project, and the Court has come to learn this and weather the ups and downs. While there are certainly reasons to grow frustrated, those who work at the CCJ understand that the non-sovereign region remains a far more hopeful, equitable, and aspirational goal than a sovereign dream never meant to be realized. And so, I conclude, the ongoingness of the region allows for an inextinguishable possibility.

2

A Myth

Paul Gupta, who was at the time of our conversation a justice at the Court of Appeal in Trinidad and Tobago, enjoyed sharing his thoughts on Trinidadian culture, Caribbean society, and the advent of the Caribbean Court of Justice. He welcomed the opportunity, he told me, to contemplate things from an "anthropological point of view," since it allowed him to engage in the type of critical thinking that he missed from his days as a student of religion. I, too, enjoyed hearing his unique perspective on issues that I had, by the time I sat down with him, already discussed many times over during the course of my fieldwork with each of my interviewees. I found it refreshing to allow our conversation to ponder more esoteric topics, such as the meaning of justice, the constitution of values, and the role and risk of technology to Caribbean ways of life. Time passed quickly, therefore, as we rambled through our conversation, and when his secretary popped her head into his office to remind him of his next meeting, Justice Gupta and I both agreed that a second interview was in order. He was a "morning person," he told me. "I usually arrive at the court at half past five," he explained, which typically left him several available hours before his court business began. Whereas I balked at a 5:30 a.m. start time, I eagerly agreed to his next suggestion: 8:00 a.m. the next week.

Our second meeting progressed similarly. I had read the materials he sent with me from our first interview, had listened to the recording of our previous conversation, and came prepared with new topics and follow-up questions, many of which opened the door to unexpected avenues of exploration, such as a foray into mythology. "What are our myths?" he asked rhetorically, referring to Caribbean people:

What are our *real* myths? What are the people's real heroes? Who are they? Mythological heroes. We have no myth. Or if we have myth, it's underground, you know? But anthropologically, that should resonate with you. And I think that's the power. When you go back to America, this myth of the Founding Fathers, and they stood for freedom, and equality; that's mythological. Is it real? Is Abraham Lincoln real, or is he now mythological? What happened in those events? When you fought against Britain, what was that about, mythologically? *That* influences you today. When the Puritans came, etcetera, etcetera. . . . Every society lives out a myth. . . . No society can exist without myth. . . . But a question is, what is our foundation myth?

This is where I excitedly interjected, believing he had done some of the excavation required to unbury this underground myth and that he might share his discoveries with me: "That's what I don't know!" I exclaimed. Justice Gupta's response, however, was not the revelation that I had hoped for. Instead, giving me perhaps too much credit, he said, "But even as an anthropologist here, that you don't know, suggests that we don't even know ourselves." He pondered further:

It's underground. It's playing itself out. . . . We just need to find it. . . . If you unleash its power in a constructive way . . . then you have the potential to change a society, because you are tapping into the visceral myth that activates, that motivates, that unites, that stimulates. We don't have to do anything. The myth, the story, does it all.

As I had hoped and expected, I left Justice Gupta's office once again with much to think about. Was there a Caribbean myth of origin? And does it do it all, as he thought it might? In the example that he offered, the myth that "does it all" does it all in the context of a nation-state, specifically the United States. He asked me about the Founding Fathers, Abraham Lincoln, the Revolutionary War, and even the Puritans' arrival to a new land, suggesting that these myths and their heroes were critical to the shaping of the United States as it exists today. He made, through this example, an explicit analogy between the work that myth accomplishes in the foundation and sustenance of a nation-state and the work that it might accomplish for a region called the Caribbean. Can a Caribbean foundation myth, once unburied and unleashed in a constructive way, to draw from Justice Gupta's words, really do for the region what he believes it has done and continues to do for the state?

In this chapter, I show how those at the CCJ narrate a Caribbean myth of origin and work to imbue it with the powers that Justice Gupta attributed to the United States' foundational myths. Though he argued that "we don't have to do anything. The myth . . . does it all," I show how the Court, in fact, has to do quite a lot to create a convincing myth and counter an unpleasant past and an inconvenient present. And the myth that it ultimately comes to shape, I suggest, hinges on a timeless and effervescent spirit of Caribbeanness—a sort of proud, acolonial sense of togetherness that has made the region a region. I use "acolonial" deliberately to describe a Caribbean identity and verve that the CCJ seems to locate outside a colonial chronology. That is, instead of a Caribbean people and a Caribbean region that developed through the machinations of colonialism, the CCJ works to tell a story that celebrates a Caribbeanness that exists independent of this history. It is acolonial and time transcendent. No longer explicable through human time, it becomes mythological. This is different from the anticolonial spirit that motivated Caribbean nationalists in the 1930s, '40s, and '50s, as described by Adom Getachew.[1] The radical thinkers of that era, including several notable Caribbean intellectuals-cum-politicians, pursued a newly imagined *post*colonial approach to "world-making." That is, their endeavors, which I return to subsequently, found a footing *within* time—that is, after colonialism, whereas Caribbeanness points to a regional spirit that *transcends* time.

As the Court tells it, the CCJ itself is at once a product of this Caribbeanness and its present-day torchbearer. Indeed, it needs a Caribbean region that exists wholly independent of a colonial past to legitimize its own existence as a Caribbean court. And it is as a Caribbean court that the CCJ posits itself as filling the essential role of reflecting, serving, and carrying forward a uniquely Caribbean people and region. In short, according to the CCJ, the region could not exist without the Court nor the Court without the region, and both are founded on Caribbeanness. This myth has a temporal dimension to it. It is less about singular heroes and notable events and more about a persistent people insisting on their independent identity and region over time. Less about an identifiable villain and more about a tragic past, unflattering present, and tenuous future still tethered to colonialism. To be sure, it would be fundamentally unwise for the CCJ to villainize the Privy Council, given the Privy Council's still highly revered role across the Caribbean. The mythological battle, therefore, is against a chronology—not a court or a former colonizer—that has been well established in history books and cemented in living memory; it is against a timeline that does little to sustain the Caribbean qua *independent* region or the Court qua *Caribbean* court. This chapter, then, is about the crafting of what I call *Caribbeanness*, a sense of place and peoplehood that lifts both the Court and the region out of the problematic timeline that continues to hamper the regional endeavor and, relatedly, the CCJ's success. Caribbeanness represents the CCJ's rereading and recasting of the past–present–future in a hopeful light, rather than one of tragedy.[2]

National Myths

Justice Gupta's understanding of a nation-state founded in a powerful mythos uncannily echoes the work of Benedict Anderson, who argued that stories and storied people, the details of which have been cleansed, embellished, forgotten, reconstructed, or selectively retold, offer a foundation for a burgeoning nation.[3] Such stories help construct a sense of nationalism, which co-constitutes the idea of the nation as "loom[ing] out of an immemorial past and, still more important, glid[ing] into a limitless future."[4] They establish the nation, in other words, in perpetuity, existing more out of time than along the measured chronology of human time. Anderson was far from the first to make this suggestion. One hundred years before his contribution, for example, Ernest Renan delivered a lecture, since memorialized in a widely read essay, in which he spoke of the necessary manipulation of the past such that the brutal origins of national unity are cloaked by a far more palatable story or myth.[5] Renan trumpeted the importance of forgetting; people must forget inconvenient aspects of the past to accept the rationality and sensibility of the nation in which they now live.[6] While politics, race, religion, geography, and more have failed to bring people together, forgetting, revising, or mythologizing a past can succeed by providing a shared banner of a common "history" of success and sacrifice.[7] The rewriting of the past in this way—with a mythological artistry—is, according to Renan, critical to bridging the vast and very real differences between the people brought together under the name of nationhood.

Neither Renan nor Anderson specifically referred to the idea of a "myth of origin," but others have. Nations are not natural, God-given, or an inherent political destiny, though they might appear that way through the work of myths.[8] Rather, as Geoff Eley and Ronald Grigor Suny observe, "nationalism, which sometimes takes pre-existing cultures and turns them into nations, sometimes invents them, and often obliterates pre-existing cultures: *that* is a reality."[9] Liisa Malkki, for example, has described how "mythico-historical" narratives told by Hutu refugees created a past that was "in distinction to other pasts, thereby *heroizing* the past of the Hutu as 'a people' categorically distinct from others."[10] The mythical quality to these narratives, Malkki explains, is that the Hutu offered a moral order to the world, aligning themselves with good and the Tutsi who drove them out with evil. And the effect of such narratives was to constitute the Hutu as a morally right people and the *true* nation deserving of disputed land.

It is this idea of a naturalizing, moralizing, and even theologically derived myth that Justice Gupta asked after. He could see for himself how myths have helped unify disparate groups with troubled pasts, and he made the logical leap that they could similarly bring together the Caribbean. He also hinted at the problematic "reality" that myths were meant to address: what *really* happened, he asked, when the Puritans arrived or when colonists fought the British in a war of independence? He knew about the brutality of these events, yet at the same time, he understood the power of American Thanksgiving and the story of George Washington to constitute the United States. I take his question about the Caribbean's myth of origin, then, to at once celebrate the potential of a myth and recognize the dirty work that it must do. As it turns out, there is plenty that a Caribbean myth of origin must do: it must address the region's turbulent past and unimpressive present, as well as the CCJ's colonial entanglements and short existence.

The Caribbean's Past and Present

In 1492, as the familiar nursery rhyme—or myth—reminds us, Christopher Columbus, an Italian explorer, sailed the ocean blue. Funded by the Spanish crown, he departed from Spain and eventually landed on the shores of what is now known as the Bahamas before continuing on to other islands. This fateful journey in the late fifteenth century initiated a long, complicated, and cruel relationship between Europe, the Caribbean, and Africa and changed the geopolitics of the world forever. Countless historical texts relay this story, and numerous nations have found fodder for their own mythological stories of origin in these colonial beginnings.

While Spain made initial contact with the New World (as it was called by the Old World European metropoles), France, England, the Netherlands, and other European states were also soon lured to the lush shores of the Caribbean, and before long, the area was thoroughly colonized by Europeans who carved up the land into large plantations worked by enslaved Africans and devasted Indigenous populations through disease and war. For hundreds of years, the triangle that linked Europe to the Caribbean to Africa through the trade of slaves, sugar, and manufactured goods remained intact, only beginning to falter in the early nineteenth century when several governments began to ban the sale of human beings. Emancipation followed the end of the slave trade and led to an increase in the practice of indentured servitude—of, primarily, Indian and Asian laborers—in some parts of the Caribbean. In Trinidad and Tobago, for instance, more than 140,000 indentured workers arrived from India between 1845 and 1917, and 2,500 more arrived from South China between 1853 and 1866.[11] By the early to mid-nineteenth century, European tussles over Caribbean colonies had mostly quieted down, with Spain,

France, the Netherlands, and the United Kingdom holding tightly to their respective territories. The United States, too, was part of the Caribbean landscape, transforming a war of independence between Cuba and Spain into the Spanish-American War and gaining, as a result, (neo)colonial control over Cuba and Puerto Rico in 1898. By the time slavery, indentured labor, and the plantation economy came to an end, in the early twentieth century, colonialism had, unsurprisingly, made an indelible mark in the Caribbean, entrenching what have proved to be enduring structures of inequality, pervasive ideas of racialized incapacity, and sharply drawn territorial boundaries. As Deborah A. Thomas has shown across her work, the affects and effects of the plantation accrete, disperse, and eat away at the contemporary Caribbean, marking its present and shaping its futures.[12]

The UK's holdings were particularly vast and widely dispersed, and administering them proved to be an exhausting, expensive, and ever-evolving operation, as archival documents and historical texts indicate. One technique that was tried in various guises was to group islands together and administer them as one colony. The Leeward Islands colony, for example—which, for a time, was itself divided into two regions—consisted of Antigua, Barbuda, Montserrat, Saint Kitts, Nevis, Anguilla, and the Virgin Islands. When Dominica joined in 1871, the colony became the Federal Colony of the Leeward Islands. Eventually, the Leeward Islands were joined together with the Windward Islands and became the larger administrative unit known as the British West Indies. From the British West Indies came the West Indies Federation, inaugurated on January 3, 1958. It included ten territories: Jamaica, Antigua and Barbuda, Barbados, Trinidad and Tobago, Grenada, Montserrat, Saint Kitts/Nevis/Anguilla, Dominica, Saint Lucia, and Saint Vincent and the Grenadines.

For the most part, the move to a federation was guided, and even decided, by the British Colonial Office, which was eager to find an ever more cost-effective way of administering the islands and gently, eventually, easing them into independence. Yet the particular structure that the West Indies Federation took was a matter of tense negotiations between several key Caribbean intellectuals—"anticolonial worldmakers," Getachew calls them—who strived to confront the racialized hierarchies instilled through colonialism with newly thought alternatives to the nation-state that could challenge "the Eurocentric character of this international order."[13] These "worldmakers" did not reject notions of sovereignty but insisted that sovereignty must be more than a juridical claim; it must also be an equalization of legislative and economic power.[14] To thinkers such as Eric Williams of Trinidad and Tobago, a federation would help accomplish just this. It would allow small Caribbean states to, as Getachew puts it, "evade the economic dependence inherent in the global economy by organizing regional institutions that were egalitarian and redistributive."[15]

While there was some coalescence among Caribbean leaders as to the economic utility of a federation, there was far less agreement regarding the balance of powers between the federation and its member states. While Williams advocated for a strong, centralized federal union that could create and sustain a "Federal Market," others, such as Norman Manley of Jamaica, argued for a looser federal model—a confederation—that could better accommodate the independence of new states and respect their national efforts to develop and modernize. This difference in opinions racked the federation before it even began; the 1956 federal constitution was up for argument and revision almost immediately after the formation of the West Indies Federation in 1958, and by 1961, political infighting and a bitterly fought compromise that leaned heavily toward Manley's vision ultimately resulted in Jamaica's withdrawal from the federation (to Manley's surprise). Jamaica soon thereafter declared independence and was followed within the year by Trinidad and Tobago, a series of consequential events that led to the demise of the West Indies Federation by 1962. Indeed, the dream of a different future that, through a regional governance structure, could escape the "informal domination" of the postcolonial world came to a quick, ugly end. If not completely destroyed, this vision of Caribbean modernity and the lofty goals of Williams and others had been embarrassingly deflated.

It is hardly surprising, then, that what has followed the West Indies Federation carries with it the weight of this disappointment and harbors the hesitation and doubts that it triggered. Specifically, a series of treaty-based economic integration attempts have followed the fall of the West Indies Federation, each with minimal success. The first of these was the Caribbean Free Trade Agreement (CARIFTA), which was formed in 1965 by four Caribbean states and dependent territories and joined in 1968 by seven additional states and territories. However, CARIFTA, like the West Indies Federation, also did not last long. By 1973, with the signing of the Treaty of Chaguaramas, the Caribbean Community and Common Market (CARICOM) had already replaced it. CARICOM created an association of thirteen states and territories within the West Indies and was intended to increase economic integration and cooperation between its member states. Progress, though, was slow, and by 1989 the heads of government of the member states reached a decision to revise the Treaty of Chaguaramas to establish the CARICOM Single Market and Economy (CSME) in a revitalized effort to integrate the region's economies. The revision process was also quite slow, and it was not until 2001 that the Revised Treaty of Chaguaramas was signed and the CSME was created. As I describe in the next section, the establishment of the CCJ was contained within the Revised Treaty.

The rapid transformations (and dissolutions) of the West Indies Federation and CARIFTA had been replaced by the sluggish—nearly imperceptible—activity of CARICOM and the CSME. Nearly fifty years since CARICOM's creation and more than twenty years since the CSME was established, both the Caribbean public and Caribbean academics offer less-than-salubrious opinions of these endeavors. Some of the most biting criticisms I cover in chapter 4. Here, I mention that discussions of CARICOM regularly elicited eye rolls and chuckles when brought up during the dinner club meetings I was part of during my fieldwork. This group of professional Trinidadian women enjoyed regaling me with stories of CARICOM's futile and failed efforts at open trade within the region. One memorable example was offered by Amelia, who worked for Trinidad and Tobago's Standards Commission. According to her, Jamaica had recently rejected the importation of toilet paper manufactured in Trinidad and Tobago because of rumors that it was causing urinary tract infections and other ailments. This sort of interstate "tit for tat" undergirded by fierce national allegiances and fanned by questionably accurate rumors, everyone agreed amid their eye rolls and laughter, was what made the CSME an ineffective endeavor.

These humorous dinnertime stories about the inefficacy of the CSME were more profoundly echoed by leading academics in the region. Norman Girvan, a widely respected expert on regionalism and economics in the Caribbean and the invited keynote speaker for the Caribbean Association of Judicial Officers' Third Biennial Conference in 2013, offered a scathing review of the CSME's progress:

> In short, 24 years after the CSME was first launched, it is not even close to completion. More to the point, we [do] not know *when* it will be completed. Progress has slowed to a virtual standstill; the momentum has been lost; interest has waned. It is not yet officially dead; but it certainly appears to be comatose.[16]

By any stretch, this is not a positive review of the region's present circumstances.[17]

Saddled with a violent colonial past, encumbered by the failure of the West Indies Federation, and troubled by a torpid present, the Anglophone Caribbean region offers little to celebrate when it comes to the reigning stories of its creation. The fact that a region can be identified at all is not because of God's will, political destiny, or a natural teleology. Instead, what underlies this region as a discernible entity—what carved out these particular islands and grouped them together—was, according to the histories most often repeated, the ugly process of colonialism, which was later supplanted by deliberate and, ultimately, disappointing projects of economic regionalism, neither of which lay the groundwork for a pride-fueled regional unity.

The Court's Past and Present

The Caribbean Court of Justice is linked to both the region's past and its complicated legal relationship to the United Kingdom in the present. For much of the colonial period, Britain's Caribbean territories used a three-tiered judicial system composed of domestic trial courts, the West Indian Court of Appeal (which served, as the name suggests, the broader West Indies), and the Judicial Committee of the Privy Council in London (often referred to as the JCPC or simply the Privy Council) as the final court of appeal. The Privy Council filled this role for all of Britain's colonies around the world, and as these colonies slowly gained independence, they, in most cases, slowly delinked from the Privy Council. Not so in the Caribbean.

Indeed, it appears that an alteration to the region's relationship to the Privy Council was never seriously contemplated throughout the Caribbean's experiment with federalism or much of its planning for independence. Independence conversations and considerations in Trinidad and Tobago, for example, worried far more about protecting the impartiality of the legal system and warding off possibilities for political meddling, both of which required, according to the Secretary of State for the Colonies in 1962, the entrenchment of the right to appeal to the Privy Council in Trinidad's independence constitution.[18] An entrenchment that did, in fact, happen in Trinidad and Tobago and elsewhere throughout the Anglophone Caribbean, as territories began to achieve independence.

Although the early 1970s enjoyed a brief flirtation with the idea of delinking from the Privy Council, a proposal made by both regional and state-level actors, the idea found little support among the general public and was more or less abandoned by 1974.[19] It was not picked up again until the late 1980s and had shifted focus significantly. The concern for CARICOM heads of government by this point was less the ongoing relationship with British law and more the need for a court that could help advance the economic and cooperative goals of the Treaty of Chaguaramas. CARICOM, after all, had made very little progress, and the heads of government were eager to make changes that would reinvigorate regional economic integration, still not ready to fully let go of the world-making aspirations that led to the West Indies Federation. To this end, in 1989, they reached a decision to revise the Treaty of Chaguaramas and mandated the formation of the West Indian Commission to conduct research and generate proposals in advance of the revision.

The West Indian Commission's nearly six hundred-page final report, *Time for Action*, was presented to CARICOM in 1992. In five of these pages, it addressed the issue of a regional court:

> We believe that [the] time is at hand for establishing the Caribbean Court of Appeal—what in an integration context we would prefer to call the CARICOM Supreme Court . . . with both a general appellate jurisdiction and an original regional one. . . . It is fundamental to the process of integration itself.[20]

The commission argued that this proposed court could further the development of the region in multiple ways by providing easier access to justice, developing Caribbean case law, fostering confidence through the appointment of West Indian jurists, and deepening regional integration by interpreting the Treaty of Chaguaramas.[21] Much, in other words, was promised by this single court.

Time for Action, in conjunction with the ongoing revision of the Treaty of Chaguaramas, appears to have been the final push to begin serious planning of a regional court, and some nine years later, in 2001, coinciding with the advent of the CSME, the heads of government of twelve Caribbean states signed the Agreement Establishing the Caribbean Court of Justice (see table 1). The Agreement established the Court with two distinct jurisdictions: an original jurisdiction to which all signatory states were automatically subject and an appellate jurisdiction for only those member states that took the necessary steps to delink with the Privy Council. While the original jurisdiction would handle claims deriving from CARICOM treaties and agreements—acting as a truly regional court deciding regional issues, the appellate jurisdiction provided a replacement for the Privy Council—serving as the highest appellate court addressing issues arising from individual state legal systems. This is a jurisdictional division of labor that leads the Court to describe itself as "two courts in one."[22]

In 2005, the Caribbean Court of Justice, long in the making, finally opened the doors to its courthouse seated in Port of Spain, Trinidad and Tobago. At the time of its opening, two states—Barbados and Guyana—had acceded to its appellate jurisdiction. By the time I began my research in 2012, one more had joined: Belize. And in 2015, a fourth acceded: Dominica. As of mid-2022, no other states have made the switch from the Privy Council to the CCJ.[23]

As should be evident, the CCJ's past is integrally entwined with both the Caribbean's ongoing relationship to the Privy Council and the region's (mis)

TABLE 1 The Caribbean Court of Justice has automatic original jurisdiction over the member states that signed the Agreement Establishing the Caribbean Court of Justice in 2001. It has appellate jurisdiction only over those states that have acceded to this jurisdiction. Those states are listed in the second column, with the year of their accession in parentheses.

Signatories to the Agreement Establishing the Caribbean Court of Justice	Signatories to the Agreement That Have Acceded to Appellate Jurisdiction of the CCJ	Full Members of CARICOM That Did Not Sign the Agreement
Antigua and Barbuda	Barbados (2005)	The Bahamas
Barbados	Belize (2010)	Haiti
Belize	Dominica (2015)	Montserrat
Dominica	Guyana (2005)	
Grenada		
Guyana		
Jamaica		
Saint Christopher [Saint Kitts] and Nevis		
Saint Lucia		
Saint Vincent and the Grenadines		
Suriname		
Trinidad and Tobago		

adventures in economic integration, in the form of the West Indies Federation, CARICOM, and the CSME (from which the CCJ sprang). Further, its current existence is marred by brevity; at the time I conducted research there, the CCJ had been open for a mere seven years. For a court, these problems of time create a host of unique challenges.

The CCJ, for instance, has had little time to create its own legal authority. Relatively few cases have been decided by the Court—an average of ten appellate jurisdiction cases and one original jurisdiction case per year throughout the Court's first ten years—resulting in a limited body of its own case law, which is, critically, the currency of authority in common-law jurisdictions, such as those of most of the CCJ's member states.[24] It has also had little time to establish reliable and predictable patterns and practices or prove its ability to outlast challenges, making it a relatively unknown and untested institution in the eyes of potential Court users.[25] During my time at the Court, for example, I witnessed the occurrence of the first judicial retreat, the rollout of the first five-year strategic plan, the pomp and circumstance of the first itinerant trial, and the excitement over the first electronically filed court documents, which were celebrated with a champagne toast by the judges and the Registry staff. Similarly, the judges regularly decided issues related to evidence, procedure, and use of law that had never previously been addressed by the Court. So many firsts underscored the human hand involved in the Court's work.

Instead of the illusion that law was merely *enforced*, a lack of time exposed, quite crudely, how law was clearly *made*.[26]

Indeed, the making of the Court was well within living memory, posing another significant challenge. My interviewees were able to give me the names and contact information of many of the founding architects, some of whom I was then able to interview. The Court, in other words, was easily recognized as an institution made by men, who, as I learned in my research, had their own motivations and inspirations for supporting the Court, having largely come of age during the rise and fall of the West Indies Federation, the wave of independence, and the initial experiments with regional economic integration attempts. Their still fresh fingerprints made it difficult for the CCJ to claim that it was an objective "rule of law" institution rather than a "rule of men" creation that brought with it a palpable agenda still linked to a regional dream of decades past. And in the Caribbean, even the slightest suggestion of human interference can be damaging. This is a region, recall, where there has long been tremendous concern over the meddling of politicians; several of my interlocutors at the CCJ half jokingly and half seriously claimed that an accusation of corruption and a resultant fracas within government took place "every nine days" in Trinidad. At times, the national courts have even been implicated in the scandal, leading to persistent suspicion that sitting governments and "big men" around the region had the ear of the courts.[27] The CCJ has not been immune to these allegations, whether founded or not, and the fact that many of the people involved in the founding of the Court are not only still alive but also remain prominent players in legal circles added fuel to the ongoing fires.

A related challenge is that the CCJ had not yet earned the *faith* of the region. Different from trust, faith is not something wholly rooted in time but in timelessness—a quality that is far more closely related to mythology than history. Unlike, for instance, the economy, which is understood to be created, managed, and manipulated by humans, law and justice tend to be associated with a more "mystical foundation"[28] that is rooted in faith and belief rather than in logic and rationality.[29] It is more readily understood as having a divine origin, and it is this that lends law, at least in part, its authority.[30] Because it is understood as coming from and existing in a time-space that is different from that of the time-space of human life, law exists (or should exist) beyond the reach of human interference.[31] This sense of timelessness and the faith it might engender, though, cannot be easily achieved when the establishment of a court is a recent event linked closely to a manmade economic endeavor, such as the CCJ's own inception. Law can be seen to made at the CCJ because of its newness, pulling the curtain back on its mysticism and seeming divinity.[32]

Finally, the omnipresence of the Privy Council—a tribunal that has been around "since Jesus was a little boy," as a friend at the CCJ liked to joke—only exacerbates the problematic newness of the CCJ.[33] While the Court has struggled to attract a faithful following, the Privy Council has enjoyed the people's faith for centuries, and it shows no sign of actively dispersing its flock. While it has encouraged Anglophone Caribbean states to establish and use a court of their own, it has never stated that it would actually require these states to leave its jurisdiction. Rather, the Privy Council has been sending mixed messages on this very point. In early 2005, just months prior to the opening of the CCJ, the Privy Council overturned an effort by the Jamaican government to join the appellate jurisdiction of the CCJ, agreeing with the Opposition's argument that the proper procedure had not been followed. Since then, Jamaica has not yet been able to muster enough support to accede to the appellate jurisdiction through the procedural avenues outlined in that decision. In 2006, one year after the CCJ's opening, the Privy Council traveled to the Bahamas, at the request of the Bahamian judiciary, for its first itinerant sitting in 170 years. It did so again in 2007, in 2009, and yet again in 2017. It has visited the Bahamas more times, in fact, than it has any other location outside the United Kingdom.[34] These frequent and continued interactions with the Caribbean suggest that the Privy Council is happy to continue to serve the region, as it has done for hundreds of years prior. Its timeless presence in the region established by an incredibly deep history and unforeseeably long future painfully highlights the precarity of the CCJ's own existence.

Considered together, the region's problematic past, the Court's complicated entanglements, and both of their unsettled present existences bring the Caribbean's future and the CCJ's raison d'être into question. The CCJ, after all, depends on the existence of the region for its very being. It is the CCJ, then, that turns to myth, which has the potential to lift both the Court and the region from their problematic timelines and place them in another temporality altogether: an acolonial Caribbeanness.[35] The Court's mythmaking work, which I turn to next, is subtle and largely unintentional. To be sure, those who work at the Court would not describe what they do as making a myth. To them, they are merely presenting the relevant history of the Court.

An Introduction to Caribbeanness

It was eight o'clock on a November morning, and, while other CCJ staff members slowly arrived, the entire Court Protocol and Information unit—Dr. Williams, Serena, and Diondra—had already been at the Court for some time. They had met, welcomed, and ushered fourteen of the twenty expected attorneys (the remaining six sent their apologies for running late) up to the first-floor courtroom in preparation for their planned tour. This visit, like other scheduled visits, had been highly anticipated by Dr. Williams and his team because opportunities to tell the story of the Court directly to the public did not arise too frequently. When there were visitors, therefore, the CCJ mobilized many resources and personnel. Depending on the size of the expected group and its importance, as determined by Dr. Williams, the chief protocol and information officer, the impending arrival of a tour group catalyzed a variety of activities in the days and hours leading up to the visit. For larger groups, numbering more than roughly ten, the Protocol and Information unit organized a reception of finger foods, juices, coffee, and tea that would be served at the conclusion of the visit. For more important groups, such as law school student associations and other assemblages of attorneys or politicians that could bring cases to the Court in the future, Dr. Williams prepared a PowerPoint presentation that preceded the tour and often recruited several CCJ judges to participate in a question-and-answer session that took place after. And, for all groups, regardless of size or importance, the Information, Communications, and Technology staff at the Court delivered a courtroom technology demonstration, and the Protocol and Information unit distributed neatly compiled CCJ-branded gift bags containing a variety of informational materials. Every visit also included a guided tour of the courthouse.

Today's visit by twenty attorneys qualified as both large and important and thus necessitated the full array of activities, beginning with a PowerPoint presentation. After finding their seats in the empty courtroom, the visitors silenced their cell phones and quieted their conversations, allowing Dr. Williams to begin his presentation. As was usual for him on tour days, his formal black suit was adorned with a CCJ-branded tie and a small CCJ lapel pin (a devotion to the Court's branding that I return to in chapter 6). He had a background in teaching before beginning a profession in court protocol, first with the Trinidad and Tobago Supreme Court, then with the CCJ. In fact, he had worked at the CCJ since its inception, and he knew a tremendous amount about the Court and had, like the Court's other inaugural employees, played a significant role in the character of the Court as it exists today. Dr. Williams was perfectly suited for his job.

His presentation, entitled "The Caribbean Court of Justice—One People, One Court," began the work of extricating the CCJ from its problematic timeline and introducing the audience to a far more hopeful, prideful, and even innate sense of the Caribbean. This began within the first moments of his presentation with a slide covering the "Genesis of the CCJ," a topic about which Dr. Williams was "not going to go into full detail," since, as he told the audience, he was sure "that most of you are aware of all of this." He moved through this slide accordingly, explaining quickly and in one breath:

> At the 22nd meeting of the Heads of Government in 2001, as a result of which the Treaty of Chaguaramas, which dated from 1974, was revised and updated to become what we call the RTC—the *Revised* Treaty of Chaguaramas. Contained within the Revised Treaty was the structure for the CSME—the CARICOM Single Market and Economy—in which the Caribbean Court of Justice is the lynch pin.

Following this dizzying account of dates and treaties, Dr. Williams paused briefly and delivered the following sentence much more deliberately:

> Make sure you understand this because it is the truth; it is a truism—it is not something I am saying because I work here. No CCJ, no CSME. Very simple.

What Dr. Williams managed to accomplish, though, was far from simple. Though he suggested that the creation of the Court was common knowledge, his telling of its past managed to obscure its origins.[36] It involved a confusing tacking back and forth in time, a reference to a conference, a couple of treaties, acronyms, and acronyms within acronyms. Following the timeline was difficult, but understanding his references was likely not; almost certainly, these Trinidadian attorneys would have recognized these conferences, treaties, and abbreviations, all of which pertain to the Caribbean: the "Heads of Government," to which he referred, are the Caribbean Community heads of government; the "Treaty of Chaguaramas," as well as the "*Revised* Treaty" are treaties signed by Caribbean states; and the "CSME" is the Caribbean Community Single Market and Economy. The Court of Justice, of course, is also Caribbean. Through this repetition, it would have been clear to these attorneys that the CCJ was thoroughly Caribbean in its origin. Its exact date of origin or its development over time, on the other hand, did not come across quite as clearly. His narration, in other words, suggested that what was truly important to know about the Court was the not the sequence of events or the dates of inauguration, but the CCJ's utter Caribbeanness, a quality that could explain the existence of the Court without clear reference to time. It is telling, incidentally, that he called this a story of the Court's "genesis," suggesting a more spiritual origin, rather than a telling of its history, thereby acknowledging its human creation.

Dr. Williams's account also gestured toward the future indispensability of the CCJ with his truism, "No CCJ, no CSME." The CSME was intended to bind the region together in an economically cohesive market and economy that could sustain the competitive onslaught brought on by globalization.

Guiding the idea of the CSME was the belief that the small island states of the Caribbean would face sure economic ruin unless they bound together, and Dr. Williams's memorable one-liner played into this doomsday scenario: No CCJ meant no CSME, and no CSME meant no viable Caribbean. To be able to make this argument, however, Dr. Williams had to switch which endeavor depended on the other for its existence. As described earlier in the chapter, the creation of the CCJ is, in fact, subsumed within a treaty that is dedicated to the establishment of the CSME.[37] If the CSME had never been created, it is questionable whether the CCJ, in either its original or appellate jurisdictions, would have ever come to fruition. But, as also detailed earlier, the CSME is not exactly the shooting star to which the CCJ would want to hitch its fate. It has met unceasing delays, roadblocks, and hesitations and has not yet led to the hoped-for integrated economic region.[38] Rather than cede its fate to the fading light of the CSME, it is far better for the CCJ to have it the other way around, to position itself as the guarantor of a Caribbean future and the protector of Caribbean people.

The emphasis on the CCJ's Caribbean origins and its position at the helm of the region continued throughout Dr. Williams's presentation and prepared the audience for the final segment of the slideshow: "What the UK Has to Say." It is here, for the first time, that he acknowledges the ongoing colonial history that the region must confront, but he does so in a way that distinguishes the Caribbean from the colonizers that, in many ways, coalesced it. He clicked forward to the first slide in this section and read from the quotation on the slide using his best British accent, distancing, by doing so, his Caribbean English from its colonial heritage:

> *It is obvious that, from the mere distance of those colonies and the immense variety of matters arising in them, foreign to our habits and beyond the scope of our knowledge, any judicial tribunal in this country*—which is the United Kingdom [Dr. Williams parenthetically reminded the tour group]—*must of necessity be an extremely inadequate court of redress.*

Returning to his Trinidadian lilt, Dr. Williams emphasized, "The Lord Chancellor of England said that in 1833, 180 years ago, but we're still up under their . . . fill in the blank." The audience chuckled, comprehending his reference to the almost embarrassing, undoubtedly awkward, and oddly anachronistic situation of the former British colonies of the Caribbean: for 180 years, according to the quote that he had read, the British have been pointing out the inconvenience and incoherence of serving a "foreign" people in the courts of the United Kingdom and, yet, and this was the uncomfortable joke, little has changed.

What made this joke even funnier and more uncomfortable was that the British, according to Dr. Williams's presentation, never budged from this position. They have long realized that the Caribbean and its people were fundamentally different. He moved to his next slide. "This is more recent," he pointed out. According to this slide, in 2003, Lord Hoffman, a member of the Privy Council, had also expressed the limitations of that tribunal in administering justice to the Caribbean, a distant and foreign locale. Then, another slide—even more recent, but without a date—that included a quote from the then-current president of the Supreme Court of England, who expressed his frustration with the amount of time that that court had to spend on Privy Council matters. And then a fourth and a fifth slide, all reiterating the basic sentiment that the UK law lords and legal academics found the Caribbean's continued utilization of the Privy Council to be nothing short of a nuisance. The message, as presented by Dr. Williams, was clear: the United Kingdom did not want the burden of deciding Caribbean cases, never wanted this burden, and would likely, and with good reason, shed itself of this burden in the future. After all, why should this British court be deciding the cases of these Caribbean islands? The suggestion, of course, was that it made no sense at all, and that the CCJ was positioned to right this wrong on behalf of the region; it was a uniquely Caribbean solution to a Caribbean problem. This Caribbean court could best serve these Caribbean people, who are, as even the British recognized, a distinct population living in a notably distant group of islands. This assertion of fundamental difference between the Caribbean and Britain helped introduce the idea of a Caribbean that somehow existed devoid of colonial influence. Dr. Williams's presentation ended with this suggestion lingering in the air.

Caribbeanness across "All-Times"

The emphasis on a region that exists independent of colonial influence continued through the attorneys' tour of the courthouse. So did the obfuscation of a clear chronology. Following Dr. Williams's presentation, the attorneys were divided between Serena and Diondra. Serena, whose group I joined, was an expert at what she did, combining professionalism with charisma to produce an informative and entertaining tour. When I met her in 2012, she had been employed by the Court for several years, first as an intern in the Public Education unit and then as a full-time customer service officer within Court Protocol and Information. Her duties had always involved interfacing with the public, a job for which she was perfectly suited. She had mastered the Court's story and could regale visitors with the basic details, the complex

FIGURE 3. A display case in the lobby of the CCJ's Office of the Registry, 2012. Photograph by author.

organization, and the fascinating biographies that constituted the CCJ. I liked Serena tremendously, and I think that visitors did, too.

After exchanging brief pleasantries with the attorneys assigned to her, Serena guided them back to the ground floor of the courthouse and into the Office of the Registry, located just as one enters the building's front door. There, she offered a brief introduction to the workings of the Registry and directed the attorneys' attention to several exhibits located within its lobby (see figure 3). She explained, "Now, a lot of people think that the idea of setting up a regional final court of appeal was a recent idea." She continued:

> *But* we have a letter . . . from as far back as 1901. It was written in the *Jamaican Gleaner* in the Letters to the Editor suggesting that the Privy Council, because of the distance from the colonies, they would have been too far to really dispense true justice. And the author suggested that we set up our own regional final court of appeal.

As the attorneys absorbed this information, she went on:

> In 1970, at a conference of heads of government, the idea for a regional final court of appeal was put forward. However, it was not until 1989 that the heads

of government agreed to establish the court. In 1999, Trinidad and Tobago announced that we would house the court here. And the heads of government approved the Agreement Establishing the Court. In 2001, the Agreement was signed.

With a wave of her hand, Serena led her audience's gaze to a series of photographs displayed on the walls. She explained:

> On the walls we basically have a pictorial depicting the establishment of the court from the very inception of the signing of the Treaty of Chaguaramas. What I find interesting about this is that even as far back as the public consultations, you see people who are involved in the court up until now.

Serena pointed out a couple of familiar faces in the photographs, including the then-president of the CCJ and one of its founding architects, and allowed the visitors a minute or so to look at the pictures. While highlighting the still living and breathing creators of the Court might seem contrary to its interest in erasing its human origins, there was something important about the people in these photos. They were Caribbean people—nearly all Afro-Caribbean—who were, in some cases, flanked by the flags of Caribbean states. Moreover, some of the photographs worked to cloak their own age. Three black-and-white photos under the label "The Beginning" helped bolster Serena's claim to the CCJ's deep history. Two of these photos, as the labels indicated, depicted the "Signing of the Treaty of Chaguaramas," an event that took place in 1973, while the third photo showed the "Signing of the Agreement Establishing the Caribbean Court of Justice," which took place, as Serena had just told the group, in 2001. This photo, too, is displayed in black-and-white, which imparted to it an air of antiquity (see figure 4).

What is also notable about Serena's narration of the genesis of the CCJ is that it added different dates and documents to those listed by Dr. Williams, but, like his story, Serena's explanation pointed to the Caribbean energy, inspiration, and efforts that led to the creation of the Court: a letter to a Caribbean newspaper, the actions of Caribbean heads of government, and the signing of Caribbean agreements by Caribbean actors. As the tour progressed, and she led the attorneys through the four floors of the courthouse, the Caribbean-inflected narrative continued. Serena highlighted the deliberate Caribbean character of the Court, which included walls painted in pastel "Caribbean colours," such as the lime-green Registry lobby, and decorated with artwork by Caribbean painters; a Caribbean-wide children's art competition; a Caribbean law school moot court competition; the second largest collection of Caribbean law books (the largest being housed at the University of the West Indies at Cave Hill law school in Barbados); the Caribbean nationalities of the staff and judges; and

A MYTH 53

FIGURE 4. A poster featuring black-and-white photographs of the Court's "Beginning." The photographs depict the "Signing of the Treaty of Chaguaramas" (1973, *top and bottom left*) and the "Signing of the Agreement Establishing the Caribbean Court of Justice" (2001, *right*). Photograph by author; permission to include images by an unknown photographer granted by Caribbean Court of Justice.

so on (much of this I return to in chapter 6). This Court, as it was presented to this tour group, practically overflowed with Caribbeanness, a point that Dr. Williams later reinforced: this Court, he stated, "wasn't anybody else's idea. It was *ours*."

After completing the tour, Serena returned her visitors to the courtroom, where they learned about the CCJ's impressive technology before moving to a conference room for their question-and-answer session with several judges. Among other topics, the judges ruminated on the Court's future. While there might not yet be a substantial caseload in the original jurisdiction, one judge thought that members of the "younger generation" had been better trained in international law and would be more willing and eager to make a name for themselves by bringing significant original jurisdiction cases. He noted as well that "things are picking up . . . especially in the appellate jurisdiction." Another judge predicted a surge in cases once Trinidad and Jamaica joined the appellate jurisdiction, a prospect he treated as unassailable fact. Overall, the attorneys heard forecasts for a brilliant future—a future that sprang from the initiative and cleverness of Caribbean attorneys, like themselves, and states, like the one they represented—told to them by the most senior people at the Court. The future was *theirs*, just as the Court was, too.

The morning's events ended with a small reception. The attorneys, judges, and several CCJ staff members mingled and chatted informally over snacks and tea. And four hours after they first sat down to hear Dr. Williams's presentation, the attorneys were at last preparing to leave the Court. As they collected their items and expressed their gratitude, Serena, Dr. Williams, and Diondra distributed a gift bag to each visitor. The gift bags contained the standard tourgoer fare: copies of several of the treaties mentioned during the visit, the Court's annual report, a judicial code of ethics, and a couple of informational booklets. These informational booklets offered more information on the history of the CCJ. Whereas one identified the 1970 Heads of Government Conference as the key date of origin, the other, also noting the Heads of Government Conference, placed the initial suggestion of the Court decades earlier, in 1947, with a meeting of West Indian governors.[39] These two booklets, in other words, offered the attorneys more dates and different trajectories regarding the formation of the CCJ. By the time the attorneys left the building, therefore, they had been exposed to at least four different renditions of the Court's beginning, multiple dates of origin, and a string of treaties, agreements, and conferences, and it remained entirely unclear which of the four stories was correct.

Providing the "right" story, however, was not the broader objective of the tour. The CCJ staff certainly could have scripted its PowerPoints, tour talks, and booklets such that they told identical stories with fact-checked dates and figures, but they had not. They provided, instead, a multiplicity of dates, which, though almost certainly unintentional, had the effect of muddying the Court's chronology, making it difficult to trace the CCJ's beginning to a particular time, place, person, or project. Indeed, as the Court presents it, the location in time of the CCJ's origin is not terribly significant. What matters— what is most relevant—is the Court's foundation in the Caribbean people, its leaders, its drive for autonomy, its indefatigable spirit, and its sense of place, something I call together "Caribbeanness." I also stress the point that Caribbeanness exists distinct from time; it is something, as the CCJ suggests through its tours and presentations, that has been present in "all-times."[40] And it is this Caribbeanness that catalyzed the creation of the Court and continues to guide, animate, and authorize its actions, as well as permeate its very existence. The Court, in turn, safeguards and showcases the Caribbeanness that made it.[41]

Transcending Time

It is important to note that the CCJ does not whitewash the colonial experience or disavow the troubles of prior regionalization attempts. It also, unlike the "worldmakers" who contributed to the making of the West Indies Federation, does not seek to locate the region in a postcolonial chronology.[42] Rather, it works to displace the region, and the region's court, from this timeline through a time-transcendent notion of Caribbeanness that exists independent of this well-known history and the predicaments of the postcolonial present. The problem is that this history—and the present that it has led to—is difficult to overlook, despite the CCJ's efforts.

Six weeks after the attorneys' visit to the Court, I met with Cynthia in her downtown office in Port of Spain. She is a twentysomething Trinidadian litigator who had been practicing law for three years, and in that time, she had already appeared before the CCJ in an original jurisdiction matter. She had also previously participated in two CCJ-hosted moot court competitions for Caribbean law schools and had been on more than one tour of the courthouse, including the one described in this chapter. She believed in the Court and its objectives, and she had been veritably steeped in its mythology.

Despite this intimate familiarity with the CCJ, Cynthia had not adopted the Court's narrative of itself. Rather than understanding the Court as the product and progenitor of Caribbeanness, she sees the CCJ as being integrally related to the economic regionalization endeavor. She positions the Court, that is, firmly in a familiar chronological timeline. To her, therefore, the CCJ is primarily an economic tribunal created to accomplish tangible goals. Its overarching objective, she explained to me, is "to revitalize CARICOM and to establish the rule of law in the operation of the CSME." Cynthia fully understands that this is not an enviable charge, given the poor performances and flagging reputations of CARICOM and CSME. Despite being a firm believer in economic regionalization, she acknowledges that there has been "consistent inactivity" over the past forty years of CARICOM, and she recognizes that the CCJ's future, as far as its original jurisdiction is concerned, rests more in the hands of private entities that might bring cases than in the state signatories that have, so far, remained mostly inactive. For the Court to fulfill its mandate, Cynthia argued, "it's really going to require an invested interest from private persons and attorneys in general who are willing to represent them in the original jurisdiction . . . which is sorely lacking." Her forecast, delivered with a shrug of her shoulders and a shake of her head, hardly resembled that of the CCJ, and it certainly had little to do with any sort of emotion associated with the Caribbean. Instead, it is starkly pragmatic, grounded, and based on the documented history of regionalization. Private interests, economic concerns, and real people who are willing to take a risk by going to the relatively untested CCJ are what will determine the fate of the CCJ, according to Cynthia.

Then there is the appellate jurisdiction. Like Dr. Williams's presentation, Cynthia's story also noted the Privy Council's eagerness to rid itself of the burden of deciding Caribbean cases. "They have been extremely careless with our jurisprudence," she said, "because they are tired of coddling us." She also similarly saw the great opportunity afforded by having a court of one's own: "We would lose this inferiority complex that we've been carrying around for a long time. . . . We would gain self-confidence; we would gain a certain degree of international prestige; and we would gain autonomy in how we conduct our affairs." Despite these possibilities and the seeming recognition of an "us" composed of Caribbean people, Cynthia remained circumspect on when or whether Trinidad and Tobago would accede to the Court's appellate jurisdiction. Attributing Trinidad's failure to join the appellate jurisdiction of the Court to "political confusion" and calling it "very embarrassing that Trinidad hasn't been able to get its act together," Cynthia stopped short of making any predictions about Trinidad's ultimate accession. "The appellate jurisdiction?" she wondered aloud, "I don't know . . ." To her, there was no overwhelming Caribbeanness that would draw Trinidad into the fold of the Court, and the Privy Council's reign could very well continue indefinitely. In her view, an abiding sense of regional pride that could propel the Caribbean—and the Court—into a bright future simply was not there.

Given Cynthia's understanding of the past and the future of the CCJ, it is not surprising that her assessment of the Court's present also differed. The Court offered an image of its current self in which its Caribbeanness was practically overflowing. It was a product of a Caribbean past, of Caribbean people, and of prolonged Caribbean initiative. Serena pointed out the Caribbeanness that was literally embedded in the walls of the courthouse, and Dr. Williams proudly announced that this Court was no one else's idea but "ours." Yet, Cynthia reflected, "the CCJ has not really impacted the general consciousness of the Caribbean." How could, she seemed to question, the Court claim to be integral to the Caribbean when it had not even registered in the Caribbean's consciousness? And, so, the newness of the Caribbean Court of Justice comes to rear its ugly head once again. The impressive narrative offered by Dr. Williams, Serena, and the others in which the existence of the Court is carefully woven together with a mythological Caribbeanness continues to be openly challenged by far better-known tales of colonial history and regional economic endeavors. For Cynthia, the CCJ is admirable but still new, still struggling, and still wrestling with a past that has not been left behind; the region is mostly inert; and a triumphant spirit of Caribbeanness simply does not exist—replaced, instead, by an "inferiority complex," "political confusion," and states too timid to bring lawsuits.

A Caribbean Myth of Origin

If Justice Gupta and I were to revisit the question of the Caribbean's myth of origin, I would direct him to the CCJ. There is no triumphant battle, like the American War of Independence, and there are no individual heroes, like George Washington, but the CCJ offers a myth, nonetheless, that seeks to explain the existence of the region. It tells a story of an ageless Caribbean people from an always-already constituted Caribbean region who have a timeless sense of Caribbean togetherness. Delinked from the passage of time, this Caribbeanness, as I have been calling it, exists not in spite of nor because of colonialization or regionalization projects but is distinctly acolonial—removed from time and somehow devoid of the complicated, violent, and failed relationships, politics, and processes that have wrought the region. Instead, in the myth of Caribbeanness, the Caribbean, as a region and a people, exists unto itself. It is *this* Caribbean that has created the CCJ. And it is *this* Caribbean that the CCJ sees itself as protecting and fostering.

Drawing on and perpetuating this myth, Justice Richards, a judge at the Court, said the following about the CCJ's role:

> The Court is important as the last bastion of regionalism. But, hidden behind that, of course, is the notion that the Court is also the remaining possibility for developing, I would like to say, a Caribbean civilization, even though not many people have used that concept, but that is the idea. It is not just that we have a regional market or common market or a single market, but in its mission as the Court of appellate jurisdiction, I think we can begin to shape and give character to a kind of regional jurisprudence that is very Caribbean in its flavor and in its essence.

It is notable that he emphasizes a Caribbean "civilization" as a "concept" (rather than a market or state) and points to its "character," "flavor," and "essence" (rather than rules, laws, and order). While still speaking of the Court's work as a modern, legal institution—it does, after all, create jurisprudence and have a jurisdiction, as Richards notes—he selects words that present the CCJ as something more, something that can transcend the coldness of modernity, markets, and law and order. Yes, it is a court of law, but it is also the torchbearer of Caribbeanness. He speaks to "regionalism," for example, as something that already exists but requires the protection and effort of the Court to develop it, shape it, and express its essence.

Yet "regionalism," I suggest, is not the most helpful gloss to the Court's mythmaking work. Regionalism connotes a scaling up of nationalism, overdrawing the similarities between the nation and the region, when, in fact, there are palpable differences that can even set the two at odds. Indeed, nationalism and the national allegiances that it generates are often problematic to regionalism. Rather than being synonyms on a different scale, therefore, they are, at times, considered antonyms (something I discuss in chapter 4). The Court's myth of origin, too, sidesteps history and offers an explanation of the CCJ's genesis that seeks to locate the Court's foundation independent of a problematic past. Myths of nationalism, in contrast, often depend on a retelling of history and a recasting of the heroes and villains within it. Justice Gupta, for example, reminded me of the interweaving of myth and fact in the story of the American War of Independence and the figure of Abraham Lincoln, highlighting the way in which the nation is sustained by stories that have come to stand in for another telling of the past. What the CCJ is engaged in, therefore, is not a form of nationalism writ large. It is a slightly different sort of myth, one that I call Caribbeanness. It is a myth that helps foster a region, a people, and a court without asking them to forget the past. It does not quite "do it all," as Justice Gupta thought it might, but it provides a way out of a deflating history and a difficult present and proffers the possibility of a prideful regional future.[43]

3

A Territory

The Caribbean Court of Justice was nearing its seventh anniversary at the time *Shanique Myrie and the State of Jamaica v. the State of Barbados* was filed in 2013 by a relatively young female attorney from Jamaica, who, perhaps just as one judge had hoped, saw an opportunity to build her reputation through the filing of a significant case in the Court's original jurisdiction. This case, known more simply as "the *Myrie* matter" throughout the courthouse and the Caribbean, put before the CCJ a fundamental question regarding the existence and definition of the Caribbean region by asking what rights are enjoyed by a citizen of a Caribbean Community and Common Market (CARICOM) member state and what responsibilities a member state has toward such citizens. It presented the Court with an unprecedented opportunity to capture the attention of the Caribbean public through the possibility it afforded the Court to issue a truly impactful regional judgment and through the salacious fact pattern it presented. In this chapter, therefore, I focus closely on the *Myrie* matter, which remains the Court's most publicly referenced and most widely recognized case, to illustrate how, through the Court's management of this case, the CCJ's judges and staff confronted the strictures of state territoriality through a reconceptualization of a juridico-political territory. I explore how the CCJ, though its use of technology, travel, and legal decision-making, provided an exemplar of regional territoriality that departs profoundly from the space-time of an idealized sovereign nation-state.

The *Myrie* Matter

This case deals with important issues of Caribbean Community law which have not previously been addressed by this Court. The most prominent among them is whether and to what extent CARICOM (or Community) nationals have a right of free movement within the Caribbean Community. The case also raises other aspects of Caribbean Community law which are of very significant doctrinal and practical relevance. First and foremost, however, this is a case about a young Jamaican woman who one day left her country, for the very first time, in order to travel to another Caribbean country and, having arrived there, found herself in a situation from which, several months later, according to Jamaican medical practitioners, she was still suffering post-traumatic stress.

The staid legal language of this first paragraph of the judgment for *Myrie v. Barbados* offers the most efficient summary of a case that can best be described as a defining moment for the CCJ.[1] The ever-so-slight emotion that creeps into the final sentence of the opening paragraph only hints at the excitement and energy generated by this case as it made its way through the Court, traveled to Jamaica and Barbados for the hearing of testimony, and culminated in two days of final arguments in early April 2013 at the seat of the Court in Port of Spain, Trinidad and Tobago. After a period of calm, the excitement reignited when the judgment was delivered in October 2013, just in time to make the Court's self-imposed six-month deadline for delivering its judgments.

The case revolved around the personal experience of Shanique Myrie, a young Jamaican woman who attempted to travel to Barbados for the first time in March 2011. As detailed in her initial filing with the Court, Myrie alleged that what began as routine questioning at the immigration counter at the Grantley Adams International Airport in Barbados quickly became a humiliating and terrifying experience.[2] Although her passport was stamped and approved for a one-month stay by the immigration agent at the counter, her passport was taken from her by another border official who escorted her from the arrivals hall to a separate room. From that point on, Myrie claimed that Barbados agents subjected her to extensive interrogation regarding her plans in Barbados and peppered her with slurs pertaining to her nationality, which accused Jamaicans of carrying drugs, stealing men, and lying. Not only were her suitcase and handbag searched but also her body. She alleged that a female officer took her to a bathroom, ordered her to strip, and performed a cavity search under unsanitary conditions. The agents did not find any drugs or contraband in any of these searches but nevertheless moved Myrie into a filthy detention cell located in the airport after taking her luggage and handbag from her. She was forced to share the small cell with another young Jamaican woman—a cell that I later toured as part of the trial. The next morning, immigration officials escorted both women through the airport, put them on a commercial plane, and returned them to Jamaica. Myrie was never provided an explanation for her treatment or deportation.

Based on these allegations, Myrie claimed that Barbados violated various rights provided to her in CARICOM treaties and agreements, allegations that allowed the CCJ to exercise its original jurisdiction over this case. Among her claims, she argued that Barbados violated her right, as a citizen of a CARICOM member state, to enter Barbados. She asserted as well that Barbados violated its obligation to implement a policy of hassle-free travel, as required under these CARICOM documents. The State of Jamaica, which joined the matter as an "Intervener," a role that evolved over the course of the case, supported Myrie's claims, while the State of Barbados vehemently denied them. CARICOM, which also joined the case as an "Observer," took a much less active role and offered clarifications on CARICOM's procedures, expectations, and intentions, which generally came down on the side of "free movement" within the Caribbean Community in furtherance of the project of regional integration. In other words, it too, though more subtly, supported Myrie's interpretation of the law but attempted to stay neutral in its interpretation of the facts.

The specific allegations made in Myrie's legal complaint were simultaneously explosive and expected. On the one hand, the accusations of intimate and seemingly unjustified incursions on Myrie's privacy at the hands of Barbados state agents drew gasps and discomfort from all who learned them. While the regional press seized on the scandalous details of Myrie's claims, repeating them ad nauseam in the many articles written about the case, the Court seemed to shy away from the sheer impropriety of the alleged actions. Indeed, the egregiousness of Myrie's experience was nearly unutterable or, at least, unlistenable throughout the trial. When cross-examining one witness, for example, an attorney for Jamaica began to read Myrie's description of the airport incident sentence by sentence. I recall feeling the tension and anticipation building in the courtroom as the attorney neared the most graphic parts of Myrie's encounter. But the judges would not allow these details to be read aloud, interrupting the attorney before the words could leave her mouth. One judge intervened, asking the attorney whether she really intended to proceed sentence by sentence, which, he thought, did not seem necessary. The attorney protested but agreed to move on to the last sentence, which she began to read: "She then pushed her fin—" Another judge intervened before she could even finish the word *finger*. He insisted, with the other judges voicing their assent, that this attorney move along more quickly by summarizing paragraphs, rather than reading sentences. The Court, it certainly seemed, could not bear to hear the particularly delicate details of Myrie's experience. Such words spoken in a such a setting would have been, it is likely true, explosively interruptive. Yet, for the media, the entire airport encounter was disruptively productive, and to the public, it was excitingly suggestive; online articles attracted a good amount of commentary, and many of the CCJ's own employees, huddled around the library counter where my desk was located, enjoyed speculating about what "really" happened.

On the other hand, Barbados's alleged treatment of Myrie came as no surprise at all to those in the region. It was just another example of what everyone had come to expect as far as relationships between nationals of different Caribbean countries were concerned. For many Jamaicans, Myrie's mistreatment at the hands of Barbadians was par for the historical course and reflected Barbadian's long-held attitude of superiority and impunity. In a blistering op-ed, for example, a Jamaican attorney called for Jamaica's withdrawal from CARICOM and its rejection of the CCJ, citing as part of his reasoning Barbadians' well-known "bombastic self-importance" and penchant for mistreating and demeaning Jamaicans.[3] "Remember . . . Shanique Myrie?" he asked, as a way to underscore his point.

Barbadians, of course, felt otherwise. For many of them, there was no question that Myrie was traveling for nefarious and illegal purposes and thus deserved deportation. "Everybody knows her pimp paid for her passage," declared a Barbadian friend of mine, echoing much of the commentary coming from Barbados. Even a Barbadian politician, a self-declared "devout supporter of regional integration," explained to me with the utmost certainty that Myrie was undoubtedly a stripper moving to Barbados for work. To them and many other Barbadians, Myrie fit into a problematic and long-standing pattern of economic migration into Barbados. "Barbados already has too many people," my friend complained. Yet, everybody continues to move there for work, she lamented.

Citizens of other CARICOM states often identified with one side or the other based on their own prejudices and perceptions. These sentiments reflected deeply felt divides within the region dating back to colonialism, federalism, and the earliest days of independence, which put Jamaica, Guyana, and other poorer, (perceived) blacker, and (seemingly) less developed states on a lower rung of a state hierarchy dominated by Barbados, Trinidad, and other wealthier, (perceived) whiter, and (seemingly) more developed states.[4] The *Myrie* matter, in short, constituted a regional crisis in that it exposed deep cleavages within CARICOM—most often along state lines—in a way that could not be ignored and that demanded some sort of resolution. Enter the CCJ.

Faced with these allegations, historical divisions, and a case that pitted one state against another—not to mention a quintessentially *regional* legal issue— the CCJ embraced the opportunity to resolve *Myrie*. From the moment the case was filed, the otherwise slow pace of the CCJ's day-to-day operations was punctuated somewhat regularly by case management conferences and pretrial hearings for *Myrie*. The energy reached a crescendo in late February 2013, as the Court prepared to begin the trial and hear testimony in Jamaica (from the Jamaican witnesses) and Barbados (from the Barbadian witnesses) and peaked again in October of that same year, when the Court delivered its judgment.

As the opening paragraph to the judgment suggests, the Court ultimately found in favor of Myrie, viewing her version of the facts as substantially true and agreeing that, pursuant to "Community law," she had been denied her right to freedom of movement as a citizen of a CARICOM state. In short, Myrie should have been allowed to travel to Barbados and stay there for an extended period of time by dint of being a Caribbean national, as defined by CARICOM. The CCJ further held that if Community law was inconsistent with domestic law, Community law prevailed, as each state "consented to the creation of a Community obligation."[5] These findings, however, were tempered by the Court's other decisions. It found, for instance, that it did not have jurisdiction to adjudicate violations of human rights, noting that its jurisdiction is "established and circumscribed" by regional treaties and agreements, which "constrain the Court to interpret and apply the [Revised Treaty of Chaguaramas] and secondary 'legislation' emanating from the Treaty." Human rights, which are delineated in international treaties, therefore, are beyond the scope of this regional court's original jurisdiction.[6] The CCJ also found that Myrie had not sufficiently established her claim of discrimination based on nationality. In the end, then, Myrie was compensated only for the violation of her right to travel and the "loss, trauma and injury [she] suffered and continues to suffer"[7]—a total package of about US$39,000, or a mere "slap on the wrist," as I heard one reporter murmur following the delivery of the judgment. This award did not nearly match the request made by Myrie, who sought a total of just over US$400,000. Yet, Myrie rightfully claimed victory, and many Jamaicans following the case celebrated the feeling of long-overdue vindication. Many Barbadians, on the other hand, including my friend, were left speechless, perplexed as to how the CCJ could have so incorrectly interpreted the facts or have been bamboozled by the likes of this young Jamaican woman, who remained, in their eyes, clearly a prostitute. In short, while the judgment was certainly a gratifying win for Myrie, it was not a landslide victory.

Myrie was not the only winner, it is important to note. In addition to the nationally rooted reactions, a third narrative developed in the wake of the judgment. This story line shifted away from the state-versus-state showdown and focused, instead, on the fate of the region following the Court's decision.

A Belizean news channel, for instance, cast the decision as a defining moment for "CARICOM citizenship."[8] And Ronald Sanders, a politician from Antigua and Barbuda and a frequent contributor to regional newspapers, trumpeted the decision as "an occasion for real celebration of Caribbean regionalism at the level of people."[9] Indeed, the Court itself gave every indication throughout the trial that this case was about a regional people—not states, not money, and not even economic development—a notable emphasis on human beings that I take up in the next chapter. As one judge said during the course of the trial, "the [Caribbean] Community is for all of us; it's for the judge and for the farmer," and in their written decision, the judges speak of "CARICOM nationals" and cite a report that supports free movement as a means "to enhance [CARICOM nationals'] sense that they belong to, and can move in, the Caribbean Community."[10]

When I ran the "region-as-the-winner" narrative by several CCJ judges, they were largely unsurprised, if quietly proud. From the beginning, this case had always been about the region and the rights that inured to the people of the region. Simply by having an opportunity to clarify these rights and the role of the region vis-à-vis the state, the Court knew that CARICOM would be the winner regardless of which party could claim victory. Thus, even before the trial had begun, those who worked at the CCJ confidently deemed the case "landmark" and "historic." And it was, as the years following the decision have proven. *Myrie* continues to garner press as a touchpoint in CARICOM immigration and travel, and it remains a turning point for the Court, not just because of its consequential judgment but also because it initiated the CCJ's newfound willingness to travel around the Caribbean—a physical movement, I argue in this chapter, that carries with it (in many cases, literally) significant symbolic weight toward the creation of a territorialized region.

The State and the Region in Time and Space

Knowing that one is *in* the Caribbean region, a discernible politico-legal entity, is not obvious. As I described in chapter 1, it is the nation-state that makes itself felt. I *knew*, for instance, that I was *in* Trinidad and Tobago. During my initial visit and even more pronouncedly after I moved there, I experienced an equally uncomfortable and exciting period of adjusting to life amid another state's laws, politics, institutions, celebrations, and mundane happenings. I worked to master a new currency, the Trinidad and Tobago dollar. I read the politically charged headlines with wide eyes. I waited impatiently as the president's motorcade with its flashing police escorts regularly clogged the Queen's Park Savannah roundabout. And I celebrated each of the national holidays. More urgently, I desperately endeavored to learn the rules of the road. I braved the notorious Port of Spain traffic, navigating the extraordinarily narrow streets and practicing (though never actually mastering) the quintessentially Trinidadian polite tap of the horn to communicate an astounding array of driving intentions, all while driving on the opposite side the road from what I was used to. I observantly noted the swiftness and agility of the tow trucks that made illegally parked cars disappear in the blink of an eye, and I was simultaneously pleased and disconcerted to find that I could fill up my tank for about US $11 because, in this oil-rich country, gasoline was subsidized. In short, I was acutely aware of the state's presence everywhere and at all times. My Trinidadian friends, though, whom I still considered "interlocutors" in those early days, were never surprised by the continual accusations of political corruption, took it in stride when the prime minister provided *one day's notice* for a public holiday to celebrate a local hero, and shrugged at my questions about the price of gas. To them, the state, as much as it was a part of their daily lives, had faded into a sort of unremarkable background; it was just the state being a state in this country called Trinidad and Tobago. With differing levels of awareness, then, my interlocutors and I experienced the state through its spatiotemporal steadiness.[11] There was no question about it: we were all living *in* Trinidad and Tobago. The state had successfully mapped itself onto the territory of these two islands, extending its legal authority to the shores of both Trinidad and Tobago and no further. Its territoriality helped it to be experienced as a reality.

But were we *in* the region? This was a much more difficult question to answer. As much as the Court's region was defined by twelve member states that we could all point to on a map, the region itself was more or less without a discernible territory. This despite the fact that the word *region*, unlike the word *state*, actually indexes physical space—a general area. But here, the Court's member states are spread over an area that is so expansive and so fuzzily defined that the region begins to lose its spatial definition. Indeed, some 1,200 miles separate the northernmost point in Belize to the southernmost border of Guyana, and nearly 2,400 miles lay between Belize to the east and Suriname to the west, amounting to almost 2.9 million square miles, or roughly the same size as the contiguous United States, which is just shy of 3 million. The CCJ's member states, though, are hardly contiguous, with both nonmember states and the glittering Caribbean Sea wedging themselves between islands and state borders, making an uninterrupted border around the region impossible. As a prominent Barbadian attorney lamented to me, "One of the greatest tragedies is that if we were not divided by so much water, we would have already been fully integrated."[12]

But water was not the only problem. It remained, in contrast to the state's ever presence, that the region is simply not experientially manifested in the same way that the states of Trinidad and Tobago or Barbados or Jamaica are. There are few CARICOM holidays, there is no CARICOM currency, and CARICOM laws have little impact on quotidian life.[13] Relatedly, and most important, the region's legal authority, which was still only vaguely defined and not yet readily accepted, struggled to cross state lines and reach the shores of any of the member states, much less one of them. There was, overall, a lack of cohesion, contiguity, or boundedness, as well as a lack of a shared, recognizable law that led to a lack of "there-thereness," to echo Gertrude Stein's reflection on the nonexistence of her childhood neighborhood.[14] It was difficult for anyone to say exactly *where* the region was (if, indeed, there was a region at all), other than on the papers that created it or in the minds of those who worked for it.

As I came to realize over the course of my fieldwork, this absence of a defined regional territory was one of the many issues the CCJ sought to address as it went about its work to constitute a region. Since actual distances could not be collapsed, the Court endeavored instead to create a feeling of cohesion and contiguity among the citizens of its member states. Creating a myth of origin based on a shared Caribbeanness, as I described in chapter 2, was one way it went about this. It also sought, more groundedly, to make the region a reality in the same way that I and my friends experienced the state of Trinidad and Tobago as a reality. It sought, as the judges wrote in the *Myrie* decision, "to enhance [CARICOM nationals'] sense that they belong to, and can move in, the Caribbean Community."[15] The region—the Caribbean Community region, more specifically—needed to be a *place* that could be traversed and to which people could belong.

The idea that a region can be or should be locatable in space and time takes a page from conceptualizations of the idealized state. In the sovereign state, law contains, defines, and governs a particular people and a given land, and that arrangement exists in a seemingly constant perpetuity[16]—a sense of stability that is manufactured and maintained through an ongoing hum of everyday activities, like those I described earlier: commercial exchanges using a national currency, law making and enforcement, national holidays, bureaucratic processes, and more. *Where* these activities take place becomes where the state is thought to exist in space. And, *when* these activities take place is when the state is thought to exist in time, which is, effectively, all the time.[17] Thus, the space and time of states is powerfully connected, in a way that helps naturalize and normalize the idea of the sovereign state.[18] As one scholar has remarked, "the maintenance of the temporal construction of the givenness of the state and its sovereignty in scholarship and popular perception, provides

A TERRITORY 67

the foundation for conceptualizing it in spatial terms."[19] In other words, the experienced steady state of the nation-state has led to a "givenness" of the territorially bounded sovereign state—a stable and seemingly permanent "state-idea."[20] The state is made to seem *really real*, not just to those people who visit it or live in it but, perhaps even more significantly, to innumerable actors on the global stage, who can negotiate and trade with a discernible, stable entity known as the state of Trinidad and Tobago, and who will respect, or at least acknowledge the existence of, its borders and jurisdiction.

This is essentially what the CCJ is after: a region that is perceived as *really real* by the people, states, governments, businesses, and more that might interact with it. That is, the Court endeavors for the region—much like a state—to be locatable in space and time and, significantly, to have regional law map precisely onto these borders.[21] One should know when they are *in* the region both by the boundaries that demarcate the territory and by the laws that rule in that jurisdiction. Yet, as I illustrate in this chapter through the Court's handling of *Myrie*, the CCJ does not strive—indeed, in the face of multiple sovereign states, cannot strive—to establish the same effect of permanence to which states aspire. Instead, the CCJ's region flits in and out of perception by not always existing everywhere at all times for all people, thereby distinguishing the reality of a region from that of the sovereign state, even while borrowing a spatiotemporal conceptualization of how a geopolitical entity should be in the world. In short, the region's space-time is realized as intermittent and itinerant. Staccato rather than steady. And mobile rather than immovable. There is a shiftiness to the region that at once allows it to exist at all within a world dominated by sovereign nation-states, thereby challenging the sovereign model, but ultimately curtailing the possibility of its own hegemony. Sometimes, after all, the region is just not there.

The Region within the Four Corners of a Screen

When I arrived at the CCJ on what was my second full day of work as a legal intern, I was greeted with a pleasant surprise: a case management conference (CMC) was scheduled to take place at 10:00 a.m. in the Training and Conference Room. Already, the technology team was busy prepping the video-conference setup, and the Office of the Registry staff was gathering files and checking case submissions. No attorneys, though, were present. As with the great majority of the CCJ's hearings, I soon learned, this one would take place virtually.

Still unsure of the Court's expectations of me and exactly how court proceedings unfolded, I arrived about fifteen minutes early to the hearing, stopping first at the Registry to see if they needed help with their cart full of documents before making my way to the Training and Conference Room on the second floor. This room is very much a multipurpose room. Some days it hosted staff meetings or question-and-answer sessions for visitors, as it did for the tour I described in chapter 2. Today, though, it was arranged for the *Myrie* hearing. Court staff had unfolded a number of tables and shuffled chairs around into a *U*-shaped setup that became familiar to me over the course of my research. On the closed end of the *U* were five folded paper nameplates and five filled glasses of water for each of the five judges assigned to the matter. There was also a long-necked microphone for each judge, as well as two triangular tabletop microphones. Two large flat screens were positioned directly across from the makeshift judicial bench with a small camera mounted on top. One screen showed the CCJ bench in its entirety and was angled such that the registrar's seat, to the left of the bench, was also visible. The other screen was divided between three courtrooms: Jamaica, Barbados, and Guyana, the locations of the plaintiff and intervenor, the defendant, and the CARICOM general counsel, respectively. Remote controls, laptops, files, and a landline telephone, as well as a couple of microphones, awaited court staff on the registrar's side of the *U*, while I was directed to sit on the opposite side, along with other legal interns and two visitors to the Court, where we would be completely out of view of the camera. The tables were simple and unadorned, leaving the seated legs of the judges visible, and the backdrop to the judicial bench featured nothing other than the yellow walls of the room and the closed greenish-white blinds of the windows. The sparseness surprised me, and as I later found out, also bothered the newest member to the CCJ's bench. Many months after this hearing, Justice Richards described his dismay over the bareness of the bench after he happened to notice it in the video screen that reflected the judges back to themselves. "Looking at the screen," he said, "I saw us on the bench and we were completely bare, bereft of any seal of officialdom. . . . The seal of the court isn't there. The flags of the countries are not there. . . . It looked as if you were in a classroom of some sort." The region, he seemed to be saying, was hardly perceptible. He told me that he raised this issue with the president of the Court, and eventually, during the time of my research, flags and the Court seal were added to the videoconference setup (see figure 5). But for this hearing, the background was stark.

Well before the ease and familiarity of Zoom, videoconference hearings were still somewhat new to the Court and its users and, from my non-tech-savvy perspective, quite complicated. It was not until sometime in 2010 that all the member states' courtrooms had been supplied with a videoconferencing system that linked them through the CCJ and sometime later before it was up and running.[22] Thus, while videoconferencing was available by the

FIGURE 5. The Training and Conference Room set up for a hearing unrelated to the *Myrie* matter. The screen on the left depicts the CCJ judicial bench *after* flags had been added to the background. The screen on the right shows the videoconference room in the Barbados Supreme Court. A judge's paper nameplate and long-necked microphone are visible at the bottom of the photograph. Photograph by author.

time that I arrived to conduct my research, it was not a smooth or problem-free process. Dark images, bad sound, frozen pictures, and other technological glitches were a regular part of video hearings. This CMC was no different. Three IT staff members were already in the room when I arrived. They were double-checking the various points of connection and communicating via video, cell phone, and landline with their counterparts in Jamaica, Barbados, and Guyana, whom I could see on the screens also moving around their courtrooms fine-tuning the audio and video resolution. Sound seemed to be the problem today, with not everyone being able to hear everyone, and it took a good thirty minutes to resolve the issue. In the meantime, CCJ staff, interns, and visitors to the Court made their way into the Training and Conference room and found their seats along the sides of the *U*. I could hear the judges murmuring in the hallway just outside the room. I could see the attorneys in their respective courtrooms shuffling their papers, many miles away from one another but, at the same time, jammed up close together in the space of one flat screen through the miracle of (still-being-ironed-out) technology. Everyone waited as patiently as possible.

At last, nearly twenty minutes after the scheduled start time, the court usher, seated at the door of the Training and Conference Room and well out of view of the camera and, consequently, the attorneys, knocked loudly on the door to the hallway and announced, "All rise for the Judges of the Caribbean Court of Justice." We in the room rose, and the attorneys, seeing only the registrar, rose soon after. The judges, wearing suits, not robes, solemnly entered, stood behind the chairs near their nameplates, and bowed ever so slightly toward the screens in front of them. This time, we—that is, all of us in the room *and* on the screen—bowed in unison back to the judges and responded as a unit to the registrar's quiet instruction to "please be seated." The hearing was officially in session, and some sort of newly formed cohesive unit had been constituted in the space of the hearing and with the assistance of a camera, two screens, several microphones, and a number of phone calls.

While this case management conference had an agenda—to review each party's compliance with a previous court order—Justice Maxwell, the president of the CCJ and the presiding judge of this hearing, could barely contain his excitement to discuss the venue of the trial. Indeed, he brought this up very early in the hearing, foreshadowing what he saw was the true task of this CMC: determining where and when this historic trial would be held. He explained that the Court wanted to discuss whether the trial should be held in Jamaica to hear witnesses there and then move to Barbados to hear those witnesses, in order to minimize the costs and inconveniences to all. He also wanted to discuss cutoff dates for the collection and presentation of evidence.

Before these more exciting topics, however, the hearing had other ground to cover, and slowly the hearing progressed, allowing each party time to discuss compliance issues. As with any court hearing, there were various failures to produce documents on time, various excuses, various requests for extensions, and various arguments for urgency. The judges patiently addressed these concerns and complaints, and in consultation with the registrar, who kept the official calendar for the Court, set new dates and deadlines for the production of documents.

After about two hours of such discussion, the CMC finally reached the issue of venue. It had been my understanding that this was something that had been long decided. When I had visited the Supreme Court of Barbados earlier in the year, the chief justice of Barbados told me, as fact, that the CCJ would be back in his country for the *Myrie* trial. He was giddy about this; he loved the publicity and the hubbub and took great pride in his beautiful courthouse. But, as I learned at the CMC, apparently the decision to take the CCJ abroad had not yet been made; instead, Justice Maxwell posed it as a question to the parties, though stating his preference unambiguously. Would the parties agree to an itinerant trial? The attorneys for Jamaica and for Myrie quickly and eagerly agreed to host the CCJ. The attorney for Barbados, however, hesitated, citing a handful of concerns, from the cost of travel to the question of security in Jamaica because of animosity against Barbadians as a result of this case. The latter objection, in particular, raised eyebrows and ire. The Jamaicans protested, and a judge noted that "this is part of the problem." The CCJ president, however, in his always quiet voice, said he was listening but reminded the Barbadian attorney that "the Court is also concerned with the issue of access to justice for ordinary folk, as this is a central charge of the Court." He wanted to show that the Myries of the region were just as able to seek justice in this Court as large corporations; if they cannot afford to bring all their witnesses to the seat of the Court, the Court will come to them. Thus, "the Court feels it is best to sit where the witnesses are, but I will not make this order without Barbados's consent," he stated. The Court, therefore, would await a submission by Barbados on this issue.

With the question of venue hanging in the air unsatisfyingly and no other matters left to discuss, the hearing ended. The judges rose, we all rose, everyone solemnly bowed, and the judges walked slowly to the back door, off camera, disappearing from the screen. For a moment longer, the attorneys remained on the shared space of the other screen, until Peter, a member of the CCJ IT staff, turned off the video feed with the flick of a remote control. Throughout the hearing, in fact, the IT staff and the remote controls played significant roles. The technological problems that delayed the start of the CMC plagued the entire hearing, and the parties had recurrent issues hearing one another because their sound wavered in and out. At one point, the video connection dropped entirely, necessitating a recess while IT staff across the region ironed out the problems. Even beyond these issues—that took fevered whispering, quiet phone calls, and remote control magic to solve—CCJ IT staff also used their powers to regulate the equipment in the room, occasionally zooming in or out, adjusting the angle of the camera, or, frequently, muting the microphones of the judges, who, because of the multiple microphones in front of them could only hold private discussions with the assistance of the "mute" button. Peter, therefore, had to pay close attention to the rhythms of the hearing and click the sound on and off as the judges spoke on and off the record. The parties, gathered together on one screen, would sit patiently through what I imagined to be awkward vacuums of occasional silence on their end.

Though at times frustrating, the whole video hearing was a strangely unifying experience. The entire technological event brought relative strangers momentarily together to hear, see, and witness the same things, from the CCJ judges entering their screens to lapsing sound to choreographed bows.[23] And perhaps most important, this group of people, gathered together within the defined space of a screen, were all subjects of the same regional law in the same space at the same time. The region, in other words, that had been constituted on the screen for the duration of the hearing was linked not only through technology but also through a shared jurisdictional space.[24]

Traversing the Region

Barbados never submitted an objection to the Court's proposal to hear witnesses in Jamaica, so the president's plan stood; for the first time in its short history, the Court, as an institution, would travel to hear testimony. From its seat in Trinidad and Tobago, the CCJ planned to pack up its essentials, of which there were many, and move three times during the course of the trial, which was to be held throughout the months of March and April 2013: touching down, with a splash, in Jamaica for three days, then, two weeks later, flying into Barbados with great fanfare for four days, and, two weeks after that, hosting all parties at the CCJ's own courthouse for two days of closing arguments. The preparation that was needed to pull off such a feat was impressive, imposing, and, certainly, interruptive to the Court's everyday activities.

The day before our departure for Jamaica, for example, was filled with packing, organizing, collating, double-checking, and logistical planning. The Office of the Registry seemed to have exploded with piles of folders, books, and office supplies waiting to be packed into open suitcases laying on the floor.

There were also boxed computers, monitors, and microphones and other odds and ends that had been requested by the CCJ's IT team, who had traveled to Jamaica a couple of days in advance to begin setting up the Court's temporary courtroom there. *Myrie* was no small matter, and its case documents were plentiful. The Registry staff struggled to fit everything into a movable mound and eagerly accepted my offer to haul as many binders and folders as would fit into my own luggage. And when I left the Court that day around 5:00 p.m. (with much of the Registry staff still busy packing), I was laden with *Myrie* materials.

After spending a good hour at home squeezing these binders into a suitcase that also held my personal items, I sat down to eat my dinner. Around 7:30 p.m., I received a phone call from the IT manager, Ms. Carl. No one, apparently, had remembered to pack the surprisingly large digital courtroom clock that kept time for the attorneys and for the transcription software used by the Court. Ms. Carl wondered whether the driver, who was scheduled to pick me up the next morning, could bring the clock with him, and if I could add it to my luggage. I agreed, of course, and I ate my dinner quickly so that I could transfer my belongings and the Court's files to an even larger suitcase that could accommodate the clock. I also did not expect a phone call an hour later. This time it was the registrar, Ms. Brown, who was still at the courthouse and still finalizing the arrangements for Jamaica. She wanted to confirm my flight details to ensure that I would have appropriate transportation once I arrived in Kingston. I gave her these details, thanked her for her thoughtfulness, and urged her to go home and get some rest before our early flight and the busy days ahead. She laughed.

Ms. Brown, Ms. Carl, the court executive administrator (CEA), and several other administrative staff members at the CCJ had had little time to rest in the weeks preceding the beginning of the trial. Everything needed to be arranged, from the judges' flights, ground transportation, and accommodations to the security detail at the trial, the procuring of office equipment, electronics, appropriate chairs and desks, and flagpoles for the judges' temporary chambers and courtroom. In fact, Ms. Carl, the CEA, and another IT manager had flown to Jamaica weeks in advance to confirm that the Jamaica Conference Centre, which would host the Jamaica segment of the trial, would be an adequate venue for the Court and to create detailed plans as to what equipment, labor, and skill sets were necessary to transform a conference room built to United Nations specifications into a courtroom appropriate for a CCJ trial. This was not an international diplomatic meeting, after all; it was a regional legal tribunal. Jamaica's own court system, overcrowded and underfunded as it was, had no courtroom that could have accommodated the full panel of seven CCJ judges. And one week before the trial was set to begin, two IT staff members returned to Jamaica once again to begin the process of wiring the conference room. The incredible mass of cords and wires hidden behind the makeshift registrar's desk was a testament to the amount of work they had put in: computer screens for each judge, more screens for the attorneys' desks and the witness stand, multiple computers for the Registry staff, overhead projectors, screens for the overhead projectors, and microphones for the judges, registrar, witnesses, and attorneys. They had also created an IT workstation in the back offices complete with a printer, fax, copier, two computers, Wi-Fi routers, and a telephone.

When additional CCJ staff members, including myself, arrived to assist with setup, the conference room–cum–courtroom was well on its way to being fully wired, but it was still in need of additional indicia of a regional courtroom, which we spent the next two days carefully adding according to Ms. Brown's detailed checklist. We created signs with the official name of the case and signs to indicate where to enter the courtroom, where the designated seating areas were for the media, the public, visiting attorneys, and counsel appearing in the case. We added partitions to keep the witnesses separate as they waited their turn to give testimony. We hung the CCJ flag on a flagpole placed directly behind the judges' bench and positioned the judges' name cards carefully. We placed the CCJ seal (a smaller one than Ms. Brown would have preferred, but the larger one was too heavy to carry with us, she explained) at the center of the Registry desk, and we placed the digital clock in a similarly conspicuous location (see figure 6). We assisted the court reporters (whom the CCJ had specially hired and flown in for this event) in finding an ideal place in the courtroom to set up their own equipment. And we unpacked and arranged the many, many case files, binders, and office supplies—staplers, notepads, pens, pencils, and official CCJ stamps—that Ms. Brown and I had brought to Jamaica. This array of materials included color-coded CCJ name badges complete with headshots—just like the ones we wore at the CCJ courthouse in Port of Spain—for all the individuals who would be permitted into the back offices and judges' chambers. It was, as should be obvious, an enormous undertaking.

When the Court traveled to Barbados several weeks later, the necessary preparations were much more minimal but no less detailed. The newly built Supreme Court Complex in Barbados (which Justice Matthews referred to only somewhat jokingly as the "Palace of Justice") was expansive, impressive, and constructed with a courtroom equipped with the same technology as the CCJ's and that could accommodate the full bench of CCJ judges.[25] Office space, however, was a bit more limited, and several Barbadian judges had to

FIGURE 6. The Jamaica Conference Centre as transformed into the Caribbean Court of Justice's temporary courtroom to host the first segment of the *Myrie* trial. The CCJ flag can be seen behind the judicial bench. The round CCJ seal is visible on the Registry desk next to a digital clock, which, along with all the paperwork and equipment visible in this photograph, was brought from the CCJ headquarters in Trinidad and Tobago to Jamaica for this trial. Photograph by author.

lend their chambers to CCJ judges for the duration of our stay there. And, despite the availability of technology and the suitability of the courtroom, we had to bring several important items with us: the judges' name cards and robes, the CCJ flag, and the (smaller) CCJ seal (see figure 7). We also transported the masses of trial documents and files that constituted the Courts' records of the case, which I, mercifully, did not have to carry with me this time.

Throughout these long days of preparation in both Jamaica and Barbados, we were assisted by staff members from the Jamaican and Barbadian Ministries of Justice, respectively, who were issued and wore CCJ name badges to ease their fluidity of movement. They had been assigned to assist the CCJ and did so with great humor, able skills, and tremendous patience, setting aside their own state-related duties for as long as the regional court demanded their services. These Jamaican and Barbadian legal assistants, court managers, and IT staff members shuttled us from place to place, showed us their cities, and

FIGURE 7. The full CCJ bench, dressed in their blue and gold CCJ robes, in the courtroom of the Supreme Court Complex in Barbados for the second segment of the *Myrie* trial. The justices allowed the media and visitors to take photographs as they remained seated immediately following the conclusion of this segment. This courtroom was designed and built to accommodate the full seven-member CCJ bench. The CCJ flag is visible behind the judges, and the CCJ seal, which cannot be seen in the photograph, was positioned on the Registry desk. *Seated, left to right*: the Honourable Mr. Justice David Hayton, the Honourable Mme. Justice Désirée Bernard, the Honourable Mr. Justice Rolston Nelson, the Right Honourable Sir Dennis Byron, president of the Caribbean Court of Justice, the Honourable Mr. Justice Adrian Saunders, the Honourable Mr. Justice Jacob Wit, and the Honourable Mr. Justice Winston Anderson. Photograph by author.

recommended the best places to eat and relax (or "lime," as they would say in Trinidad) during the CCJ's short stays in their countries.[26]

The intent of all of this labor in both Jamaica and Barbados was to create a region-idea, to make regional law as real as it had ever been, and to distinguish the authority of the region from the authority of the state. A key point here is that to accomplish this, the Court *emplaced* the region through its movements and actions. That is, the CCJ's efforts worked to manifest the region in particular places—putting roots down and a flag up—by physically hauling the stuff, symbols, and people of regional law and authority to new lands. It is quite likely that the Jamaican Ministry of Justice had a stapler to spare, a court reporter to hire, and maybe even a digital clock for us to use, but the CCJ took it upon itself to bring its own office supplies, transport its own court reporters, and arrange for a driver to bring the digital clock to my doorstep so that I could shove it into my luggage at the last minute. There was something different about the "stuff" that we had toted with us: it was regional stuff, regional law, a regional court, and regional governance. With its binders, documents, wires, monitors, and, especially, its seal, stamps, ID tags, flags, and robes, the Court endeavored to constitute something different and new, yet eminently locatable, which appeared for three days in Jamaica and then four days in Barbados.

Indeed, although the Court's presence was brief in each location, it was notable—and not just to those who participated in the trial. As we deboarded the plane in Jamaica, for instance, CCJ staff, including myself, were ushered through Immigration, past long lines of curious onlookers; escorted swiftly through Customs, despite the massive amount of equipment we were carrying; and, to my surprise, seated in chauffeured SUVs. Several of the judges, who were also on the flight, had also been guided through the same effortless movements and were comfortably seated in BMW sedans that were lined up and awaiting their arrival at the front entrance of the airport. The troubles associated with state borders—the very state borders that had proved so troublesome to Shanique Myrie in the first place—dissipated at the presence of this regional court. Even local traffic laws, it seemed, were suspended in the presence of regional law. Our motorcade, led by the BMW sedans, departed the airport from a separate exit and raced through the crowded streets of Kingston with the aid of police escorts on motorcycles, which held traffic at bay as we cruised through the intersections, unimpeded by stop signs or traffic lights. Throughout the hearings in Jamaica and Barbados, the police escorts continued to guarantee the unobstructed travel of the judges from hotel to courthouse and back again and continued to attract attention as they cruised through crowded rush hour traffic in both Kingston and Bridgetown.

The privileges and immunities provided to those traveling for court business paved the way for our trouble-free travel. However, the point had been adeptly illustrated to those bystanders who witnessed our movement through the airports and the cities that the law of the region trumped the law of the state, allowing for judges, attorneys, staff, and Myrie alike to move from island to island. The very borders that had kept Myrie from traveling freely and that were at the center of this case had become porous, with their porosity synchronized to the Court's movement. As the Court moved, the regional space that it inhabited and the regional law that it embodied moved with it, supplanting state space and state law for the period of its incursion.

This regional authority, moreover, was something that the Court exercised overtly during the trial itself, making sure that the viewing audience knew that this Court wielded this authority in this place at that moment. The

CCJ, for example, called its *own* witness in Barbados, a recalcitrant immigration officer—*the* immigration officer, in fact, who had purportedly performed the cavity search on Myrie. When the State of Barbados failed to include her on its own witness list, the Court stepped in and commanded her presence and conducted its own direct examination. Whereas this practice is not unheard of under international law, it is unheard of in either Jamaica or Barbados, where common law is practiced. Through this move, therefore, the CCJ announced its departure from familiar state law. On another occasion, an expert witness in Jamaica did not show up on time to give her testimony, and the president of the CCJ, clearly frustrated with the seeming lack of respect, threatened to "compel her presence." After learning that the witness, an academic, was currently delivering a lecture and could not be reached by phone, the president stated with severity in his voice, that "being in a lecture" was no excuse, and he insisted on pausing the trial while the Court prepared a subpoena that would force her immediate appearance. When the witness at last arrived, before the subpoena was issued, the president castigated her in open court for failing to take her obligation to the Court seriously. Here, the region could be seen flexing its muscles.

The CCJ, in other words, landed on the shores of Jamaica and Barbados with some impact. Bumping the state, briefly, off its own territory by disrupting its sovereign control over the populace, over its borders, over its courtrooms, its conference centers, and its civil servants. The CCJ worked laboriously to construct a regional presence and to exert its regional law over these people in those places at those times. The unfortunate academic expert witness, for example, was absorbed or interpellated (as we will see in chapter 4) into the fold of regionhood as she stood before the Court and apologized for her transgressions. This was regional territory that answered to regional laws, and she had become a regional subject.

But it was all momentary, never intending to be permanent. The judges were eager to hurry the trial along and showcase the efficiency of regional justice. The Jamaica segment of the trial finished a day earlier than expected, and, in Barbados, the president of the Court was able to move his departure time earlier in the afternoon on the last day of the trial. The region territorialized this land only temporarily. When the Court departed the shores of Jamaica and Barbados, having repacked its belongings, lowered and carefully folded its flag, and retraced its route back to the airport, the emplaced region, which it had so painstakingly and consciously created, dispersed. The land, law, and people that had been drawn together by the CCJ's presence shifted out of alignment as the Court moved to its next location, where—there and then—land, law, and people once again came together in the presence of the

Court. In contrast to this, the state persisted. The Barbados flag remained flying even as the CCJ flag came down, Jamaican traffic resumed just as soon as the motorcade had passed, the expert witness returned to giving lectures and, presumably, to following state laws, and our able and enjoyable friends from the Ministries of Justice returned to their positions as state civil servants working for state judges in state courts as soon as the region no longer demanded their service.

A Region in Law

Six months after the closing arguments, which were completed during a brief meeting in Trinidad following our visits to Jamaica and Barbados, the *Myrie* trial came to an end with the delivery of the judgment in early October 2013. The CCJ had done much over the course of this case to make real the region. Its judgment, as well as the way in which it was delivered, was no different. It was the, perhaps, inevitable conclusion to a trial in which the existence of the region had been painstakingly performed. Once again, the reading of the judgment was staged in a regional setting—this time in CCJ's own courtroom in Trinidad—replete with indicia of the region, including the CCJ seal; CCJ, CARICOM, Barbadian, Jamaican, and Trinidadian flags; blue walls signifying, as the Court tells it, the Caribbean Sea; and the blue and gold robes of the judges, which similarly stand for the Caribbean Sea and sun (as we will see further in chapter 6). Alerted through a "Media Invitation" issued by the Court in the preceding week, about a dozen representatives of local and regional media outlets were present with their video cameras, still cameras, and notebooks, and nearly twenty members of the public, many of whom looked to be of university age, jostled for a seat in the public seating area. The president of the CCJ's wife also joined the viewing public for what I believed to be her first time, whispering to me that she "couldn't miss this." Notably absent in person, though present on videoconference, were the lawyers and the parties to the case. They were seated in their own courthouses, which had attracted their own media and public spectators, and they were gathered together within the four corners of the video screens, which were visible throughout the courtroom.

Five minutes after the appointed start time, the judges solemnly entered and took their seats at the bench. Despite malfunctioning sound in Jamaica and near inaudibility in Barbados, the president announced that he will be reading the executive summary of the official judgment and then proceeded to do so, with the other judges reading along on their own copies. As the president read, it became clear, as indicated by the faintest of murmurs from the audience, that Myrie had prevailed in her case against Barbados. The CCJ found Myrie's version of the facts to be substantially true and that she had been denied her right to freedom of movement as a CARICOM national, but it simultaneously determined that there was not sufficient evidence of discrimination based on nationality, a claim made by Myrie and supported by Jamaica. The Court also found that it lacked jurisdiction to adjudicate her claims relating to violations of her human rights, the broadest of Myrie's allegations. Lastly, the judgment awarded Myrie a somewhat small amount of money in Barbadian dollars (totaling BBD$77,240, or about US$38,620), which fell far short of her request but still elicited a subdued smile from Myrie to her attorneys, visible on the video monitor.

While the work of justice demanded that the CCJ make a final determination on Myrie's case, the Court, through its judgment, did so in a way that posited the existence and triumph of the region rather than the winning or losing of either party or a particular state. By determining that there was not sufficient evidence of discrimination based on nationality, for instance, the judgment avoided acknowledging (and, possibly, having to reiterate and reinscribe) deep-seated national prejudices and perceived differences that tend to separate rather than unite. The relatively meager monetary award to Myrie, moreover, helped temper Myrie's individual success. The judgment, it seemed, was directed instead to an abstract person, to whom the CCJ repeatedly referred in its judgment as the "CARICOM national." The CCJ was clear on this. It was the region and Myrie's status as a national of this region that mattered. The Court's finding, "that it lacks jurisdiction to make the Declarations and Orders sought by Ms. Myrie relating to breaches of her human rights," emphasized this;[27] as much as this case, this Court, and this law were not about specific state-based nationalities or even particular people, they were similarly not about more broadly universal matters such as human rights. In other words, the Court circumscribed its jurisdiction to the region. It was no bigger and no smaller than the Caribbean; its law reached the shores of its member states and touched the people of its region but extended no further.

The Region Comes, the Region Goes, and the Region Comes Back Again

As I described at the beginning of this chapter, *Myrie* was celebrated as a triumph of the region. Not only had the Court outlined the rights of citizens of the region to travel unimpeded, but it had, more literally, outlined the region, mapping it out through its movements in space and through the limits of its jurisdiction. It etched the bounds of the regional territory. Yet, the emplaced region existed only temporarily. Video feeds turned off, the makeshift courthouses closed shop, and the waves of press following the *Myrie* judgment eventually died down, though they never vanished completely. As momentously as the region came into being in place and time, it quietly slipped back into near imperceptibility. With this dissipation, state borders once again hardened, and border crossing by citizens of CARICOM member states was, as before, subjected to the rigidities and proclivities of state sovereignty. Citizens of economically less-advantaged states, such as Jamaica and Guyana, continued to be denied entry into economically more-advantaged states, such as Barbados and Trinidad and Tobago, at much higher rates than the other way around. Indeed, only six weeks after the *Myrie* decision, newspapers reported that Trinidad and Tobago border officials denied entry to and deported thirteen Jamaicans in a single night.[28] These denials of entry, moreover, continued to make headlines for several years after *Myrie*, and they occasionally pop up even now, some eight years later.

Yet, all has not remained completely the same. The region's presence, as constituted through the Court's actions in *Myrie*, might have been transient, but its effect was lasting. Certainly, sovereign state borders still exclude in somewhat predictable patterns, but the region has been exemplified as a possibility. It *can* exist, fleetingly but critically. Nearly every article that discusses ongoing denials of entry also offers the CCJ's decision in *Myrie* as the other, better possibility. It is what should have and could have happened in these other cases. In other words, the work that the CCJ did in *Myrie* to demonstrate the actuality of the region—that is, by emplacing it—made this region come to life in a way that it had not yet been fully imagined; namely, this region has law, and those laws apply to the people who occupy that particular space. The region, thus, became invocable on this land for these people.

4

A People

It was early in the morning on March 18, 2013, and I was aboard a crowded Zed-R minibus—named for the *ZR* appearing on its license plate—heading toward downtown Bridgetown, Barbados. I had planned to walk from the Bridgetown bus terminal to the magisterial Supreme Court Complex in time to observe any action preceding the first day of hearings in Barbados for the *Myrie v. Barbados* original jurisdiction trial before the Caribbean Court of Justice. As discussed in chapter 3, the legal issue at the heart of this case, stripped of its salacious facts, was the principle of free movement by Caribbean Community (CARICOM) nationals between CARICOM member states, a principle that is, as was argued by the State of Jamaica and the plaintiff Shanique Myrie, included in CARICOM agreements and treaties and fundamental to the project of regional economic integration. It put before the Court, in other words, a critical question: to what extent was this region really a region for the people who lived there?

One of my fellow passengers on this morning commute already seemed to have an answer to this query. I disembarked the minibus at the crowded open-air bus terminal at the edge of town, peered at my crumpled maps, and quickly decided to seek the assistance of a young woman who had been riding the same Zed-R. Alicia, a Barbadian university student, was heading in the general direction of the Supreme Court Complex and kindly offered to walk with me part of the way. On our short walk through Bridgetown we discussed the *Myrie* trial, which came up naturally as Alicia wondered why I was in a suit (and sweating) and making my way to the courthouse. She had, like many Barbadians, heard of the case and knew that the CCJ judges were in Barbados to take the testimony of Barbadian witnesses. Though she, admittedly, did not know the details of the case, Alicia knew that Barbados

Customs and Immigration officials had been accused of mistreating and deporting a young Jamaican woman with debatable justification. This factual scenario, Alicia felt, made Barbados look "real bad." It was hard to disagree. But, Alicia said, "every country has prejudices . . . this Caribbean Community thing, it's just on paper." As an example, she pointed out that there are many Barbadian students attending university in other Caribbean locations, and, she insisted, they must stick together, or they will have to face various sorts of discriminatory acts. Alicia suggested that I spend some time at the Cave Hill campus of the University of the West Indies (UWI) while I was in Barbados. "Just look around at how the students from other countries all stick together," she instructed, apparently presuming that I would be able to differentiate between students of various nationalities simply by looking at them.[1] Regionalism? Alicia thought not. An integrated Caribbean? Not in her experience. From Alicia's perspective, whatever it was that had been recorded on paper had not actually resulted in a community of people that recognized themselves as belonging to a Caribbean region, and whoever this Court thought it was serving, it was not her or the students at UWI, who, Alicia insisted, continued to suffer at the hands of national prejudices.

Yet, it is precisely Alicia and people like her that the CCJ sees itself as serving. In the Court's 2011–2013 *Court Report*, the President of the CCJ somewhat poetically wrote, "the Caribbean Court of Justice is part of the soul and spirit of the human beings who call these shores of the Caribbean home. . . . It is my steadfast belief that the raison d'être of this Court is to serve our Caribbean people. This Court belongs to the people."[2] In this same "Message from the President," he also insisted that "the justice we deliver must touch the likes of the ordinary man."[3] Indeed, this idea of the CCJ as a people's court is echoed throughout much of what the Court does and says.[4] The Court's website, for example, links people to the region and to the court with a tagline, just beneath its name, proclaiming, "Your people. Your region. Your Court."[5] And to illustrate exactly who "your people" are, a collage of what might be described as "ordinary" Caribbean men and women accompanies the text. A similar demographic mix featuring some of the same faces appears on the cover of the Court's first and second annual reports.[6]

As one of the Court's managers explained to me, the selection of which faces, races, ethnicities, and ages to include on the cover of the very first annual report required a great deal of thought. The challenge, she said, was how to include the "whole Caribbean" on the cover. "This," she remarked as she held up the report, "was a big accomplishment," since it handily represented the Caribbean that the Court sought to serve, from Maya Indians to dreadlocked Rastafarians (see plates 2 and 3). Much like the president's message, the "whole Caribbean" to which this administrator referred is not composed of contracting parties, which could have been graphically depicted with a map or the flags of the member states, but of smiling everyday Caribbean people who were not unlike those sharing the Zed-R with me on that hot Barbadian day. People, in short, are at the center of the Court's mission.

There is, then, a disconnect between the people the CCJ proclaims to serve and the people, like Alicia, who disclaim the region entirely. To understand this gap, this chapter takes *people* as its central focus. I examine the CCJ's work in appealing to particular people in an effort to populate the conceptual and territorial region it works to construct through other means. In chapter 2, for example, I described how the Court posits a myth of Caribbeanness from which the region and the Court have originated, and in chapter 3, I discussed how the CCJ etches the porous boundaries of a region through its own travels across it. But who, exactly, is supposed to believe in this myth or live within these boundaries? The simple answer is Caribbean people. However, these people—as Alicia demonstrates—are not necessarily a self-conscious or self-constituted population. They do not necessarily see themselves as belonging to the CCJ's region. Instead, the Court must create a regional public; it must enroll them into the idea of the Caribbean as it is mythologized and bounded and transform them into subjects of the law the Court represents. It seems clear, though, that whatever it is the CCJ is doing, it is not quite attaining this objective; it is not reaching Alicia and others like her and enrolling them as steady subjects. What, I ask, is it doing wrong? When, if ever, does it get it right?

Interpellating Publics

The Court communicates all the time. Well beyond its official legal work, the CCJ communicates through its decor and dress, its bench and its travel, and its website, speeches, and publications.[7] When it broadcasts "Our people, our region, our Court" on its home page, when the annual report portrays the faces of diverse peoples, and when the president explicitly mentions "ordinary people" in his speeches, the CCJ can be understood as saying something to somebody for some reason. In this chapter, I take the Court's multifarious communications as interpellative speech acts. Interpellation is an act closely associated with the making of nations by states. Here, however, I show how the CCJ—a decidedly nonstate apparatus—communicates in ways that work to create and enroll a regional public, rather than a national one. As with its other region-making efforts, this is not mimicry but indexicality at work; the

CCJ aims not to copy but to point to and build from a quintessential technique of nation-state making in its pursuit of a region.

Louis Althusser described the process of interpellation in his quest to understand how state ideology could transform individuals into subjects.[8] To illustrate this process of transformation, he turned to a "most commonplace" occurrence: a police officer hailing an individual by calling out, "Hey, you there!"[9] The correct individual, he wrote, will almost always turn around, responding to the state agent's call and thereby transforming into a subject of state discourse. In its most stripped-down sense, this is interpellation.

In the decades that have followed Althusser's attractively straightforward example, the basic idea of interpellation has been complicated by work that explores the full scope of the interpellative process and considers the challenges of interpellating not just an individual (or even a group of individuals) but a public, which is, ultimately, what the CCJ is after. Instead of "Hey, you there!" directed at a particular individual, the Court's speech is aimed at "indefinite others."[10] "To address a public," writes social theorist Michael Warner, "we don't go around saying the same thing to all of these people. We say it in a venue of indefinite address and hope that people will find themselves in it."[11] In other words, a public does not form by hailing one thousand souls individually but by speaking impersonally to a totality of people, however that may be defined, who then, in some way, respond.[12] Someone might become a member of a public merely by reading a public address, for example. But what if they don't? What if they read the headline and reject it? Or read it and decide that it is not meant for their eyes?

This is the paradox intrinsic to the interpellative transformation of both individuals and publics—a paradox that leaves open the possibility of failure.[13] The police officer in Althusser's example speaks to a subject who does not yet exist but is made only through the interaction, just as public discourse both presupposes and entails the very public it is addressing. This is to say that the not-yet-subject and the not-yet-public must do *something*—"no matter how somnolent"—to become the subject or the public that the addresser intends.[14] And the fact is, increasingly perhaps, public discourse is not always received in the way or by the people that the speaking institution intends, resulting in an "interpellative misfire."[15] There are "gaps" between the envisioned publics and the actually-interpellated publics, which ultimately lead to failures in "pragmatic enactment" such that the institutional endeavors do not work or public discourse creates an unintended public.[16] It certainly seems, as I discuss in this chapter, that the CCJ suffers from various interpellative misfires. While "misfire" suggests a certain level of intentionality, here I stretch it somewhat to account for the challenges that the CCJ encounters in both its intentional and unintentional interpellative communications. Alicia, for instance, is a Barbadian who was being hailed by a regional court that was currently putting the State of Barbados on trial (and later finding Barbados liable). It was within reason that Alicia might not identify herself as part of the public the CCJ is hailing. In this example, the CCJ's intentional acts misfire. However, in other examples offered in this chapter, the characteristics of the CCJ's interpellative acts are far less purposeful—sometimes taking shape by dint of having an English-speaking staff. Yet, these acts, too, misfire, in that they turn away prospective subjects rather than hail them.

But there is more to the CCJ's difficulties. Not only does the Court experience its share of interpellative misfires, it also wrestles with what I call *interpellative dissonance*. The CCJ's address to indefinite others is merely one hail among many others across time. These competing calls have the benefit of fine-tuning with experience and have already successfully interpellated large swaths of the same public that the CCJ addresses. Alicia's comments provide a succinct overview of the dissonant calls that "ordinary" Caribbean people encounter; at the same time she disavowed the existence of a region, she pointed me in the direction of one of the most widely recognized regional institutions—the University of the West Indies—and acknowledged the possibility of interregional travel among students. Even then, she pointed to the most familiar and enduring publics of the modern era: a national public. In effect, her comments reveal that she has responded to one regional hail (that of UWI) over others (that of the CCJ or CARICOM) and that, above all, she and other students remain steadfastly responsive to their own national hails. It is this noisy field of cross-firing calls that leads to interpellative dissonance and in which the Court struggles to make its own voice heard, especially as it moves out of the courtroom and into the Zed-Rs and minibuses of the broader Caribbean. And this is very much a risk when indexing practices of nation-state making, such as interpellation; in doing so, the CCJ implicitly points to similarities between what it is doing and what a state is doing, thereby positioning its interpellative acts within an already crowded field of public hails.

This chapter, then, tracks the Court's calls to a Caribbean public. Sometimes these calls are carefully scripted and deliberately deployed, other times they are accidental and implicit. In both cases, though, the CCJ's call is itself quite revealing and provides clues as to the precise characteristics of the public the Court intends to interpellate. Envisioning the public in this way often leads to an alienation of Caribbean people rather than their conscription—interpellative misfires that have contributed to the Court's struggle for support across the region. Also contributing to the CCJ's troubles is the sheer number of Caribbean hails coming from other institutional sources and, even more profoundly, the now-hegemonic hail of the nation-state. Within this crowded arena of Caribbeans and states, the CCJ's call is frequently lost among the interpellative dissonance. Within an enclosed courtroom, as I describe at the end of the chapter, however, the Court's hail reigns supreme. If not able to fully constitute a regional public, the CCJ manages to stoke an ember of regional affinity and intimacy.[17] If not the end point to its efforts, it marks a beginning and a possibility.

Talking to Ordinary People

> We got poor marks from our stakeholders on how we went about our public education exercises, because in the first couple years of the Court's existence, we thought that it was very important to have public education sessions with people throughout the region. So, we went to a number of different countries, that's the judges in the main, and we had what we called "town hall meetings" where we spoke about what the Court is about, the decisions that the Court had already given, the respects in which it was important to have a Court like this. And many of our stakeholders thought that this was a little vulgar, that the court should not be, um, what's the word, selling itself . . . like a preacher. So, we've cut back on some of that in that overt sense. But what we started to do is to try and devise mechanisms for reaching the public in different ways, so that we have this CCJ Corner program.
>
> INTERVIEW WITH JUSTICE MATTHEWS

The "CCJ Corner," a short and simply worded column offering a summary of CCJ judgments, began to appear in such regional newspapers as Trinidad's *Express*, Jamaica's *Observer*, and Barbados's *The Nation* sometime during the latter half of 2013. The exact date and circumstances of its origin, though, like much at the CCJ, was somewhat shrouded in mystery; among my friends at the Court, I was far from alone in thinking that it had just appeared one day. Of course, there was more to it than that, and I was determined to find out the story behind this new form of mass communication. It was, in my experience, the Court's most visible and widely reaching public education effort. After asking around to no avail, I was finally able to schedule a meeting with Justice Matthews, who, it turned out, was largely responsible for its creation and operation.

To the best of his memory, the idea for the "CCJ Corner" began when President Maxwell, as the new president for the Court, made a trip to Jamaica in 2012. There, he spoke casually to a writer for the *Observer*, who complained to him that the media often did not know about the Court's decisions when they came down. The president felt that this was something that needed to be addressed. Following this encounter, Sara, the senior public education and communications officer for the CCJ, tried to follow up with the *Observer* journalist with a proposal for a recurring short column that summarized CCJ judgments, but, according to Matthews, Sara "did not get far or did not get through" to the journalist. It then dawned on them (Matthews did not say who "they" were) that this was probably something they could offer to multiple media sources—not just one newspaper. They saw in it, as the quotation at the start of this section indicates, an opportunity to address the public in a far less "overt" or "vulgar" way than the Court's earlier public education attempts. And so the "CCJ Corner" was born.

When it began, the work of its production fell into Maria's lap. She was a judicial research assistant at the Court who was just completing her tenure when mine began. From Maria, it passed to Tabitha, an intern, then to Sydney, another intern, before it arrived on Rhianna's desk. It was Rhianna, also a judicial research assistant, who made the greatest strides with the "CCJ Corner," bringing more media on board and working closely with regional law schools to attract more law student contributors. The idea was to make it as deeply regional as possible: regional law students preparing summaries of judgments from a regional court to be published in regional newspapers for consumption by a regional public.

The production process, as far as Justice Matthews described and Rhianna augmented, began with a careful selection of which judgments deserved summary and publication. As Justice Matthews explained, those dealing with more "esoteric" issues were not included, but the ones that had a "story" and that dealt with issues of law that were "applicable to everyday people" or "judgments from which you can extrapolate some sort of lesson" were sent to law students to be turned into five hundred-word summaries. These included cases that touched on issues of personal property, commercial mortgages and loans, criminal confessions, trade unions and wrongful termination, and a right to a fair trial, among other topics. Even those cases that inevitably delved into more "esoteric" issues were handled in a manner that highlighted their more general relevancy. As one "CCJ Corner" column explained,

> While the Caribbean Court of Justice (CCJ) case of Roseal Services Limited v. Challis [2012] CCJ 7 (AJ) deals with quite a bit of procedural and technical points, it still offers assistance to the *general public* on what matters may appropriately be appealed to the CCJ and how to make specific appeals.[18]

After the appropriate cases had been selected, Rhianna sent the judgments to either the principals, the students, or some other designated contact at the law schools. Law students then prepared the summaries and sent them back to Rhianna, who edited them and forwarded them to Justice Matthews for his final approval before she distributed them to the newspapers. Rhianna kept a list of newspapers that participated in the "CCJ Corner"—fourteen English-language papers in eight Caribbean states by the time I was wrapping up my research—and she was actively trying to attract more media outlets to the program. The problem, she learned, was that many of the papers wanted the CCJ to pay for publication space, treating the summaries, it seemed, akin to advertisements, which the CCJ would not do (as we will see in chapter 6). Rhianna also prepared a brochure to help attract more newspapers and law students into participating. The brochure explained, "The vision of The CCJ Corner is to ensure that justice is not isolated in an ivory tower but instead is accessible to the ordinary person in the street, the maxi, the ZR or the mini bus engaging in that hallowed Caribbean tradition of reading the morning newspaper."[19] It is worth noting that the maxi is to Trinidad what the Zed-R is to Barbados and the minibus is to Jamaica: a sort of every person's inexpensive public transportation.

Justice Matthews underscored the plebian intent of the "CCJ Corner" in my conversation with him. It fit squarely into the CCJ's new five-year strategic plan as a way to make the Court accessible to as many people as possible. It was a way, he said, to "popularize the Court." While he admitted that five hundred words—the maximum length of each summary—could not expect to do much, he did hope that it could accomplish three basic goals: "pique the attention of someone who is interested"; "give the flavor of what the Court is doing"; and demonstrate that the "Court is working." Modest goals, indeed, but crucially important for this new court that enjoyed very little recognition.

For next year and a half or so (that is, for as long as Rhianna served as a research assistant), the CCJ continued to manage and encourage the publication of these tidy, digestible summaries that focused on pedestrian issues and appeared in highly available regional newspapers. Instead of addressing an elite audience of lower courts and members of the bar through densely written legal decisions, the Court made a concerted effort to speak to everyday people in a more familiar register and showcase issues that people could more readily accept as being applicable to them. Indeed, accompanying most of the "CCJ Corner" columns was a short statement making this intention evident: "This summary is intended to assist the Caribbean public in learning more about the work of the CCJ."[20] In addition to this explicit goal, the precise format of the "CCJ Corner" was poised to accomplish something more. Specifically, if people read these summaries and understood them as applicable to their own lives, they would effectively be interpellated as subjects of the Court's region. Equally powerfully, by publishing the "CCJ Corner" in an eminently accessible and widely read medium—the daily paper—the Court positioned this project as a means to constitute a border-crossing imagined community, in yet another indexical reference to nation building; Trinidadians could read and find relevant what Jamaicans, Guyanese, and Belizeans could also read and find relevant, establishing some sort of bond with strangers distributed across the Caribbean Sea.[21] Through the "CCJ Corner" and with the aid of newspapers, they could be connected to one another as members of a regional public.

It is impossible to know, though, how many people actually read this short column. It has proven difficult, as well, to gauge how regularly or for how long the newspapers actually published it. From what I have found, it was not published on a reliably weekly basis and did not remain in publication for more than one and a half years. What I do know, however, is that the "CCJ Corner," when it was running, was published only in English-speaking papers; the recruitment brochure, also written in English, made localized references to Anglophone Caribbean forms of transportation; and the student participants came from English-speaking law schools. The CCJ, in other words, spoke to a very specific Caribbean public throughout the publication process. Because Rhianna, an English-speaking Trinidadian, was at the helm of the "CCJ Corner" for the majority of its existence, her language abilities likely had something to do with the Anglophone audience to which the column was directed. Yet, this does not change the fact that the Court's Caribbean—that is, the indefinite others that it hailed through this public address—was composed of English-speaking people from Anglophone states.

Jamaica, Trinidad, and All the Rest

While it was evident from the "CCJ Corner" that the Court might have inadvertently hailed an English-speaking Caribbean public, other forms of its public speech affirmed its affinity to Anglophone publics and revealed that within this population the Court had hierarchically organized preferences. When I arrived at the CCJ for the first time, its publicly accessible areas—the library and the Office of the Registry—were donned with festive bunting in the colors of the Jamaican and Trinidadian flags. The desktops and countertops, too, decoratively displayed small flags from these two countries. It was August 2012, and both Jamaica and Trinidad were celebrating their fiftieth year of independence from Britain, and the CCJ was eager to celebrate along with them. Unquestionably, fifty years of independence is important and worthy of celebration, but, given what I later learned about the importance of Jamaica and Trinidad to the CCJ's mission and success, there might have been more to these supportive gestures. Indeed, the Court did not celebrate the independence days of any other member state while I was there, not the thirtieth year of independence for Saint Kitts and Nevis in September 2013 nor the thirty-fifth of Dominica in November of that same year. The office manager had posted a list of each country's day of independence in his office to remind himself, as he explained to me, when to put up and take down the relevant flags and decorations for each country. However, it appeared that only Trinidad and Jamaica earned this level of attention.

As it turned out, the judges and staff placed a great deal of stock in the (presumed) eventual accession of Jamaica and Trinidad and Tobago to its appellate jurisdiction, and, in many ways, the breadth of the Court's impact rests on this happening. These two countries have historically paved the way to and away from prior regionalization projects. Jamaica's withdrawal from the West Indies Federation, followed soon after by Trinidad and Tobago's, for example, led to the quick demise of that region-building effort in 1962, while it and Trinidad and Tobago's initiative led to the creation of CARICOM in 1973. Having these two states on board the CCJ's project of regional development was—and still is—seen as vital because of this well-established pattern in which Jamaica and Trinidad lead and the rest of the Anglophone Caribbean follows. Additionally, and not insignificantly, Jamaica and Trinidad and Tobago are two of the most populous states among the CCJ's signatories. Larger populations mean more litigation, and more litigation means more opportunities for the Court to exercise its authority, display its legitimacy, and develop a body of Caribbean law. Lastly, there is also the motivation to smooth over the awkwardness of having a Court seated in Trinidad without having Trinidad and Tobago participate as a full member. In short, the CCJ's favoritism toward Jamaica and Trinidad can be explained largely in pragmatic terms.

To persuade these states to accede the CCJ's appellate jurisdiction, the Court must entice their citizens. While neither Jamaica nor Trinidad and Tobago constitutionally requires voter buy-in by way of a referendum, in both states, a referendum is viewed as a necessary component to accession. In Jamaica, the government has occasionally offered to hold a referendum on the issue as a means to appease the opposition.[22] In Trinidad and Tobago, a report issued by a Constitution Reform Commission in late 2013 urged the use of a referendum because of the particularly sensitive nature of this issue. Given that the CCJ has become a politically divisive topic in Trinidad and Tobago, the commission argued that a referendum has become necessary to fully air the issue across political lines.[23] Thus, the CCJ adjusts its public discourse, displays, and activities to appeal *in particular* to Jamaican and Trinidadian national publics. It hangs their colors, it publishes in their papers, and it mentions their most popular forms of public transportation in its brochures because it is critically important that whatever public the CCJ can attract includes the citizens of Jamaica and Trinidad.

Where does that leave the English-speaking citizens of the Anglophone Caribbean states that are considered less vitally important, less litigiously populous, and less historically strategic? It leaves them in a far less stratified group, which the CCJ addresses through far less specified discourse and display. Instead of directing its speech to citizens of a particular state, the Court, instead, speaks more generically to "our people" through its website, annual reports, and other public materials. Yet there are occasions when the CCJ speaks more pointedly to a particular national public. After Dominica acceded to the CCJ's appellate jurisdiction in 2015, for instance, the president of the Court congratulated "the people of Dominica" (which is particularly interesting, since Dominica did not require or ask its people to vote on the issue, needing only government action to make the change) for "their resolve to make this final step in their own independence arrangements and in the enrichment of our Caribbean civilization."[24] Clearly, the president was speaking to the people of Dominica as newly interpellated members of a Caribbean public. But other than these occasions in which the Court calls to specific state publics, the CCJ tends to speak to the "whole Caribbean" en masse, giving a preferential edge to Jamaicans and Trinidadians. Meanwhile, Barbadians, Guyanese, Belizeans, and Saint Lucians alike are spoken to equally and indistinguishably. And this is a problem. Both the fact of preferentially calling to Jamaicans and Trinidadians and the act of hailing the citizens of all of the other CCJ member states as equals does not match up with historically felt and widely held hierarchies or acknowledge deeply felt wrongs.

"NOT a Caribbean Man"

> There comes a time when the only thing to do is make clear, definitive, unambiguous statements about things of importance. Here goes. I am a Jamaican, I am NOT a Caribbean man. I want no part of the totally useless creation we label CARICOM. The peoples who populate those islands 1,000 miles away from my home are not brothers and sisters. There has been some cross-breeding, but it's statistically insignificant to warrant the familial term "brothers."[25]

Jamaican attorney Ronald Mason's short article "Kick CARICOM to the Kerb" was published in the Jamaica *Gleaner* newspaper in May 2013 and soon circulated throughout the major papers in the Anglophone Caribbean, attracting substantial public commentary along the way.[26] In his article, an irate

Mason put forth an argument as to why Jamaica should leave CARICOM. He highlighted the unbridgeable differences between the nationals of Caribbean countries, the slights received by Jamaicans region-wide, and the failures of CARICOM to actually benefit Jamaica's trade and economy. Of all of CARICOM's objectionable qualities, Mason seemed to find its insistence on grouping people together in some sort of Caribbean family to be the most repulsive of all, as evidenced in the quotation that begins this section. This family was not his.

Mason's article, as well as many of the public comments that it inspired, focused on CARICOM, but to him, as to many others, CARICOM was largely indistinguishable from its affiliated institutions, such as the CCJ. Instead of considering the Court on its own terms, Mason rejected it, too, as a nonessential and possibly replaceable institution should Jamaica really "kick CARICOM to the kerb." After all, the CCJ, in Mason's view, suffered from the same fantasy of Caribbean familiarity as its mother institution. His rejection of CARICOM, the CCJ, and the so-called family they represent illustrates the "gap" between the Court's envisioned public and the public to which it actually speaks.[27] Even though the Court speaks preferentially to Jamaicans, the idea that Jamaicans would still be lumped together as part of a broader Caribbean public—"brothers and sisters" within the same family, to use Mason's analogy—is enough for Mason to refuse to be interpellated in the way that the CCJ intends. Yes, he heard the hail, and he did, in fact, turn around to acknowledge that it was addressed to him (as well as indefinite others), but the crude gesture he made upon acknowledgment suggests that if the Court is successful in calling forth a public, this public is not the supportive group of people it envisions or requires. Mason, in other words, will not be voting to accede to the Court's appellate jurisdiction should a referendum be held. And he is hardly alone in his refusal and rejection of the proffered regional public.

While Mason took issue with the familial bond implied by CARICOM and the CCJ, others find the racial makeup of the Court's region objectionable. In 2012–2013, many of the Indo-Caribbean citizens of Trinidad and Tobago and Guyana remained wary of the racial demographics of the Court's member states, which have overwhelmingly Afro-Caribbean populations. Some Trinidadians of Indian descent wondered how a Caribbean Court that served a predominantly Afro-Caribbean public could or would serve them. How would the Court's jurisprudence reflect *their* values, histories, cultures, or social circumstances?[28] The proof of the Court's inability to represent them, they argued, was in the makeup of the judicial bench itself, which was, at that time, composed of five Afro-Caribbean and two white European judges. The CCJ was well aware of this concern and, on occasion, spoke directly to the issue. For instance, the president of the CCJ acknowledged the link between this racial division and Trinidad's acceptance of the Court in a speech he presented at the 2013 International Bar Association Conference in Boston. He noted that "the absence of an Indo-Caribbean judge on the CCJ bench has led to a host of concerns published in Trinidad's newspapers as to the ability of the Court to render impartial, apolitical, independent decisions [citations]."[29] In fact, as the president instructed me as I began the research for this speech, which focused on diversity in the judicial selection process, he hoped that his words would help the Indo-Trinidadian population feel included in and represented by the Court and, at the same time, "satisfy" the Afro-Trinidadian population. Delivered in the United States and receiving little coverage within the region, I doubt, however, that this speech reached much of the public the president had intended.

Still others objected to the CCJ's hierarchical ordering of its public, in which Jamaicans and Trinidadians appeared to receive special attention. While not many people actually saw or heard the Court's subtler hails to Jamaicans and Trinidadians (the Independence Day flags in the courthouse, for example, were largely unseen and unnoticed), it did not escape notice that the Court was seated in Trinidad, raising concerns of hometown preference. Moreover, large swaths of the region read about and reacted to the Court's judgment in the *Myrie* trial. The Court's ruling in favor of Myrie, a Jamaican national, did not square with the prevailing stereotypes and hierarchy held by large segments of the non-Jamaican Caribbean population, who often attributed unsavory characteristics and nefarious activities to "ordinary" Jamaicans like Myrie. The insults allegedly directed at Myrie by the Barbadian immigration officials and the rumors that circulated among Barbadians in the prelude to the trial—that Myrie traveled to Barbados to steal their men, that she was transporting drugs, that she was a prostitute and a stripper, that she had paid a pimp to arrange her travel, and so on—were unassailable truths to many Barbadians, who had naturalized these stereotypes of their neighbors to the north, and were totally unsurprising slurs to many Jamaicans, who had come to expect this treatment from Barbadians. What surprised many Caribbean citizens, then, was that the Court ultimately ruled in favor of Myrie, finding her actions to be innocent and her story to be believable. While the judges carefully justified their decision with law and evidence, the Court's ruling also happened to reflect its prioritization of Jamaica within the region.

For some people in the Caribbean, this was the first indication that the CCJ, perhaps, did not view the region in the same way they did. Consequently, it was their first opportunity to reject the Court's region and the subjecthood it required. As the *Myrie* decision made evident, the Court's region was one in which Jamaicans could be found truthful and wronged and where Barbadians could be found to be liars and liable. This was a region in which Jamaica could win over Barbados, and this was simply too much of a reversal for some people to accept. "Time to leave the CCJ," read one succinct anonymous comment on Nationnews.com, a Barbadian online news portal.[30] Another commenter warned: "Regional Integration has always been about finding the lowest common denominator . . . and we are well on the way there . . . ," suggesting that the Court's regional integration project was not one he wanted to join.[31] Although a much greater number of people expressed their acceptance of the CCJ's decision, debated its merits, or even celebrated it as a win for the Caribbean, it is important to recognize that certain members of the CCJ's potential public wholly rejected the Court and the region it hoped to create.

The regional hierarchy that is revealed in these newspaper comments, written under the cloak of online anonymity, were echoed in many of the conversations I had with others in Trinidad. Mr. Naidoo, a long-practicing Trinidadian attorney, matter-of-factly explained to me the "hierarchy of nations" in the Caribbean. Jamaica, he told me, would like to be at the pinnacle of the Caribbean, but, according to Naidoo, they simply do not have the finances to back up this claim. Trinidad, though, does, he stated confidently.[32] The smaller islands that constitute the Organization of Eastern Caribbean States are often treated by the larger Caribbean islands as somewhat inconsequential entities who will just "follow along," Naidoo explained.[33] While the hierarchy that he presented was not shared exactly by everyone with whom I spoke, I found that almost every conception of the Anglophone Caribbean I encountered offered a window into the presence of some hierarchical organization. Naidoo attributed this ordering to the varying financial circumstances of the states, but many others pointed to cultural stereotypes—such as Barbadians being more British, Jamaicans more troublesome, and Guyanese just "backwards" —as an explanation for their feelings. The overall sense that I gathered was that, at least for Trinidadians, Barbados and Trinidad stood historically and happily at the top of a regional ladder, while Jamaica and Guyana regularly fell to the bottom, a position that Jamaicans and Guyanese felt all too keenly. In other words, the hierarchy that the CCJ communicated through everyday speech, Independence Day decorations, and a landmark decision did not resemble these widely held hierarchies, nor did it acknowledge deeply felt wounds. With good reason, then, Mason might reject a "family" of Caribbean people that failed to atone for its history of wrongs, while Naidoo might decline to join a Court that holds a hierarchy that does not reflect his own ideas of Caribbean order.

All the Caribbeans

Mason's commentary was not limited to CARICOM, though that was his primary target. Not only is the CCJ also dragged into it, but later in his article, he adds the West Indies cricket team (the Windies) into the mix, arguing that it, too, fails to provide an adequate source of "bonding." Mason thus manages to consider together, without notable distinction, CARICOM, the CCJ, and the Windies, rejecting them all in short order. What these three institutions have in common is that they are all regional and are all focused on the Anglophone Caribbean, commonalities that serve as the basis for Mason's sweeping rejection. What they do *not* have in common is the same regional membership or the same regional goals.

CARICOM is a treaty-based group of fifteen member states and five associated states committed, fundamentally, to regional economic integration. The CCJ has twelve member states (representing a subsection of CARICOM) and is devoted to deepening regional integration and developing a Caribbean jurisprudence. The Windies includes fifteen states and territories (not the same fifteen as CARICOM but with significant overlap) and represents the region in international cricket test matches. And there are far more regional institutions serving different memberships and different goals and vying for the attention and allegiance of a slightly different but in many ways similar Caribbean public. My Zed-R friend, Alicia, mentioned UWI, one of most widely recognizable regional institutions. There is also the CXC—the Caribbean Examination Council—which oversees educational standards and testing in sixteen participating states; the Caribbean Development Bank, with nineteen full members, four nonborrowing members, and five nonregional members; and numerous other regional institutions, such as the Caribbean Premier League of Cricket, the Caribbean HIV&AIDS Alliance, and the Caribbean Disaster Emergency Management Agency. This is not to mention any of the organizations that span much broader swaths of the Caribbean and more readily include Spanish-speaking, French-speaking, and Dutch-speaking states. Institutionalized understandings of the region, in other words, abound.

So do *folk understandings*, by which I mean individual imaginings of what constitutes the Caribbean. Lynette, my friend and coworker at the CCJ, explained that her idea of the Caribbean was "a group of countries with a shared history and in the Caribbean Sea. A group of small islands . . . [with] a similar culture across the board in terms of how we treat people, be it foreigners, each other, whatever." She continued, "when I think 'Caribbean,' I think Barbados, Grenada, Trinidad, Saint Lucia, Saint Vincent, Jamaica." She proceeded to exclude Guyana and Suriname, both located on the South American continent, and to include Belize, located on the Central American isthmus. She also, without further explanation, excluded the Bahamas, Bermuda, the British Virgin Islands, and the US Virgin Islands from her understanding. And while she included French-speaking Haiti and "kind of" included Martinique, she excluded Spanish-speaking Dominican Republic and Cuba, the mere suggestion of which prompted Lynette to exclaim: "No! Definitely not!" Lynette, it seemed, could confidently identify a core group of countries that constituted the region (influenced, it seemed, by CARICOM) and several that most certainly did not, but she struggled to provide a cohesive explanation of what it was that bound together certain Caribbean nation-states but not others, which led to the meandering boundaries of her Caribbean.

Mr. Banks, a well-respected Jamaican attorney, was no different. Language was the first mark of distinction he noted. "Let's start with the English-speaking Caribbean because they are closely related in a number of ways. We play cricket together, colonial territories, common experiences, similar governmental system, similar culture..." He remarked that Dutch-, Spanish-, and French-speaking countries share some of these characteristics, but then there were outliers. Despite having "a lot of sympathy for Haiti," Mr. Banks explained that it simply does not have the same democratic traditions shared by the rest of the Caribbean Community. He thought that the Dominican Republic, on the other hand, might in time become part of the Caribbean, presumably because it had democratic traditions. Notably, Mr. Banks, who is a firm believer in the CARICOM regional economic integration movement, shifted from a discussion of one region (his) to another (the Caribbean Community), illustrating the fluidity of the Caribbean.

Indeed, the boundaries of the Caribbean proffered by Lynette and Mr. Banks were redrawn over and over again over the course of my interviews, where it became standard practice to ask what one thought of or imagined as 'the Caribbean.' This question led to a surprisingly bewildering diversity of responses, contemplation, self-contradiction, and, frequently, rejection of the institutional definitions of the Caribbean, though UWI, the Windies, and even CARICOM were sometimes used as a starting point. Regardless of the stated reasons for constituting the Caribbean in a particular way, my interviewees always made exceptions that they were often unable to explain. They also revealed hierarchies that echoed Naidoo's much more explicit spelling out. Lynette's "kind of" inclusion of Martinique, Mr. Banks's "sympathy" for Haiti, or the frequently voiced concerns over Guyanese immigrants taking over Trinidadian jobs vertically organized Caribbean states and territories in a more personalized ordering.[34]

The point in describing all of these Caribbeans—both institutionalized and folk—is to draw attention to the heavily trafficked, messy field that the CCJ entered in constituting a regional public. Each regional institution works to hail its own regional public, crowding the airwaves along which the CCJ's own hail must travel. If the CCJ's hail is to successfully reach the ears of the potential public, it must still navigate each member's own imagined Caribbean. In the end, some regional hails are heard, while others are not; some calls are distinct and defined, while others are confused and combined; and some potential members respond selectively, while others reject wholeheartedly. Regularly falling on the losing end of these equations is the CCJ, with its new and yet-to-be-honed hail and its ever-evolving public education efforts. As one CCJ judge acknowledged, "it's quite clear that UWI occupies a very central place in the psyche of the West Indian people. . . . I don't think the Court has managed to attain something equivalent. Not yet." In short, the interpellative dissonance of cross-firing regional calls to subjecthood has proven to be an extraordinary obstacle in the CCJ's regional endeavor.

The Siren Song of the Nation

While the existence of multiple regions poses a problem for the Court in that it creates confusion and clogged interpellative airwaves, it is the unflappable devotion to the nation-state that seems to cause the biggest hurdle of all. Ronald Mason, for instance, rejects the region's call, but passionately takes up the hail to national subjecthood. He opens his article, after all, by powerfully declaring: "I am a Jamaican. I am NOT a Caribbean man," and continues by elaborating the vast differences and prejudices that will forever distinguish Jamaicans from other Caribbean peoples. Many of the public online comments following his article agree with him. Though less incensing, Walter B. Alexander, a lecturer in the Graduate School of Social Sciences at the University of Guyana, reminds the readers of the *Stabroek News*, a Guyanese newspaper, that "we still have a nation to build,"[35] and Trinidad's National Foodcrop Farmers Association complains that "local agriculture is not getting the push it needs" because "Caricom goods are taking up most of the market"[36]— comments that similarly emphasize national pride, independence, state sovereignty, and the nation as something distinctly other than, in competition with, and preferable to the region.

There are also subtler calls to a national public that are perhaps even more effective in their power to distract from the regional call; these are often state sanctioned. Trinidad and Tobago, for example, marks its Independence Day with parades, revelry, flags, floats, speeches, and a day off work. The citizens respond each August 31 by decorating the landscape with red, black, and white—the colors of the Trinidadian flag—a palette that greeted me on my first visit to Trinidad. The state and its national public celebrate Republic Day, on September 24, in similar style with comparative zest. And the 2012 Olympic gold medal won by javelin thrower Keshorn Walcott also earned a work holiday for Trinidadian nationals and inspired seemingly endless Trinidadian national pride that, at times, defined itself against other Caribbean nation-states (e.g., a quintessentially Trinidadian double entendre was printed on local T-shirts: "Jamaican men run rel fast, but Trini men throw rel wood"). In sum, Trinidadian (and Jamaican, Barbadian, Saint Lucian, etc.) life is rife with moments of national verve in which one's belonging to the nation—not the region—is reinforced.[37] National subjecthood is considered an alternative to regional subjecthood, and people like Mason passionately argue that it is the better and only alternative, rejecting the very notion that a region exists in the first place. Others, like Alicia, bemoan the exclusivity and cruelty of national belonging but see regional subjecthood as nothing more than a paper promise.

A Public of a Regional Courtroom

Despite the interpellative struggles described in this chapter, the Court has managed, on occasion and only temporarily, to constitute something like—or the beginning to—a regional public within the confines of the courtroom. Here, the CCJ has the ability to transform a captive audience into regional subjects who understand themselves as belonging to the same region the CCJ envisions. The numbers are small, the occasions are rare, and the time frame is fleeting, much in the same way that a regional territory comes and goes, but a regional public, as the Court has demonstrated, is a possibility, as I learned over the course of *Myrie*.

It was the third day of the Jamaican segment of the trial, and, by now, everyone involved had more or less established their routines. I reserved a spot for myself in the "Visiting Attorneys" section of the public seating area alongside eight or so other attorneys; the presenting attorneys arrived and arranged their things at the front tables; law students flowed in and found seats amid the general public; and about four media personnel set up shop in the "Media" area. The day's session began at 9:05 a.m.

On the heels of two Jamaican witnesses who testified to their own rough treatment at the Barbados border, the State of Jamaica called its first expert, Epheium Allen. Allen was the deputy director of Immigration at the Passport, Immigration and Citizenship Agency for Jamaica. He was called as a witness to provide statistics on entries, exits, and "turnarounds" by the Jamaican border control at the airport. "Turnarounds," as an earlier witness had explained, was the term applied to those hopeful international travelers, such as Myrie, who had been denied entry at a border and were returned to their home state, usually within twenty-four hours. Among the various statistics Allen offered was a comparison between states that denied entry to—or "turned around"— the most visitors and those that turned around the fewest. He provided this information during his direct examination:

ATTORNEY: . . . how would you assess the turnarounds from CARICOM jurisdictions?
MR. ALLEN: There are some CARICOM jurisdictions where the numbers are very high, and some where the numbers are very low.
ATTORNEY: And would you wish to identify the CARICOM jurisdictions in which the numbers are very high?
MR. ALLEN: Sure. Barbados, Trinidad, Antigua, and, I believe, The Bahamas.
ATTORNEY: And where would you consider [the numbers] to be very low?

At this point, Allen's quick responses slowed just a bit. He paused for about ten seconds while he filled his lungs with a couple of deep breaths as he contemplated his answer: "Suriname." The CCJ judges, audible to everyone in the courtroom, laughed quietly at this response. Allen then thought some more. "Ummm . . ." he said, before pausing for another five seconds. "Hai . . . ti," he added haltingly. To this response, the judges, the questioning attorney, and much of the courtroom audience laughed aloud. Amid this laughter, Justice Matthews interjected, "Haiti, you said?" And Justice Meyer added, "That doesn't seem very surprising!"

What I had witnessed was a moment of Caribbean cultural intimacy.[38] "Haiti" was so funny because, as Lynette later explained to me, "*who* would want to travel to Haiti?" In other words, everyone in that courtroom seemed to share the belief that few travelers would be turned around from Haiti because so few people would actually want to go there. Allen's response, therefore, was amusing in its obviousness. Indeed, the Court—its employees and judges alike—regularly held out Haiti as the CARICOM member state that does not really belong. In describing the cohesion among CARICOM states, Justice Meyer noted, these states are "basically, English speaking except Suriname and Haiti, and Suriname people can understand English usually. Haiti is a little difficult, more difficult, but that's kind of outside still." By noting that Haiti was "outside," Justice Meyer was likely referring to the fact that Haiti has not signed the Agreement Establishing the Caribbean Court of Justice and thus could not use the CCJ. The fact remained, however, that from the Court's perspective, Haiti was more "difficult" and became the punch line of jokes that Haitians almost certainly would not find humorous. And despite its membership in CARICOM, Haiti received no interpellative attention from the Court. The CCJ, after all, does not speak French.[39]

It also does not speak Dutch. Despite the fact that Suriname is a signatory to the Treaty Establishing the Caribbean Court of Justice and despite the fact that attorneys from Suriname have been some of the more frequent users of the Court's original jurisdiction, Allen's mention of Suriname also elicited laughter. But only from the judges. Their soft chuckles from the bench stood as an open invitation to the viewing audience, implicitly posing the question: are you "in" on the same joke? Are you part of this same English-speaking Caribbean Community that can see the humor in the obviousness of Suriname having few turnarounds? Their laughter, in short, was a hail to an audience who could understand jokes built on a specific hierarchy of languages, states, and peoples that is broadly shared across the English-speaking Caribbean. When those in the courtroom laughed alongside the judges following Allen's second response, "Hai . . . ti," they accepted the Court's tacit invitation to join the fun and to share the intimacy of being part of the same community; within the walls of that courtroom on that day, they had been interpellated as subjects of the Court's region.

It goes too far to claim, though, that this was an enduring regional public. Rather, it was a fleeting affinity, a humorous effervescence that hinted toward the possibility of something different. Not unlike the porous ephemerality of the region's territory, described in chapter 3, the region's public also appeared to be limited in space and time. It was there and then, in the courtroom during a moment of shared laughter, that these primarily Jamaican observers became regional subjects. It was a moment that delivered the region from the paper on which it was conceived and transformed it into an embodied emotion (albeit at the expense of one of its own member states) for those in the room. Despite Alicia's critiques, Mason's rebuke, Naidoo's hierarchy, and the multiple comments asserting national exclusivity, a regional public, it appeared, could exist for some people, in some places, at some times.

5

A Language

Though other high-profile cases have since made their way through the Caribbean Court of Justice, more than ten years later the *Myrie* trial remains the highlight of the Court's existence. Through its remarkable handling of the trial, the CCJ managed to make thinkable something special: a territorialized region and an interpellated people that existed in a nonstable space-time distinct from that of a sovereign nation-state. But as momentous as *Myrie* was, it was, in the end, only one case, lasting less than one year. Region making, as the ensuing decade has highlighted, is a far more expansive task that, more times than not, required far less exciting and often less obvious work. Some of this work took place during the tours of the courthouse, which I described in chapter 2. Other work happened through seemingly mundane decisions that carried with them the potential to craft a region. Decisions about language fall into this category and constitute some of the most profound, most prevalent, and most persistent region-making efforts at the CCJ.

Very early on in my research, I met with the court executive administrator (CEA) of the Court, Master Jacobs, as she was called with reference to her former position as a master in the Trinidad and Tobago national courts. Master Jacobs had had, arguably, the strongest influence in getting the Court up and running and shaping it into the institution that it is today; she was one of the first employees hired to work at the CCJ and, at the time we spoke, continued to exert considerable authority in how it operated. I met with her at the suggestion of several staff members who thought that she would be able to share interesting information about the formation and functioning of the Court. They were right. Master Jacobs had her finger on the pulse of the institution.

During our conversation, she offered me fascinating details of the decisions she and others made leading up to the CCJ's opening in 2005. There was particular attention, she noted, to present the CCJ as a *regional* court, not just a court for Trinidad—a misunderstanding that might arise from the Court's location there. One way this was done, she told me, was to utilize the diversity of regional accents of the CCJ staff when creating the telephone menu for the Court.[1] For instance, she explained, "when you call the Court, we made sure that you do not hear a Trinidadian voice. You will hear a Bajan [Barbadian] voice. Deeper into the system you hear a Guyanese voice." While "outsiders" might not catch these nuances, "these differences matter" to people from the Caribbean, she assured me. Hearing these differences, she suggested, would signal to in-the-know callers that this Court was, in fact, theirs: a court for the insiders. Indeed, this linguistic choice was directed to defining the region that these callers could believe themselves to be part of, one that was inclusive of national difference, as represented by the differences in nationally associated accents.

As the CEA suggested, language and careful linguistic decisions mattered in the earliest days of the Court, and, as I learned, continued to matter to those who work there in the years that followed. Explicit discussions of language wafted in and out of my research at the CCJ, making it one of the more notable leitmotifs of my fieldwork. Many of those who worked there, from judges and high-ranking administrators to customer service representatives, seemed to understand that language could play a critical role in the CCJ's accomplishment of its goals. While not everyone was as explicit and intentional about language as Master Jacobs, a good number of judges, administrators, and staff members commented on language's ability to do something for the Court *beyond the accomplishment of law itself.* Precise language, in other words, was not reserved for the drafting of a judicial decision or the pronouncement of a particular law. It could do far more, which they seemed to well understand. Indeed, it was as if they had read and digested the wealth of legal linguistic scholarship that has expertly shown how language, through law, has the capacity to craft a veritable world.[2] In other words, my interlocutors at the CCJ proactively sought to constitute something through their thoughtful use of language. This was clear.

In this chapter, then, I explore the CCJ's decisions about and use of language as another technique to craft a region. Like a myth of origin, a territory, and a people, language has also long been associated with the making of sovereign nation-states, but, again, the Court co-opts this tool in service of the region. More than this, it is through careful attention to language that we can see best how the CCJ works to assert the *non*-sovereignty of the region, while attempting to link this non-sovereignty to the law. As noted in chapter 1, Bonilla has defined *non-sovereignty* "as both a positive project and a negative place-holder for an anticipated future characterized by something *other than* the search for sovereignty."[3] And this is precisely what the CCJ is attempting to accomplish through language; as a positive project, the Court works to signal a distinct break from persistent British colonial legacies and logics, and, at the same time, it gestures toward a yet-to-be-fully-defined Caribbean future that, whatever it is, is certainly not sovereign—a negative placeholder for something yet to be realized. The subtlety, possibility, and flexibility of language allow the CCJ to navigate the path to non-sovereignty with a necessary sensitivity, for both its rejection of a (post)colonial past and present and its embrace of an unknown future must take into account the profound tension between regional cooperation and national autonomy, the long-held familiarity with and comfort in British law and legal practices, and the acute awareness of the Caribbean's relative place in the global geopolitical hierarchy.

Constitutive Power of Language

In one sense, what the CCJ hopes to accomplish through language is nothing new. Language has long been associated with the making of polities. Specifically, the ideology that one (usually, standardized) language represents one people with one shared culture has played a critical role in nation-state making for centuries.[4] To say this otherwise, by speaking the same language, requiring people to speak the same language, or acting *as if* everyone is speaking the same language, differentiated groups are brought into being—namely, a nation of insiders and everyone else.[5] As this process of language standardization often takes place through the work of a state, this is frequently a way in which a nation becomes sutured to the state. It is an ideology that allows us to say, even while simultaneously recognizing the overdrawn inaccuracies of such statements, that citizens of England speak English, while citizens of Spain speak Spanish, and that they are distinct cultures. Even the notion of "translation," as Susan Gal has pointed out, reinforces the idea of linguistic, territorial, and cultural boundaries and difference.[6] The CCJ's orientation toward language as a tool to build a polity, then, is not misplaced, as it draws from a well-trodden and widely shared ideology that links language to people to place.

Legal language, which I also discuss in this chapter, takes the creation of the nation-state one step further: it works to establish it in law as a *sovereign* nation-state. This linkage, too—between legal language and sovereignty—is also well covered in academic literature. As Justin Richland and others have argued, it is within the details of legal discourse that law establishes the boundaries of its authority.[7] And when we begin to talk about the limits of law's authority, we verge on canonical understandings of sovereignty à la Thomas Hobbes, as well as Giorgio Agamben and Carl Schmitt, wherein sovereignty is defined by its legal authority within (but no further than) a particular territory, and it is the sovereign, solely, that has the authority to decide the exception to the legal order.[8] Thus, it is through attention to jurisdictional details—that is, the speech and practices through which law announces and delimits its own authority—that the theoretical conceptualization of sovereignty becomes legible "as the real effect of a more mundane process of administrative distribution and management."[9] In other words, when we understand "jurisdiction as a bundle of social practices" constitutive of sovereignty, the construction and maintenance of sovereignty itself becomes observable.[10]

Given the very close associations between language and the making of a sovereign nation-state, it is especially intriguing and innovative that the CCJ looks to language to create a non-sovereign region. To show how it goes about this work, in which it redirects language's potential, this chapter explores a series of examples that illustrate how those who work at the CCJ understand language as having the ability to deftly respond, at multiple levels, to crosscutting national, regional, and global pressures, at the same time they strive to establish the Court's own authority. Although the range of the CCJ's linguistic techniques may give the impression of an unfocused approach—such as claiming that linguistic differences matter, on one hand, as in the opening vignette, and silently eliding linguistic difference, on the other hand, as suggested in a later example—the Court's use of language is cohesive in one important respect: it is directed toward a future that departs from a model of classic state sovereignty.

Identifying a People, Justifying the Court

After I had been at the Court for nearly a year, the CCJ initiated a new public education campaign in Trinidad. Whereas the "CCJ Corner" column, discussed in chapter 4, targeted a broad English-speaking, newspaper-reading audience across the region, this new endeavor remained narrower and closer to home. Stymied by the slow accession of states to its appellate jurisdiction, the Court hoped that educating schoolchildren would improve the public's awareness of the CCJ and sway already-existing biases against it. The campaign was designed, then, to educate and, the CCJ hoped, also, though more subtly, persuade by offering justifications for the Court's existence and demonstrations of its excellence.[11] The CCJ was already quite practiced in providing these types of explanations, and among the justifications it regularly offered for itself was a recurring theme; a shared language, I was told on numerous occasions, made this region a region and made a regional court a necessity. This familiar argument featured prominently in the newly developed education program.

Following several months of organizing and a few hurried days of preparation, I joined two CCJ staff members on their first of several planned school visits: a morning trip to Saint Andrew's Convent, a secondary school in Port of Spain. Chauffeured by one of the Court's drivers in a Toyota SUV (rather than one of the CCJ's Lexus SUVs), we were dressed in ironed, blue, CCJ-emblazoned shirts and jeans, while a judge, wearing a suit, joined us at the school in a separate CCJ-chauffeured Toyota SUV. Our clothes and cars had been carefully planned, as we strived to present the Court as professional, yet approachable, and well financed but not "stush" (a Caribbean term for snobbish) to this youthful audience. After waiting a short time at the school's front desk, we were ushered to an open-air assembly hall where we quickly set out our supplies.

The hall slowly filled with about eighty students. Serena, introduced in chapter 2, and Sara, the senior officer and sole member of the Court's Public Education and Communication team, moved through the program they had thoughtfully prepared while I assisted as I could. The highlight of the visit—a loosely scripted enactment of an appeal—was something that they, with the encouragement of a CCJ judge, eagerly anticipated, believing that it would resonate particularly well with the junior high school–aged crowd. The objective was to have students first act out, with the assistance of narration and prompting, the process of a case moving through Trinidad courts and eventually arriving at the Privy Council, and then to contrast that experience with an appeal to the CCJ.

As our student volunteers stood in their assigned positions, Serena explained the hypothetical scenario, one designed to be widely relatable to young audiences across Trinidad: a young man and a young woman were at a school dance when the young man tried to "teef a wine" (Trinidadian creole for attempting to intimately dance) with the young woman. The young woman was not happy with this behavior and filed a case against him in the Trinidadian courts. As Serena continued to narrate, the female student walked to a series of students standing with premade signs that identified them as judges of various courts. At Trinidad's "high court," the young woman pointed to the young man and argued, "he tried to teef a wine from me," to which the "judge" responded, to the amusement of the spectators, "No!"—firmly rejecting the woman's argument. After appealing her case and offering the same argument, the young woman received the same adamant "No!" from the Trinidad "court of appeals," which also rejected her case. She then appealed to the "Privy Council," after spending a good deal of time and money flying to the England, as Serena explained, and presented the same argument. The "Privy Council judges," Serena pointed out, had no idea what "teefin' a wine" meant and incorrectly and comically assumed that it had to do with stealing or "thiefing" wine, the alcoholic beverage. Based on this misunderstanding, the "British judges" said "Yes!" to the woman's case and, in a perversion of justice, jailed or fined (it was not clear nor wholly important) the young man. The message, as Serena spelled out, was that the "Privy Council" got it wrong; no one should be punished for merely trying to dance with someone, but because the Privy Council judges are not from the Caribbean, they could not understand.

To drive this point home, the enactment continued. Serena invited the audience to imagine what would have happened if the young woman could have appealed her case to the CCJ. On this prompt, the young woman walked up to the "CCJ judge" and, as before, pointed to the young man, stating that "he tried to teef a wine from me." To this, the "CCJ judge" responded, looking at the young man, "Oh! You were just trying to dance." The onlookers laughed, and Serena made sure they understood: the fictional case was correctly dismissed this time, and justice was properly served because this Caribbean court, unlike the Privy Council, understood Caribbean people. Notably, the fictional Trinidadian case had morphed into a Caribbean one.

Indeed, there are two slippages in Serena's message.[12] First, the differences between national creoles and accents—differences that were celebrated and showcased in the Court's phone menu and differences that had caused genuine difficulties in understanding the testimony of some witnesses in the *Myrie* trial—were erased and transformed into a shared regional language spoken and understood by a regional people.[13] Although the phrase "teef a wine" is one that is recognizable throughout the region, it is strongly associated with Soca, a Trinidadian genre of music, and throughout the hypothetical case, it was uttered in a Trinidadian accent to Trinidadian courts. Yet, the Trinidadianness of this linguistic example was quietly elided in Serena's punch line. That is, the boundaries of difference were redrawn in a way that grouped citizens of various Caribbean states together while differentiating them from the British.[14] By way of clever storytelling and subtle erasures, Serena and Sara drew on classic strategies of multicultural nation making by drawing together one people out of many, to echo Jamaica's national motto ("Out of Many, One People"), which reflects its own multiracial nationalist project.[15] Indeed, the melding of many accents into one voice is reminiscent of language standardization projects that offer up a single "authentic" national—here, pan-Caribbean—dialect, masking difference in the name of cohesion.[16]

FIGURE 8. A large portable banner displayed at conferences and workshops hosted by the Caribbean Court of Justice. It, like much of the CCJ's promotional materials, features the Court's signature blue color and includes the tagline "One People. One Region. One Court." Photograph by author.

Second, Serena's message slips from a commentary on misunderstood Caribbean creole to a critique of unbridgeable cultural divides. It is not just that British judges cannot understand the meaning of the words but that they cannot understand the culture of the Caribbean, where "wining" is a commonplace, acceptable, and socially important form of dance.[17] A shared language, in the CCJ's view, is reflective of and analogous to shared cultural traditions, and shared cultural traditions are indicative of the existence of a Caribbean folk, an equation of language-culture-region that mirrors classic nation-making techniques.[18] Significantly, by suggesting a shared Caribbean language-culture, the CCJ works to constitute the region against the relief provided by the British. Even more, by understanding language in this way, the CCJ's own reason for being becomes self-evident. There *is* a Caribbean people, which this Caribbean court can *naturally*, in part because of a shared language, understand. It shares a cultural essence with this particular community.[19] As the CCJ claims in a tagline that appears on much of its promotional material, the people, the region, and the Court are singular and united (as depicted in figure 8; see also plates 2 and 3 in the inset illustrations at the start of chapter 7).

Yet the CCJ's language standardization work has to navigate more than the diversity of English-based creoles that distinguish one Anglophone state from another. Though marginalized and deprioritized in many ways, as discussed in earlier chapters, the region that the CCJ is meant to serve contains non-English speakers, too. Again, the Court minimizes and erases these differences, following the same logic that it displayed in the public education performance. On the one hand, the Court boasts three official languages—English, French, and Dutch—representing the three primary languages spoken by citizens of the Caribbean Community (CARICOM) member states, which include, in addition to the majority Anglophone states, French-speaking Haiti and Dutch-speaking Suriname. On the other hand, English is the only language that is ever actually used by the Court, as I noted in chapter 4. There, I argued that the linguistic decision to speak and publish in English indicates a strategic preference of the Court. Here, I add that at least one of the CCJ's judges views the predominant use of English at the Court as supporting the Court's claim to serve the Caribbean region; that there are not, in practice, multiple language differences to contend with means, to this judge, that there is, in actuality, the possibility of a region.

Acknowledging that I was being provocative in my choice of words, I asked Justice Meyer, "Do you think there's a certain vanity in . . . the CCJ calling itself 'the *Caribbean* Court' . . . when it's partial?"

"I don't know that it's vanity," he responded, before explaining how he thought the "Caribbean" appellation might have come to describe the Court in the first place and why it remains justifiable today: "I don't think it's vanity, but it's a big name. Maybe too big for what we are. But it's as it is. In a sense we cover most parts of the Caribbean. Yes, is it the 'Caribbean Court'? Or is it the 'CARICOM Court of Justice'? . . . I think 'CARICOM Court of Justice' would be the most proper, but then what means CARICOM? Caribbean Community."

"Perhaps it's an aspirational name," I suggested.

"Yes," he agreed. "Certainly, potentially it's possible to cover almost the whole Caribbean. But that I don't see happening. But maybe we are planting the seeds now. In fact, it's easier for us to do it than in Europe, because there they have thirty languages. Here we have four." He was referring to English, French, Dutch, and Spanish, as he later clarified. He noted, moreover, that the Dutch-speaking Surinamese attorneys who have appeared before the CCJ speak English when they are in court, obviating the need for the interpretation booth that is present in the courtroom but has never been used. "The Surinamese lawyer says, 'Let me talk English,'" Justice Meyer explained to me. "And this is fine. There's no problem there. So, that is significant. But even if you had to use [the interpretation booth], you only have four languages. . . . That would cover all [of the Caribbean]. That is doable." Thus, much as in the "teefin' a wine" reenactment, Justice Meyer erased the true breadth of linguistic difference in the Caribbean to make an argument about the possibility of a region. From the many Romance, Indigenous, and creole dialects and languages spoken across the Caribbean, Justice Meyer references four. From these four, three are included as the CCJ's official languages. From these three, Justice Meyer points out that only English—one, undifferentiated form of English—is used. From many voices and many people come one.[20]

Defining the Court's Caribbean

As my conversation with Justice Meyer suggests, the contours of the Court's region are purposefully unsettled to allow for more states to join as members. This means that while the CCJ's membership is, to some extent, bounded by those countries that signed the Agreement Establishing the Caribbean Court of Justice, the Court's jurisdiction exists in a state of constant evolution and open possibility. While all twelve state signatories of the Agreement are automatically included within the Court's original jurisdiction, only four states have acceded to its appellate jurisdiction. Of those yet to accede, there are a variety of complicated stories involving partial, failed, or promised accession, leaving space for much misunderstanding as to which states actually belong to which of the Court's jurisdictions. The clarity of the CCJ's jurisdiction is further complicated by an open invitation for other CARICOM member states or even states from the broader Caribbean to join the Court in any capacity. It is this possibility—facilitated by language—in fact, that, according to Judge Meyer, helped justify the Court's claim to be a "Caribbean" institution.

What this amounts to is that while the Court is certainly aware of its own jurisdictional membership, few others are. Even some attorneys and several judges in national courts do not have an accurate understanding of whether their own state falls within which (if either) of the Court's jurisdictions, making the question of whom exactly the CCJ serves at any given point in time a live and valid issue. In the midst of this uncertainty, though, there is at least one bright line: those who appear before the CCJ are expected to call its judges "Your Honour," while those who remain with the Privy Council continue to use "My Lord," a point that was concisely made to a group of Caribbean attorneys visiting the Court.

Following a tour of the courthouse, this group of attorneys had the opportunity to meet several CCJ judges for a prearranged question-and-answer session, much like the one described in chapter 2. As they waited for the judges in the conference room, Dr. Williams, the CCJ's chief protocol and information officer, offered advice to the attorneys on how to interact with the judges and encouraged them to use the opportunity to ask questions. It was in this vein that someone asked, "How should we address the judges?" Matter-of-factly, Dr. Williams responded that they can be called "Judge or Your Honour." He added, with a raised eyebrow and a wag of his finger, "We don't use 'Lordship.' That is for the Privy Council." With this comment, underscored by a cautionary gesture, Dr. Williams etched a line through the confusing jurisdictional terrain of the broader Anglophone Caribbean.

In much the same way the public education visit emphasized an "us" (Caribbean) versus "them" (British) divide, "Your Honour" versus "Lordship" creates a distinction between those Caribbean people who appear before the CCJ and those who continue to use the Privy Council.[21] While both are terms of judicial address used in many courts around the world—"Your Honour," for instance, is the preferred mode of address in a number of former colonies—Dr. Williams made the relevant distinction crystal clear; "Your Honour" is *ours*, he suggests, while "Lordship" is *theirs*, thereby refining the definition of "us" as opposed to "them."[22] Dr. Williams insisted that "we" do things differently, and that this difference could easily be heard through the choice of judicial address. Therefore, in selecting a term of judicial address that is deliberately *other* than the term of address used at the Privy Council, the CCJ established categories of insiders and outsiders—not just between British and Caribbean, but among Caribbean people themselves: who is with the Court and who is not, who is on board with the regional agenda and who is not, who is ready to move toward an acolonial future and who remains tethered to the colonial past.[23]

"Your Honour," though, does not offer a clean break from colonialism. As many in the region know through widely available American television shows and via general public knowledge, "Your Honour" is used throughout the courts of the United States (a state with its own British colonial past, no less). The CCJ's adoption of this term of address, then, could well be taken as a move toward an alternative (neo)colonial relationship. This is not entirely wrong; CCJ judges and staff did occasionally point to the Supreme Court of the United States or the US president at that time, Barack Obama, as desirable models for Caribbean law and governance. Nevertheless and despite the potential (neo)colonial connotations, "Your Honour" remains, most important, *not* British. It is gender neutral, distinctly unmonarchical, and far less deferential than the (post)colonial "My Lord" and "My Lady." Further, whereas "My Lord" might signal continued dependence, "Your Honour" can index revolutionary independence. In the end, even if "Your Honour" might have the effect of aligning the Court and its members with the United States, it is far more preferable than "My Lord" calling to mind the British because, of all things, the CCJ and its constituents are certainly not that. The switch to "Your Honour," then, though seemingly inconsequential, contributes to the creation of new categories of personhood at the same time it cuts through the unsettledness of the Caribbean to delineate the Court's region.[24]

Developing a Caribbean Jurisprudence

A court's primary role, though, is not to justify its own existence or even to circumscribe a region (in ideal circumstances, those foundational matters would have been long settled); rather, it is to resolve disputes and develop jurisprudence. As explained to me during a visit to the CCJ in 2018, words matter here, too. I had, during this visit, been invited to present my research at the monthly CCJ judges' meeting, and it was after my presentation that one of the judges, Justice Abel, explained to me how he became aware of the jurisprudential possibilities available through thoughtful word choice. He offered the story of his epiphany, beginning, "Let me share with you a little gem you might find interesting," as he proceeded to describe an event that occurred during the earliest days of his tenure at the CCJ.

Speaking in a judiciously anonymized way, Justice Abel described an occasion where he was drafting a judgment, one of the first he had written as a judge at the Court. As is standard practice in common-law legal systems, Justice Abel relied on *precedent*—or prior legal decisions—to draw his conclusions and reach a decision. Referring to his use of precedent, he explained that he had wanted to draw a parallel between a prior case decided by the Privy Council and the case that he was presently deciding. He said, "So I wrote something like, 'Much like in the Privy Council case, *A v. B*, the case now before this Court similarly has . . .'" Justice Abel explained that he had not given this remark much thought until he showed his draft to the president of the CCJ, who, according to Abel, found the judgment to be in fine shape but for that one sentence. "He asked me, 'What if we change "in the Privy Council case" to 'in the Jamaican case"?'" Such a change was feasible, Justice Abel explained, because the pseudonymized case, *A v. B*, had been *decided* by the Privy Council, but it had *originated* in Jamaica among Jamaicans and had been heard by at least two Jamaican courts (a trial court and a first-tier appellate court) before heading to the UK. It could, therefore, be accurately cast as either a Privy Council case or a Jamaican case. Although the historically habituated tendency is to do what Justice Abel had done and refer to it as a Privy Council case, the president, who had been at the CCJ since its inception, suggested a shift in language that emphasized the Caribbean origins of the matter—a "small suggestion," as Justice Abel remarked with a wondrous shake of his head and broad smile, that "made such a difference. It is amazing how changing one small word can really change an entire mind-set."

As his story ended, another judge chimed in to offer his own example. Justice Meyer, who, like the president, had been with the Court since 2005, noted that he, too, had rethought citational practice in a way that could emphasize the CCJ's contributions and the jurisprudence it produced. It is common in legal writing to cite earlier judgments that bolster a particular finding; a judgment, for instance, might make a legal point then cite: "see *A v. B*" for precedential support. Justice Meyer explained, however, that rather than writing "see Privy Council case *A v. B*," he insists on writing "see *also* case *A v. B*" (his emphasis). As he put it, writing "see Privy Council case *A v. B*" gives the impression that the Privy Council is the progenitor of all rules, holdings, and legal arguments, and this is not the impression the CCJ would like to reinforce. "It is not like the Privy Council is the only one to have made this point or to have been the first one," he insisted. Thus, according to Justice Meyer, "by writing 'see *also*,' it says that 'we have it [this point or rule or holding], and they also happen to have it, too.'" In other words, he chooses his words carefully and consciously to put the CCJ on par with and contemporary to the Privy Council. More than this, Justice Meyer, Justice Abel, the CCJ president, and the other judges view language—here, common-law citational practices—as a means through which law and lawmaking can be repatriated or, in this context, newly "regionated."[25] Not only did the Caribbean have law, but it had its *own* laws, a critical step in "closing the circle of independence"[26] and edging toward a sovereign-like polity defined through its lawmaking powers.[27]

Refusing Sovereignty, Constituting a Region

There is much in the CCJ's reliance on language to suggest that it is, in fact, aspiring to be sovereign. After all, through its creative use of language, it works to define a distinct people, carve out a discernible territory, and claim its own jurisprudence—classic techniques in the construction of a sovereign nation-state, if ever there were any. Yet, the Court is adamant that sovereignty—as a "North Atlantic universal" and as a model passed down through colonialism—is not at all what it desires on behalf of the Caribbean, as noted in chapter 1.[28] And, in an interesting twist, it is again through language that it signals its departure from sovereign aspirations. Specifically, its rejection of a recognizably British model of law and sovereignty comes across, to return to an example discussed earlier, in the Court's decision to address its judges by a title other than "My Lord." It comes across as well, perhaps counterintuitively, in its failure to enforce this decision.

While Dr. Williams offered one take on why the CCJ uses "Your Honour" rather than "My Lord," the Court's inaugural annual report provides an additional perspective on how and why it came to this decision. In creating a new institution, the annual report states, "Decisions must be made on seemingly simple issues such as . . . how are [the judges] to be addressed?"[29] In making each decision, as Master Jacobs explained to me and the annual report affirms, the CCJ understood itself as "creating traditions and each tradition must be created with thought and consideration for the future of the institution being created and what it means to the development of the Caribbean region."[30] Thus, when the annual report later set forth—in an eloquently subtle manner—exactly what judges will be called at the CCJ, it was clear that this decision was made with the Caribbean region and the development of the "Caribbean legal tradition," as the passage also claimed, in mind: "We are not Lords over serfs, we are Honourable men and women of the Caribbean, working for *our* Caribbean and we bow in unison to the Caribbean people whom we serve."[31]

In this one poetic sentence, the Court announced to its audience not only how its judges would be addressed but also how it sought to fundamentally transform the relationship between law and society in the Anglophone Caribbean; namely, the CCJ claimed that it will tip the historically feudal experience of law on its head. Instead of British judges "lord"-ing over their Caribbean subjects, a Caribbean court now served a Caribbean people humbly and honorably. Instead of justice coming from without and being imposed from above, it was now *of* a Caribbean people and existed *for* them. In short, by selecting "Your Honour" rather than "My Lord," the CCJ does more than distinguish itself from the Privy Council. More profoundly, it intends to shift the relationships between law, the court, the region, and society; as much as the Court has jurisdiction over the people, its people have jurisdiction over it. As much as the CCJ speaks the law, so too will its people be afforded this opportunity.

It is this rationale, exemplified in part through this linguistic decision, which essentially devolves the jurisdictional monopoly that courts traditionally enjoy, that upsets classical notions of sovereignty. Jurisdiction, as has been cleverly argued by Richland and others, can be productively considered through its component parts *juris-* (or its Latin form, *iuris*) and *-diction* (or *dictio*). Doing so highlights its meaning as "law's speech" or a "speaking of the law" and focuses attention on "the ways in which the scope of law's power and authority are announced and delimited in the everyday details of legal discourse."[32] In proclaiming its jurisdiction over a case (or even when denying that it has jurisdiction)—that is, when speaking the law—a court simultaneously presupposes, entails, and limits legal authority.[33] It is in this way that jurisdiction speaks sovereignty into existence. By sharing or devolving its jurisdictional authority, the CCJ, therefore, invites others into the project of delimiting law's power, which unsettles sovereignty as it has been conceived by the Global North. The Court does so, as the annual report suggests, knowingly and purposefully as a response to the region's experience living under the lording tendencies of the British.[34] The CCJ, in order words, exploits a weakness in the relationship between law and sovereignty—namely, that they are *not* inextricably linked.

In addition to undercutting the possibility of sovereignty, the CCJ's rearrangement of jurisdictional authority also reverses long-established expectations of legal "scaling" inherited from the British experience.[35] As Susan Philips observed in another (post)colonial state, Tonga, "higher" courts are typically associated with more serious and complex cases, more highly educated judges, stricter enforcement of the law, superior use of the English language, and a greater exercise of authority over all.[36] Yet, the CCJ—the *highest* court in the region—through its decision to address its judges as "Your Honour," explicitly disrupts this familiar scaling by ceding some of its jurisdictional authority and rejecting the quintessentially English "My Lord." Instead of being more authoritative and more English, it intentionally becomes less so or at least differently so. It also relaxes rather than reinforces the Court's authority in controlling the courtroom, another inversion of the British scales of justice I turn to next. Specifically, despite the apparent and multiplex significance of "Your Honour," the CCJ never corrects attorneys who revert to addressing the judges as "My Lord." I offer one example from the many I observed.

Some ten months into my research, I, like others at the Court, still eagerly anticipated courtroom proceedings at the CCJ. These were, after all, somewhat of a rarity given the Court's rather light caseload and its reliance on videoconferencing technology for most of its hearings. Adding to the excitement, the matter scheduled for this particular day was bound to be quite interesting. It was a high-stakes, complex matter that was part of a series of appeals coming from Belize, one of the Court's member states. Already present in the courtroom when I arrived were six attorneys representing both sides of the case: three from England and three from Belize.

Though British counsel did not regularly appear before the CCJ, this was not the first time. This series of appeals in particular brought with it a small rotation of silks and solicitors from the UK. These same hearings and appeals also established a familiarity among the attorneys, and those attending this hearing seemed to know one another fairly well and carried on casual banter as they awaited the judges' arrival. The most senior attorney from Britain, Mr. Goldsmith, was especially chatty, asking his Belizean opposing counsel, Mr. Errol, about the nationalities of each of the judges and, significantly, what he should call them. "Justice or Your Honour" was the succinct and correct response offered by Mr. Errol. "Justice" or "Your Honour," however, was not what Mr. Goldsmith called the judges throughout much of the hearing. Mr. Errol, too, occasionally got it wrong.

Within the first five minutes of the appeal, Mr. Goldsmith was already calling the presiding judge "My Lord." This was just the beginning. Throughout the day's arguments, he could not seem to get it right. Regularly and, for some lengths of time, he exclusively called the judges "M'Lords." Mr. Errol, for his part, was far more careful with his words. It took nearly an hour before he eventually stumbled, addressing a judge as "My Lo . . .—Your Honour." Not quite "My Lord" but not cleanly "Your Honour," he had managed to introduce a new term of address, a rendition of which I had heard before and after in other hearings, appeals, and cases, uttered by attorneys from Belize, Barbados, Britain, and beyond.

The verbal missteps of both Mr. Goldsmith and Mr. Errol were commonplace at the CCJ, with attorneys from all backgrounds periodically lapsing between "My Lord," "Your Honour," and the hybrid "M'Lord–Your Honour." Yet there was not one occasion during the full expanse of my research that anyone ever corrected the attorneys who got it wrong. The judges never flinched, winced, or corrected them, and the Registry staff, who are charged with managing the courtroom, never took the opportunity presented by a break in the arguments to officially announce, quietly inform, or even offhandedly mention that the CCJ policy was to address judges as "Your Honour." Just when the judges might be expected to "giv[e] instructions: sharp instructions to subordinate the mind, voice, and body to authority," as has been observed in Trinidad and Tobago's, Jamaica's, and the United States' national courts, the CCJ judges refrain from doing so in their regional court.[37] There may certainly be pragmatic reasons for a relatively new court to permit some latitude on a seemingly trivial courtroom policy, yet I suggest that more is at play.

The judges are clearly aware of the attorneys' violations. When I discussed this with them during my 2018 visit, they rolled their eyes and chuckled, adding their own examples to my already long list of observations. Justice Ramnarine, in particular, laughed aloud as she remembered a certain attorney who called her, flawlessly, "My Lady" throughout the entire course of a hearing. When the room had settled, I added that what I found especially interesting about the Court's decision to use "Your Honour" was that this decision was never actually enforced. As I said this, I could see the look of disbelief creeping onto some of their faces. I hedged slightly and explained further that "at least for the time that I was at the Court—and I attended most hearings—no one ever corrected any attorney that used the wrong term of address." The judges looked around at each other, murmuring, "Is that true?" until the president of the Court spoke up. "No," he said, definitively, "we never correct it." Several of the judges appeared taken aback, and there were whispers suggesting that perhaps they *should* start to correct attorneys, but, ultimately, the president's certainty on the matter ended the discussion and seemed to serve as a directive for the future: the judges shall not, going forward, correct the attorneys. Just as the Court proclaims in its annual report that these judges do not "Lord" over their subjects but allow them to speak for themselves, the Court does not demand subservience but is there to serve. It is within this logic, I submit, that the judges do *not* speak the law. They do not state an exception,[38] they do not exercise absolute power,[39] and they do not speak the sovereignty of the region into existence.[40] Though far less intentional than its other linguistic decisions, the Court's abstention from language becomes an important technique in the rejection of sovereignty and the pursuit of a non-sovereign region.

While the Court employs language as a means to legitimize the CCJ against a history of Privy Council dominance, carve out the Caribbean that constitutes its region, and create a jurisprudence according to the Court's own vision, the CCJ, ultimately, refuses to require others to use language in precisely the same way because to do so would undermine the Court's own broader project. To say this otherwise, the Court relies on language to set itself apart from the lording tendencies of the Privy Council and the strictures of sovereign statehood. If it were to exercise its authoritative legal voice in such a direct manner over such a seemingly trivial issue—namely, how to address the judges—the CCJ would become the very lords exercising the same domineering authority it abhors.[41] Instead, it allows attorneys to speak uncorrected.

What the attorneys' misspeakings amount to, then, are the necessary oppositional forces that save the Court from the sovereignty-making tendencies of language and law. Instead of the CCJ unilaterally determining what the Court, the region, and the law will be, "M'Lord" and "M'Lord–Your Honour" constitute the dialectic that does not derail the regional project but, in fact, makes it a possibility—for whatever is created through the absence of law's speech and the presence of attorneys' voices from Belize, Britain, Barbados, and elsewhere, it is decidedly non-sovereign.[42]

Navigating a Fine Line

The Court is wise to pay close attention to its language use, as it is the adeptness and agility of language that allow the CCJ to claim two things at once. It can celebrate the diversity of its members by featuring their accents on the phone menu and, at the same time, organize educational programs that erase these very differences. It can offer an interpretation booth and tout three official languages, while it only ever publishes or speaks in one. It can carefully adjust its citation practices in a way that asserts the primacy of Caribbean law, yet still benefit from the jurisprudence of the Privy Council. And, perhaps most important, it can intentionally indicate a departure from a British relationship between judges and society through a strategic change in judicial address but never actually enforce this change. The seeming incoherence of these linguistic decisions, actions, and inactions highlight the tricky sociohistorical landscape on which the CCJ must establish its own authority and construct a region.

This incoherence, though, is only seeming. That is, it only seems incoherent if the end goal is a sovereign nation-state, where the typical expectation (though certainly not the reality) is a single, standardized language that signifies a single, united culture, where a national court might predominantly cite only national jurisprudence and where judges exercise authoritative juris-diction. For the CCJ, though, what might seem like incoherence from the perspective of nation-state making, might be understood as a uniquely coherent approach to non-sovereign region building. The Court navigates a fine line between a colonial past and a regional future, proudly independent states and a united region, and a desire to be an authoritative and respected court that also refuses to be domineering. And it is in the space of this fine line in which non-sovereignty can exist. It taps into the constitutive potential of language and law but leads to the creation of something quite different from sovereignty or nation-statehood.

6

A Brand

During my time at the Caribbean Court of Justice, I became quite close with Serena, the customer service rep who appeared in several earlier chapters. We spent many hours chatting and laughing in the library where I worked and equal time talking in her small ground-floor office, which was really the front mail room for the courthouse and served as the one of the first points of contact for visitors to the court. This is where we were when I learned about the CCJ's now defunct gift shop. I was perched on a step stool, which had often served as the guest chair for Serena's visitors, and listening intently as Serena told me about the early days of the Court, when customer service reps wore a bright yellow tailored jacket as part of their uniform and when the Court had a gift shop located right here in her office/mailroom/customer service desk. Serena explained that the flamboyant uniforms had long been retired, but she pointed to various niches in her office to indicate that much of the merchandise that once stocked the gift shop's shelves remained. She was eager to show me, and I was just as eager to see what the Court had once hoped to sell. With some anticipatory delight, she hopped down from her chair, stepped around my step stool, and reached up the back wall of her office to a shelf containing small cardboard boxes that I had not noticed in the months prior. She brought them down, one after another, for us to inspect. Inside each box were stacks of smaller jewelry boxes, and we lifted the lids of many of these forgotten treasures. There were copper and bronze brooches, some bejeweled, with the CCJ insignia artfully integrated into their designs; there were more staid pins with *CCJ* emblazoned across them, perhaps imagined for a more masculine wearer; and there were CCJ lockets, intended to be hung on chains adorning Caribbean necks (figure 9). A small token of the Caribbean's vast biodiversity—a sea turtle, a hummingbird, a flying fish—decorated each piece of jewelry, and

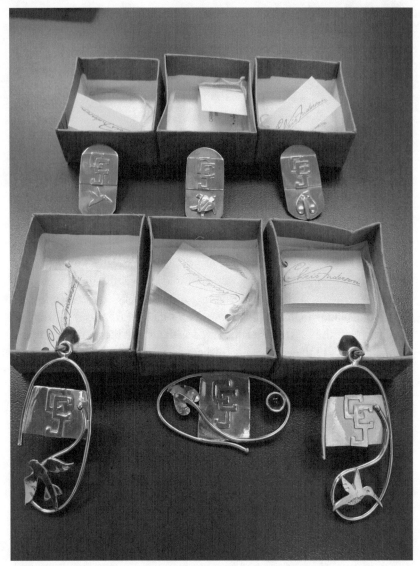

FIGURE 9. A selection of the CCJ-branded jewelry that had been for sale at the Caribbean Court of Justice's now closed gift shop. These brooches and pendants are made of fine metals and gems and feature Caribbean wildlife, such as hummingbirds and sea turtles. Photograph by author.

a card with information about the artist, a Caribbean man whose handcrafted work was "Caribbean Made," accompanied them as well (figure 10).

After marveling at the jewelry for a moment, Serena then produced a trove of other goods, stashed in other locations around her office: lapel pins, men's neckties, stationery, T-shirts, polo shirts, and gift bags, all featuring the

A BRAND 121

now-familiar-to-me signature blue of the Court and overlapping letters: *C-C-J* (as shown in plate 4 in the inset illustrations at the start of chapter 7). None of these items was inexpensive, and Serena and I wondered aloud at who would buy such gear at such prices and thought we knew the answer to why the gift shop had closed. It was not so much that US$57 for a handcrafted, high-quality metal brooch or US$55 for a Caribbean-made pendant was outlandish; rather, it was that these items prominently displayed *C-C-J*. There was something strange about the pairing of decorative accessories with the solemn administration of justice, something awkward, even objectionable, about this commodification of the Court, which, we thought, explained the eventual demise of the gift shop.

The closing of the gift shop, however, hardly meant the end of the CCJ's efforts to build a brand. To be sure, the CCJ's brand—that blue circle with overlapping *C-C-J* letters cascading down the scales of justice—appeared everywhere related to the Court: on the security guards' jackets and ties, on brochures and pamphlets, on the seal affixed to every document filed with the Court, on the desk calendars distributed to each employee, on the Court's flag, on the Court's website, and on the exterior and interior of the Court itself. A small Court seal (in gold) accompanied the CCJ when it traveled (as

FIGURE 10. Each piece of jewelry sold in the CCJ gift shop is accompanied by a small card that underscores the Caribbean origin of this wearable art. Photograph by author.

described in chapter 3), and a larger version remained housed in the Court's front display case. Employees regularly wore CCJ-branded accessories, as Dr. Williams did when hosting visitors and many judges did when delivering speeches. In short, as Dr. Williams once noted to a group of visitors, while pointing to his own CCJ lapel pin: "the CCJ is very much into branding." It is this, the Court's embrace of branding, that serves as the focus of this chapter—both *what* it is branding and *why*.

As I show, the CCJ adopts a strategy of branding to address the problem of being a court located in the Caribbean. However much the CCJ depends on the Caribbean for its existence and legitimacy (discussed in chapter 2), the fact remains that things Caribbean do not always command a great deal of respect in the Caribbean, which I discuss in this chapter. The idea of a reputable, respectable, high-quality Caribbean court is, for some local inhabitants, laughable and, for others, unthinkable. The CCJ, I suggest, seeks to remedy this problem of incommensurability through branding. Specifically, I show how the CCJ adopts a branding strategy that aims to update the image of the Caribbean as a region capable of producing and upholding the highest quality of law, such that a Caribbean court producing Caribbean jurisprudence is accepted as a legitimate and believable enterprise. It is to this end that the Court finds itself involved in a project of *place branding*. This is a practice that has been increasingly pursued by nations, states, and ethnicities looking to rehabilitate, redefine, reclaim, or protect their reputations and economies.[1] Once again, the CCJ cites and adjusts a technique that has become associated with the project of nation-state building and puts it to use in service of region making. The particularities of the regional brand, in which law and the region are married, however, demonstrate how, in its use of this technique, the Court reassigns the role of law. In other words, the Caribbean brand demonstrates how the law can play a critical and legitimating role in the constitution of a modern region; law is not the exclusive property of the modern, sovereign nation-state.

Place Branding

Whereas earlier chapters explored the CCJ's efforts to constitute a Caribbean region through classic nation-making and state-building technologies—creating a myth of origin, establishing a territory, interpellating a people, and mobilizing a language—this chapter illustrates the Court's use of branding, a more recently recognized addition to the methodology of sovereignty. It is only since about the beginning of the twenty-first century that scholars have identified branding as a key technology in the project of nation-state making, maintaining, and remaking, and they note that the seeming rise in the popularity of branding might be attributed to the ever-complexifying geopolitical landscape combined with a rise in neoliberal ideologies in which people become, first and foremost, potential customers, and history, ethnicity, culture, and patriotism are recast as commodities.

> States as well as international organizations (IOs) vie for political authority and loyalty in a dense and highly competitive market, embarking upon a quest for the hearts and minds of people both at home and around the world. . . . Patriotism—let alone nationalism—cannot be taken for granted.[2]

Cultivating a brand that crystallizes, emphasizes, and even materializes just the right characteristics of a particular place can reposition a nation-state within the world market in any number of ways by appealing to residents, tourists, investors, thrill-seekers, entrepreneurs, or simply those desiring peace, stability, law, and order.[3] Such competitive advantage is achieved through the uncanny ability of a well-conceived and strategically deployed brand to (re)shape a reputation, to give value, to bestow authenticity, and, fundamentally, to formulate a place, and what it has to offer, as a branded commodity.[4] That is, a brand can "sell" a place as a desirable "product." More than this, a successful brand can make consumers *feel*, it can make them *loyal*, it can draw them into a community of like-minded brand aficionados.[5]

In many ways, then, nation branding is like the branding of consumer products more generally.[6] It differs, however, in that nation brands are not selling nation-branded goods. For example, Andrew Graan, in his analysis of place branding in Macedonia, points out that "neither Macedonia brand wine nor France brand baguettes exist as such."[7] Instead, nation branding works to create a branded identity that "extend[s] indefinitely across a range of possible experiences and products."[8] Controlling exactly how and to what the brand extends becomes the business of those who created and deployed it in the first place, such as government officials or branding consultants. Through their talk about and commentary on (also known as *metadiscourse*) the nation's brand, these officials help sanction the application of the brand to particular products and experiences and refute its application to others. While linking the Macedonian brand to wine or the French brand to baguettes might be acceptable, for instance, linking them to political instability or a propensity to strike may not. Successful place branding, in other words, depends a great deal on making sure the brand is attached to certain products and experiences but not others.

Notably, courts and justice, much like wine and baguettes, can also be identified with the brand of the place from which they supposedly come.

Christine Schwöbel-Patel has described the branding efforts of the International Criminal Court (ICC), which worked to respond to a serious crisis that developed as a result of the ICC's record of only ever prosecuting individuals from the African continent.[9] She describes how the ICC, faced with the prospect of having African states withdraw from the court en masse, pursued a "brand of global justice" by shifting its focus to prosecuting environmental crimes[10] and vigorously asserting its assiduous adherence to the rule of law.[11] The ICC, in other words, aimed to affix the "global" prefix to the type of justice it produced. More than this, it aimed to (re)define the "global" in a particular way: as broadly interested in the health and well-being of the planet, as containing people who are viewed equally before the law, and as *not* favoring the North over the South. What Schwöbel-Patel describes might be accurately glossed as the ICC's efforts at place branding; hoping to rectify its own image problem, the ICC worked to hitch itself (and its justice) to the brand of "the global" (which it worked to define in a very positive light).

A similar marketing attempt can be detected at the Supreme Court of the United Kingdom. While it is true that a UK brand court does not exist as such, there is, I believe, a real effort by the Supreme Court (which, it is important to note, is also the seat of the Privy Council), to apply a particular branding of the United Kingdom to itself. As I learned on visits to the Supreme Court and as can be gleaned from its website, the court commissioned a Scottish artist to create an "official emblem" representing the sovereign state of the United Kingdom. The design features colorful flowers intertwined in a circle and is meant to represent the three jurisdictions of the UK—"the rose interwoven with the leek leaves for England and Wales, the thistle for Scotland and the flax plant for Northern Ireland."[12] This emblem—or brand—appears everywhere through the Supreme Court: it is handed out to visitors on stickers that identify them as tourgoers; it covers the floor of the courtrooms in a repeating pattern on custom-made carpet; it flies from the flag of the courthouse; it punctuates each page of the website; it decorates its informational brochures; and it adorns the numerous items sold in the gift shop. The Supreme Court, in other words, works hard to brand itself as a UK court and, in doing so, works very hard to define exactly what the UK brand stands for. The interconnected, unbroken circle of flowers, which serves as its brand emblem, is, I suspect, in some way meant to respond to the United Kingdom's reputation for having tense relationships and political fractures within its borders; the emblem pushes back against this image with its own statement of interwoven, unbroken connectivity. The UK (of the Supreme Court's branding creation), therefore, is a united, flowing, and beautiful, even natural, sovereignty. Again, it is a court that is leading the effort to create a brand for a place and then applying this brand to itself for one beneficial reason or another. What I explore in this chapter is how the CCJ goes about similar work on a regional level. What vision of the Caribbean is it attempting to establish through the creation of a regional brand? And what vision of the Caribbean is it working to overcome? How does it do this?

Caribbeanness, Revisited

In the myth that the Court creates, the CCJ works to address problems of its past, present, and future by creating an alternative story of the Court's origin founded in a notion of Caribbeanness (as explained in chapter 2). The Court offers Caribbeanness as a timeless sense of regional togetherness and pride that defines the Caribbean people and the land they live on. This myth of origin, in which the region is rooted in an acolonial spirit, paints a lovely picture and offers the Court as the quintessential manifestation of this authentic Caribbean region. But this mythologized version of the region's origin and the CCJ's lifeblood is not widely shared. The documented chronology of the Caribbean and the ongoing struggles of regional endeavors, as well as the CCJ's own very slow start and seemingly tenuous future give pause to even the most faithful regionalists, who do not readily buy into the myth of Caribbeanness. The Caribbean, it turns out, has a widespread image problem among the Caribbean population. Far from the glowing vision of Caribbeanness offered by the Court, many people in the region see the Caribbean as capable of producing second-rate goods, offering subpar services, and possessing inferior intellect. I learned of this reputation from a multitude of sources.

Lynette, who worked in the library with me, had also become a close friend of mine over the course of my research, and we also shared many conversations about any number of topics. I trusted her opinion, valued her insight, and looked to her for measured feedback as my research developed. On one occasion, I sought her thoughts on a fellowship application I was preparing. The fellowship was for work related to law and inequality, and I had been thinking of how to accurately cast my research at the CCJ in this light. I explained to Lynette the angle I was taking: that the CCJ faced a thorny problem with public perception. Specifically, it was often directly compared with the Privy Council and was then regularly determined to be on the losing end of this comparison. I read to her some of the online public commentary that followed a *Trinidad Express* newspaper article, since this commentary, I believed, supported my argument.[13] Many of the comments strenuously objected to the idea of Trinidad and Tobago joining the CCJ in its appellate jurisdiction with one commenter writing that the Privy Council has "constantly displayed a far more mature level of judicial thinking than local judges" and another asserting, "I have much, much more confidence in the white man's level of jurisprudence tha[n] all the legal luminaries of the Caribbean put together."[14]

Lynette was dismayed by these comments, sucking her teeth in an extended "steups"—a classically Trinidadian gesture of disapproval—as she shook her head and mentioned, perhaps as some solace to herself, that she had heard that local political parties paid university students to post incendiary remarks on newspaper websites, suggesting that these comments might be the product of such dubious activity. Nevertheless, she agreed with the argument I had proposed. These comments did reflect a prevailing sentiment of inferiority in Trinidad society. In fact, she said, this was not just regarding the Court. "People here just believe that everything foreign is better. No matter what it is: clothes, food, courts, education." To provide an example, she told me about one of her friends who insisted he did not drink orange juice, which is fairly inexpensive, readily available, and locally grown and squeezed in the Caribbean, but, Lynette learned, he did admit to drinking Florida Gold, a mass-produced, made-from-concentrate American juice product. He also does not drink apple juice but rather Mott's (a US brand of that same beverage). "Nothing local," she punctuated.[15]

In the quoted commentary from the *Express* article, Lynette's example of her Florida Gold–drinking friend, and numerous other instances that I witnessed, it became clear that being of and from the Caribbean is often not viewed as a positive quality for, at least, consumer products, courts, or judges to possess. Indeed, throughout my time in Trinidad, I listened to numerous denigrations of Caribbean law and Caribbean judges, which were typically viewed as inferior to North Atlantic law and legal luminaries, or as deserving of inexhaustible, sharp criticism, or as wholly ineffective institutions and actors. More than once, for example, the CCJ was described to me through a comparison to a useless, defective canine: a "toothless bulldog" and "all bark but no bite." There are historical reasons for this attitude, some of which I discussed in chapter 2; British administrators involved in independence negotiations repeatedly sought to protect the sanctity of Caribbean courts from the perceived corruptibility and incompetence of Caribbean jurists, a demeaning paternalism that has resulted in a long-lasting relationship with the Privy Council and a crushing "inferiority complex," as Cynthia, in chapter 2, called it. Today, then, the law that emanates from Caribbean courts is often seen as so tainted by Caribbeanness as to make the concept of "Caribbean justice" entirely implausible.

"It is quite interesting that proponents of the Caribbean Court of Justice (CCJ) have failed to take into consideration the value of justice," begins a letter to the editor written by Marvin Forbes to the *Gleaner* in Jamaica.[16] Forbes goes on to suggest that it is the very Caribbean nature of the Court that makes it unlikely to provide justice to Jamaicans. He notes that "there is a hush-hush rivalry between Jamaica and other Caribbean countries," something that has "played out in the treatment of Jamaicans in The Bahamas, Trinidad and Barbados, just to name a few." Thus, by dint of being a Caribbean court steeped in these interregional rivalries, Forbes argues that there is no possible way that the CCJ could administer something akin to justice. Only the Privy Council, he explicitly says, can do this. Forbes, like so many others in the region, including the commenters to the article I discussed with Lynette, continue to understand true and trustworthy law, justice, and jurisprudence as undivorceable, perhaps even indistinguishable, from the British brand of law, justice, and jurisprudence that arrived centuries earlier with colonization. By definition, according to this belief, justice—that is, a *British* brand of justice—cannot be provided by a *Caribbean* court.

Yet, the CCJ is adamant in its Caribbeanness. It stakes a good deal of its legitimacy in the fact that it is a Caribbean court for Caribbean people and that it is "Caribbean Made," much like the jewelry still stored in the mail room. Forgoing its Caribbeanness would be just as detrimental to the CCJ as giving up on justice. In other words, it cannot stop being Caribbean any more than it can stop being a court. It faces what might be seen as a double-identity problem; it is adamantly Caribbean when Caribbeanness is devalued, and it is held to a standard of providing British justice when it is determinedly not British.

One solution to this problem is to revalue the Caribbean. This is not so that the region can become more British and, thereby, capable of producing British law; it is not, in other words, an example of the "mimicry" of which so many postcolonial efforts have been accused.[17] Rather, it is a matter of rebranding the Caribbean such that the region can be accepted as capable of producing law of a particular quality: Caribbean law that can be viewed by Lynette's friend, Forbes, the newspaper commenters, and all the CCJ's potential users as legitimate, authoritative, effective, and eminently unassailable. The CCJ cultivates this regional brand by shaping itself into a shining example of the Caribbean brand that it necessitates. As Constantine Nakassis, a linguistic anthropologist, might describe it, the Court offers itself as a token of the Caribbean type—a materialized "brand instance" of the qualities associated with the "brand identity."[18] In this way, it performatively enacts a newly revalued region. That is, by *being* high-quality, modern, and thoroughly Caribbean, the CCJ performs a high-quality, modern Caribbean region into existence. The Court, then, expended much energy in cultivating and displaying these qualities—qualities, ironically and inconveniently, that required the Court to curtail its own marketing efforts.

A High-Quality Court

It took little time for me to appreciate the Court's startling lack of recognizability within the region, even within its own backyard. It took me longer to understand why the Court seemed to be doing very little to proactively remedy the situation. As I learned during the initial months of my research—before the "CCJ Corner" newspaper column was launched or school visits had been organized—nothing was on the Court's calendar that could be discernably identified as "public education." In fact, just before the start of my research, the CCJ had canceled three previously planned public education trips to as many of its member states. At that time, it had no school visits planned, no town halls scheduled, and no outreach programs in the works.[19] Save for an occasional media release or Tweet by @CaribbeanCourt, the CCJ's approach to educating the public primarily consisted of waiting for groups to request a tour, which the Court eagerly accommodated (as described in chapter 2). Public education, in short, appeared to be a low priority. Indeed, the Public Education and Communication unit was composed of exactly one person, who went by her first name, Sara. Sara was part of the Court Administrative Leadership Team, but did not share equal status with her counterparts, who held manager titles to her senior officer role, who were deferentially called by their titles and surnames to her more casual form of address, and who occupied private offices outfitted with locking doors, bookshelves, and sometimes televisions to Sara's shared office space. Thus, when the time came for my interview with Sara, I was eager to hear her perspective on public education at the Court. I expected some grumbling, but I was mostly wrong.

As she saw it, I had misinterpreted the role of her unit. It was not that public education was unimportant, it was just that a court—a *proper* court—was very limited in what it was able to pursue in terms of outreach. Sara explained:

> I think that, and this is—this is my perspective as a communications professional—*court* communications professional: the Court should not be involved in saying [knocks hand on desk] to the public [knocks hand on desk], "You need to come to the Court." We cannot be persuasive. It is not persuasive advertising; it is not persuasive communication. From where I stand, I think the Court needs to provide the information to the public. . . .
>
> We need to prove, we need to prove—not persuasive, but more informative—that we are a top-notch court; that we do have the ability, the skills, the expertise, the resources to bring a particular level of justice to them.

What is interesting here is Sara's rationale against conducting public outreach: that it does not fit within the image of a "top-notch court." In other words, she tacitly acknowledges the identity that the CCJ is working to cultivate. The critical feature of this identity is not Britishness but "top-notchness," the former is something this Caribbean court could never have, while the latter is something, Sara insists, the CCJ already possesses and displays, in part, through its refusal to pursue "persuasive advertising." Another characteristic of being a "top-notch court," according to Sara, is its ability to provide "a particular level of justice." Again, the key feature to this justice is not its Britishness but the fact that it is of a "particular level," which is a standard that the CCJ can attain and has, according to Sara, already attained.

Indeed, Sara's is not the only voice at the CCJ that asserts the Court's ability to provide justice of this level. At that time, the official "Vision" of the Court, posted on its website, spoke of the CCJ as a "leader in providing high-quality justice"; the judges often explained their job as "producing judgments of a high quality and in a timely manner," to quote Justice Meyer; and the Court's website, similarly, mentioned the "high-quality service" provided by the Court.[20] Through such talk of "top-notch courts" and justice of a "particular level," the CCJ works to present itself and its justice as possessing highly desirable qualities—a collection of characteristics that can engender trust and faith in the Court and thereby attract loyal users of it. People come to top-notch courts, Sara suggests. Moreover, high-quality judgments, such as those the judges work to produce, muster confidence in the CCJ, establish its visibility in the region, and strengthen its claim as the authoritative legal voice of the land. Being high-quality, in other words, assists the Court in its efforts to constitute itself as a legitimate and authoritative tribunal capable of administering the law and resolving disputes throughout the region. Thus, as it pertains to public education, Sara explains, the Court simply has to provide proof of its top-notchness.

Sara states that the CCJ's excellence can be exhibited in part through "the ability, the skills, the expertise, [and] the resources" of the Court and its employees. Within the Caribbean and beyond, characteristics such as advanced skills and training, specialized legal expertise, and relatively robust resources are broadly and historically recognized as indicating a high-quality court. Aware of this, in its minimal public education activities, such as tours, the CCJ emphasizes the advanced degrees and extensive courthouse experience of the CCJ staff, the impressive accomplishments, education, and international reputation of its bench,[21] the US$100 million held in its Trust Fund, and the vast resources located within the Court, including an impressively high-tech courtroom.[22] Serena, for example, repeats the tagline "the best and the brightest" multiple times as she describes to tourgoers the qualifications of the Court management team, many of whom have MBA degrees, several of whom have certifications in court management, and two of whom have a doctorate. She also regales them with the life histories, educational backgrounds, legal accolades, and language skills of the judges. Dr. Williams, too, always spends an extra moment when talking about the funding structure of the Court. He explains that not only does the Court have US$100 million in a Trust Fund that insulates the CCJ from funding shortages experienced by many of the other courts in the region, but the funding structure of the Court is so ingenious that even the chief justice of the United States personally complimented him on it. He met the chief justice, he adds, when he graduated from the Institute of Court Management, a program that is known, according to Dr. Williams, as the "holy grail" of court management training. Wrapped up into this tidy anecdote, this representative of the Court underscores the financial stability and creativity of the CCJ, highlights his own advanced training, and alludes to the CCJ's personal connections to other high-quality courts.

While the CCJ was quite restricted in its ability to promote its high quality to a broad public, largely because of its inform-not-persuade policy, it was able to adhere to the strictest standards within the Court. Though often unwritten, these standards of high quality often surfaced in the way they were policed. Interns were no exception to such enforcement. The CCJ regularly hosts several summer legal interns, and the year I spent there was no different. In early June 2013, the first of the interns began to arrive, and by early July, the full panel of law students had been assembled: two from Jamaica, one from Trinidad, one from Guyana, one from Canada, and one from the United States. While all the interns took some time to find their footing at the Court—learning where to sit, when to stand, and what to do—Amanda, the Canadian, and Justin, the American, had a substantially sharper learning curve. They had arrived in Trinidad with entirely the wrong wardrobe. Knowing the Caribbean as a place of sun, sweltering heat, and sandy beaches, they had packed accordingly: sleeveless floral shift dresses for her and khaki pants and polo shirts for him, clothes that might be considered appropriately business casual to a North American audience. The Court was definitively *not*, however, business casual, something they learned almost immediately through observation and through the Internship Programme manager's introductory remarks. At the Court, Ms. Paul explained, one was expected to wear full suits in "sober colors," such as dark gray or black. She noted, further, that they might occasionally see someone in a bright-colored shirt, such as red, but this would only be acceptable on days when there were no court matters scheduled. This information had the newly arrived interns scrambling, as Amanda contacted her roommate in Toronto, asking her to rapidly and very expensively ship several suits to Trinidad, while Justin opted to undergo a pricey emergency shopping excursion. By the end of their first week at the Court, they each had a full complement of sober-colored suits, leaving their casual vacation wear for the weekends.

While Amanda and Justin were able to quickly meet the image requirements of a high-quality court, Mark, a visiting American college student, was not. Perhaps he had arranged a visit to the Court in advance, but when he arrived at the CCJ's front door in late 2013 wearing a T-shirt, shorts, and flip-flop sandals, everyone was surprised—casting furtive glances with raised eyebrows. It seemed clear that he, like Amanda and Justin, had attributed the *wrong* Caribbean brand to the CCJ. It was not a casual court for laid-back beachgoers; it was a high-quality court for a professionalized population. Mark's misattribution and the potential for brand damage caused his association with the CCJ to be rather abbreviated. He had, as he explained to me during his brief visit, wanted to conduct some sort of research at the Court. He had, as I later learned, managed to schedule an interview with one of the judges. But he had not, as I also heard, been able to arrange a longer stay at the Court. This judge had not been impressed. There was, after all, a top-notch image to maintain, and it did not seem that Mark met this standard.

Maintenance of this image went beyond the clear infractions by newly arriving North Americans. The CCJ's own staff policed one another, too. Although there was no written dress policy, I became aware of additional rules and regulations through the intermittent scoldings by, most commonly, female Court managers directed at female members of the permanent staff. There was endless gossip, for example, among my friends at the Court about who had been *'buffed* (Trinidadian creole for "rebuffed") for wearing a skirt that was too short or too tight, for exposing their arms, or for not wearing a jacket. Serena explained to me that high heels, too, were often expected by management. Using herself as an example, she told me of the time that her manager insisted she change out of her flat shoes and into her heels prior to interacting with visitors. The "buffing" extended beyond the walls of the courthouse, too. Any ID-wearing Court employee walking within the general vicinity of the CCJ was at risk of eliciting a critical comment from certain members of the managerial staff should they be spotted wearing "inappropriate" attire. So, pursuant to the advice of my coworkers, I, like them, kept my suit coat on and buttoned even when venturing into the extremely hot Trinidadian sun for my lunch break, hid a pair of high-heeled shoes under my desk for when I might have to interact with the public, wore a cardigan sweater only on days when hearings were not scheduled, and selected shirts in the most subdued colors to wear on days when there were.

This image policing had a purpose. It was directly related to creating an image of the CCJ as an extremely respectable institution. Serena told me of the time she proposed the idea of "dress down Fridays" at a staff meeting. Her suggestion was met by a flurry of objections, which included the seemingly self-explanatory statement, "we're in a courthouse," before her idea was quickly quashed. Clearly, the message was that courthouses—top-notch ones—do not take a day off from an outward show of impeccable professionalism. But there is more than just the professionalism of the CCJ that is at stake in the careful curating of Court attire. The extremely professional attire worn by Court employees—nearly all of whom are from the Caribbean—begins the work of linking the "high-quality" descriptor to the region itself. Much as Carla Freeman observed in Barbados among the "pink-collar" female workforce there, the clothing worn by CCJ staff contributed to an emerging sense of what it means to be a modern Caribbean person who belongs to a modern Caribbean region—a region that is fully capable of creating and sustaining its own jurisprudence.[23]

The CCJ's aesthetics and what counts as "high-quality," however, do not come from thin air. While there are certain widely accepted indications of quality, such as ample resources, a professionalized staff, advanced education, and slick facilities—all of which the CCJ could boast—there are other indicia of high quality that are far more contextually bound. What counts as "high-quality" is what a particular audience has been acclimated to recognize as high quality. What this means is that the CCJ has had to consider its audience: a region that has, for centuries, been told that the Privy Council and its judges, justice, and staff are exemplars of a top-notch court. Thus, the Caribbean Court of Justice's presentation of itself must include at least some references to the Privy Council for its own brand of top-notchness to register with the audience that matters most. The CCJ does this, with circumspection. While many lower courts in the region retain "considerable imperial nostalgia," the CCJ is subtler and more selective.[24] There is certainly no photo of the queen. Instead, the Court displays regionally recognizable signs of quality by including waistcoats and neckerchiefs as part of the judicial costume, requiring a ritual of bowing in the courtroom, retaining the use of formal terms of address ("Your Honour" but not "My Lord," as discussed in chapter 5), preserving certain administrative positions, such as the indispensable position of the registrar, and featuring a familiar courthouse layout, including the centrally located Registry Office. Just as much as the CCJ relies on a display of being flush with resources, overflowing with expertise, and staffed by the utmost professionals to prove its quality, it also depends on the communicative value of regionally recognizable signs and symbols of a top-notch court. Again, it is not to make itself more

British that the CCJ does this; it is to present itself as high quality by indexing indicia of "high-qualityness" that are widely recognizable to its regional audience. For the brand to work, it must resonate.

A Modern Court

In addition to insisting that it is a top-notch court capable of high-quality decisions, the CCJ also insists that it is a "modern court" adhering to and promoting modern legal administration, legal practice, and legal thinking. Less hemmed in when it comes to announcing its modernity, the Court has even produced a short video, which for many years appeared on its website, in which it spelled out its modern features as a modern court for a modern region.[25] As the video shows, the Court, in many ways, defines and then hitches its own modernity by and to its high-qualityness. Specifically, as a well-financed court, it can house cutting-edge technology. And, to be sure, its technological prowess goes a long way toward convincing court users of its "up-to-dateness," or its "modernity," in other words. Unfailingly, attorneys visiting the Court for the first time marveled at the impressive array of high-tech courtroom features. In fact, anyone entering the Court through its mirrored facade, walking into its icily conditioned air, encountering its highly professionalized staff, and attempting to master its complex technology cannot help but notice that this Court is not at all deficient or delayed. Rather, it is quite modern.

Modernity, of course, can mean far more than having cutting-edge gear and gadgets, and those who work at the CCJ fully recognize this. Modernity is also embracing particular ways of thinking about the law and its application, of relating to the law across society, and of shaping the law and legal practice. It is about cultivating a particular legal culture. In her study of the passage of Trinidad and Tobago's domestic violence law, Mindie Lazarus-Black notes that the adoption of "contemporary cultures of legality constitute postcolonial nations like Trinidad as 'modern,' 'progressive,' and 'civilized,' places."[26] In constituting the Caribbean region as modern, the CCJ similarly pursues a contemporary culture of legality, in which the "rule of law," "access to justice," "timely justice," "standards of practice," and notably progressive priorities, such as "going paperless," are at the top of the Court's strategic agenda.

Not only does the CCJ strenuously hold itself to these practices, policies, and priorities, but it is devoted to bringing the entire Caribbean legal field into the fold of a modern legal culture. Much of this work takes place through conferences and workshops held by the CCJ's affiliated organizations, such as the Caribbean Association of Judicial Officers (CAJO), the CCJ Academy for Law, and the Canadian-funded Judicial Reform and Institutional

Strengthening (JURIST) Project. At events hosted by these organizations, to which Caribbean legal professionals are invited, liberal modern topics tend to dominate the panels and keynote speeches. The 2019 CAJO conference, for example, featured discussions and presentations on the rights of Indigenous persons, environmental pollution and human rights, eliminating delay in judgments and justice, developing the rule of law, eliminating gender bias in adjudication, and other issues that have become widely recognized markers of liberal modernity. In many ways, these conferences in which the CCJ is intimately involved can be seen as brand outreach. Not only do they encourage the audience to buy into these contemporary approaches and concerns of legality, but they do so in a particularly high-quality way. They are hosted at nice hotels with excellent facilities, complemented by exciting evening cultural events and afternoon excursions, and sustained through plentiful food and drink. They are unquestionably high-quality events that revolve around modern legal concerns.

In addition to these high-level, high-participation events, the Court is also involved in more personalized interactions that are similarly aimed at showcasing the Court's own modernity and helping to modernize the practice and administration of law throughout the region. Several of the judges, for instance, take their pedagogical roles quite seriously, as was evident during numerous hearings in which they patiently—and sometimes impatiently—guided attorneys through courtroom procedure, instructed them as to the timeliness of filings, and even assisted them in formulating appropriate arguments. In one hearing, for example, in which an attorney was seeking permission to appeal a case to the CCJ, Justice Neeley, the presiding judge, offered extensive advice. After listening to the ill-prepared attorney fumble through his arguments, Neeley stepped in to explain, "When you come to the CCJ . . . you have to show a realistic chance of success" before the CCJ will grant leave to appeal. He reiterated later, when the attorney continued to veer off topic, "You have to persuade us that you have a realistic chance of success," to which Justice Meyer, also sitting for this case, reemphasized again, "as the presiding judge explained quite clearly . . . we have to see if there is any merit in your case, and you have to show us." In the end, unfortunately, the attorney was not able to persuade the judges that an appeal of his case had a realistic chance of success, and Justice Neeley, who delivered the opinion of the court after a short discussion between the judges, once again used the opportunity to give a lesson on how to make an application for leave to appeal a case to the CCJ.

While other judges also participated in pedagogy in the courtroom, Justice Neeley was notable in this regard. During one interview, I asked him about his penchant for teaching. "I think it's very important," he explained, noting that the Court's jurisdiction is new. He saw it as his duty to guide attorneys back on track if

> they appear to be going in a direction that is not the correct direction. . . . I think that's very important because one of the difficulties about having all of these disparate jurisdictions [meaning, the court systems of the various member states] is that you don't have a common consensus as to what is done in a particular situation or what the law is in a particular situation. . . . It's so diverse in terms of standards, that there is no common consensus.

It was the judges' job, then, as I understood him to mean, to foster the development of shared standards and a common consensus that could draw the region together under the Court's jurisdiction. I also understood that he was not referring to just *any* standard of practice. Rather, he expected and guided attorneys to achieve a high standard in the practice of law—a practice of law that was indicative of a modern region. "We have a normative role," he said.

The Court's normative role goes further than teaching moments during the course of a hearing. At times, the CCJ's judges openly castigate state courts for their failure to adhere to modern expectations in the administration of justice—namely, the issuance of timely decisions. The courts of Barbados are a frequent recipient of such critique. In a 2021 appellate judgment by the CCJ on a case coming from Barbados, both the majority decision and a concurring decision harshly criticize the lower Barbados courts' delay in the delivery of their judgments on this case.[27] In leveling this critique, the CCJ echoed earlier admonitions it had made about the sloth-like pace in the delivery of justice by Barbadian courts. In 2016, the CCJ, in another appellate decision on a case from Barbados, noted that that case provided "another example of the inordinate systemic delay of the Barbados judiciary. Too frequently we have been forced to bemoan this unacceptable situation. . . . Steps must be taken to address this for the proper administration of justice in Barbados and a better perception of the system by the public."[28] Through these words, the Court points out that the image of Barbadian and, by extension, Caribbean-brand justice suffers when the administration of law falls short of modern expectations. The Court, therefore, takes it upon itself to set an example of the modern practice of law, to educate its users and to extract, if necessary, adherence by its member states through public reprimand.

A Caribbean Court

It is not enough, though, for the CCJ to brand itself as a high-quality, modern court providing justice of a particular level. It must be more than this.

Integral to its founding purpose and identity, this court must also be a distinctly *Caribbean* court. Its brand, therefore, has to be recognizably Caribbean, in addition to high-quality and modern. One way the Court went about gaining this recognition during its initial years of operation was to make itself as obviously, aesthetically Caribbean as possible. What exactly this effort entailed was not immediately obvious to me.

The "morning talk show," as we had begun to call it, was something I looked forward to every morning as I arrived at my desk in the library of the CCJ. Lynette and I, as well as one or two other Court employees, chatted casually about pop culture, news items, social events, or Court gossip as we booted up our computers and organized our days. Often, our morning talk shows, at my prompting or in answer to my questions, turned to discussions of the Caribbean, such as what foods were good, what fruit was in season, what a certain expression meant, or how I should interpret a recent interaction. Though never explicitly addressed, these conversations unfolded as if there were some shared understanding of what constituted "the Caribbean." Given that the participants in our morning talk show, excluding myself, were all from independent English-speaking Caribbean islands, the contours of "the Caribbean" were shaped by these same features: English-speaking, independent, and islands, thereby creating sufficient common ground to carry on productive but lighthearted conversation. It is through these truly enjoyable conversations, which frequently continued on and off throughout the day, that I gathered a great deal of information about what Trinidadians, Tobagonians, Barbadians, and Jamaicans (as the most frequent participants in these morning chats came from those islands) thought about what it meant for something to be from or made in the Caribbean. As I had already learned from Lynette, there were a great number of Caribbean things that were viewed as being subpar—local orange juice as compared with Florida Gold, for instance. What I learned during the morning talk show, though, was that there were also a good number of Caribbean qualities that induced pride among Caribbean people.

On more than one occasion, for example, we discussed Caribbean food. While everyone had their favorite cuisine, with Trinidadian and Jamaican food being the most preferred, and each cuisine had its own idiosyncrasies, such as Trinidadian food using more spice and Jamaican breakfasts being startlingly large, the overwhelming consensus was that Caribbean food was delicious. It was seasoned well, it was rich in flavor, and it was creatively prepared. Creativity also peppered colloquial Caribbean expressions to prideful effect. My fellow conversationalists took great delight in discussing Caribbean vernacular, and we frequently turned to the dictionaries on Caribbean creole, slang, and colloquialisms that were housed on the library shelves to get "authoritative" information on certain turns of phrase. Just as with food, my friends had great fun discussing the linguistic diversity in the Caribbean. What one said in Trinidad may not be understood in Barbados, for example.[29] Yet, they could all agree on and get a good laugh out of the playful, creative, and at times impishly confusing (to outsiders, such as myself) expressions of particular Caribbean cultures. To the amusement of my friends, for instance, I struggled to acclimate to the paradoxical temporality of the Trinidadian expression "just now," which might mean five minutes from now, one hour from now, or even one day from now but definitely did not mean right at this exact moment. The Caribbean joke was on me, it would seem. As one CCJ judge described it, Caribbean speech is "colorful," and this, he implied, and my talk show cohosts agreed, is a valued trait.

As can be gleaned from these casual conversations, there is some work involved in extracting shared Caribbean characteristics that rise above the differences that distinguish specific Caribbean cultures. While it would do damage to the Court's claim to Caribbeanness to have a red, black, and white color scheme, as these are colors of the Trinidad and Tobago flag, the CCJ can claim Caribbeanness by being more generally colorful. Similarly, the Court would struggle to establish its Caribbean status by favoring a Jamaican musician or a Guyanese artist, but it can, and does, display Caribbean creativity. Indeed, color and creativity—along with the Court's insistence that these are distinctly Caribbean traits—play a large role in the CCJ's presentation of itself as a Caribbean court.

The CCJ's first annual report, published in 2006, for instance, explains the bright color of the judicial robes: "Blue robes signify the Caribbean Sea which touches our shores and binds us together—the pure and strong gold band signifies the strength of the Caribbean sun which warms us all."[30] (See plate 1 of the inset illustrations at the start of chapter 7.) This brilliant blue color, in particular, which often serves as the backdrop to the CCJ seal, appears everywhere and on everything related to the Court: its website, flag, stationery, informational materials, gift bags provided to each tourgoer, polo shirts worn by staff during school visits, and more. The vivid color scheme, more broadly, is carried out across the CCJ courthouse and, like the robes, is intended to represent Caribbeanness, as visitors (like those in chapter 2) are told. The pale lime-green Registry lobby, the pale aqua library, the two-tone blue courtroom, and the pink judges' chambers are "Caribbean colours," the tour guides explain (see plate 5). When I once pushed for a further explanation as to what made the pastel color scheme distinctly "Caribbean," Serena and Lynette could only repeat what they had been told: that it was meant to look like the colors of houses in the Caribbean. The resemblance, I could see, was there.[31]

The CCJ also meant to sound Caribbean, primarily through the accents of the courthouse staff and judges, which were evidently Caribbean in origin (a point discussed in chapter 5), but also through a CCJ anthem, which I learned, on April 16, 2013, was equally, though not as obviously, Caribbean. Soon after I arrived at the CCJ that morning in April, I found out, along with the rest of the staff, that a last-minute meeting had been planned to celebrate the Court's eighth anniversary and that we were to be in the Training and Conference Room by 11:00 a.m. Serena was busily trying to rally people into action, hustling them up to the second-floor conference room. Despite her best efforts, by 11:00 a.m., the all-staff meeting had noticeably light attendance, with many people standing huddled by the door. The president of the Court was away on business, so another judge stood in as master of ceremonies. He offered brief remarks before turning over the speaking duties to the president, who appeared before us on a prerecorded DVD.

The president's remarks were also brief. He began with a short overview of the history of the Court and its successes. He pointed out the "innovation and independence" of the Court and the importance and prestige of the judges. He commended the "unfailing support" of the CCJ's administrative units and their dedication and hard work. He also, rather surprisingly, quoted cultural anthropologist Margaret Mead. "Never doubt that a small group of thoughtful, committed citizens can change the world," he said, referring obliquely to the staff of the CCJ and the monumental task of (re)making the region. He further urged the staff to commit to carrying out the newly introduced strategic plan and noted that the people of the region "look to us to provide a high quality of justice." The president's speech ended, and we all looked around, waiting for what would happen next. This is when Dr. Williams made the embarrassing announcement that there was supposed to be cake and ice cream, but it had not yet arrived. Doubtful that it would show up anytime soon, Lynette and I returned to the library to work. A few moments later, Serena called us to say the cake was there, so we went back upstairs, we ate our cake, and then the celebration was officially over. I remember thinking at the time that the whole event was rather odd, sort of a pep talk combined with a birthday party with an added exhortation to "get to work."

Back in the library once again, I was debriefing the experience with Lynette and Mandy, one of the judge's secretaries, when we were interrupted by a couple of loud, sharp beeps over the building-wide intercom. Nothing followed, so we resumed our conversation. Another set of beeps had us wondering if there was a problem with the intercom, which I had only ever heard in use once before, to notify staff that they could leave work early to avoid heavy rains and potential flooding. And that is when it started: an easy-listening tempo with a female voice. It was a ballad about the CCJ. An anthem celebrating the accomplishment that this regional court represented, that touted its appellate and original jurisdictions, that held it out as a symbol of independence. Lynette, Mandy, and I stood there with our conversation suspended, looking awkwardly up at the speakers in the ceiling as the song ran its course. There was no explanation that preceded it or followed it, and, neither Mandy, who had been at the CCJ since its inception, nor Lynette, who recently celebrated three years there, could recall ever hearing this song before. I later asked Serena about the CCJ song. It turns out that it was the winning entry in a songwriting competition run throughout the CARICOM region, and the song had been around since the beginning of the CCJ. The anthem, then, was made in the Caribbean, for the Caribbean, and about the Caribbean. Given that no one recalled having heard it before, though, I remain uncertain why the song had been produced, other than having yet another creative and Caribbean-made feature in the Court's repertoire.

To be sure, the CCJ anthem joined a rather large collection of artwork, competitions, and books that are housed in the Court and offered as being "Caribbean." Adorning the pastel walls (already Caribbean in their color) are works of framed fine art by Caribbean artists. Brightening the otherwise subdued mood of the judges' lounge are colorful children's drawings, which had been the winning entries in a Caribbean-wide competition sponsored by the CCJ. The competition asked primary school–aged students in the Caribbean to submit artwork to be displayed in a calendar published by the Court in its earliest years. Serena, in explaining this competition to me, admitted that the Court had made a slight miscalculation in running the competition. It turned out that students from a single classroom at a school in Antigua, a member state of the CCJ, dominated the competition. The problem was that this happened to be an international school, and most of the winning entries had been submitted by British and American students—a detail that I only heard once and that was easily cured (and omitted) by emphasizing that students *in* the Caribbean participated in this Caribbean-wide competition, thus retaining the Caribbeanness of the calendar. The CCJ also hosted an annual moot court competition to which only Caribbean law schools were invited. It was an event that took over the entire courthouse for two full days, as three members of the bench participated in judging the arguments, staff busied themselves hosting the teams of students, and visiting dignitaries from the region attended the closing ceremonies and the presentation of the winners' shield. The president of the CCJ described the moot court competition as an opportunity to "grow the region."

The Court, as can be seen (and heard), asserts its Caribbeanness through the story it tells of its origin and through the sounds and sights of the courthouse, which it insists, through much repetition, capture the celebrated color and creativity of the Caribbean. The robes, the walls, the song, the competitions, the Court's seal (also the result of a Caribbean-wide competition), and even the judges and staff themselves, who boast long associations with the region, become the insignia of the Caribbean. Whereas high quality and modernity are displayed through brilliant résumés, ample resources, judicial standards, rule of law, and even waistcoats and neckerchiefs, "Caribbean" is captured through a multitude of things deemed—by the Court—as being Caribbean.

A High-Quality, Modern Caribbean Court

The final challenge is to link these three qualities—high quality, modernity, and Caribbean—together, such that a "particular level of justice" can be believably associated with a Caribbean court of law. This final step is what makes this a rebranding and revaluation of the region itself, rather than simply a branding of the CCJ, though it is that, too. It is not just that the CCJ is high-quality, modern, and Caribbean, it is that these three valued qualities exist indistinguishably. Thus, what comes from and is created by the Caribbean will necessarily be high-quality and modern. This goes for Caribbean jurisprudence, Caribbean judges, a Caribbean Court, and Caribbean jewelry, artwork, and songwriting. They are modern and high-quality not in spite of but *because of* their Caribbeanness.

To achieve this, the CCJ is steadfast in its branding, using the courthouse, judicial costume, conferences, presentations, and personnel to performatively display the high-quality, modern Caribbeanness of the Court. It is, after all, Caribbean bodies (or, at least, bodies associated with a Caribbean court) that don superprofessionalized clothing. It is only the winning (or highest-quality) entries to various Caribbean art competitions that are featured on the CCJ's walls, sound system, and official seal. The Caribbean-made jewelry featuring Caribbean biodiversity that Serena and I ogled in her office is made from high-quality metal and high-quality stones; even their prices suggested that they were top-notch. It is also important that the judges' uniforms combine waistcoats and neckerchiefs with the blue and gold of their robes. And the modern, high-quality conferences hosted by the CCJ's affiliated institutions take place in Caribbean locales for Caribbean legal professionals and feature Caribbean experts highlighting Caribbean issues. In short, high quality, modernity, and the Caribbean are laminated together in a sensible (quite often, literally, sense-able) way at the CCJ. They are also projected by the Court as inextricably linked through the way that the CCJ talks about its own work.

Somewhere toward the middle of his 2011 speech to the attendees of the Organisation of Eastern Caribbean States Bar Association's Eighth Regional Law Fair, the president of the CCJ turned his attention directly to the development of Caribbean jurisprudence.[32] "Now I will take a brief look at just six of the cases that came before the CCJ to point out the way in which ordinary citizens have benefitted from the development of Caribbean jurisprudence," the text of his speech reads (I was not present at its delivery), and, as promised, the remainder of his talk focused on the details of six cases. What is remarkable about the president's discussion of these cases—these emblems of Caribbean jurisprudence, as he had identified them—is that neither the Caribbean nor the Caribbean content of the Court's decisions was at all a focus. In fact, the president uttered the word *Caribbean* just once during his extended discussion of these judgments.[33] Instead, for each of the six cases, he included a rundown of the legal issues, an overview of the Court's reasoning, and a summary of the CCJ's final decision. The emphasis remained squarely and dispassionately on the sophistication, complexity, and objectivity—all markers of a modern, high-quality legal culture—of the Court's jurisprudence. Even the president's nonpersuasive but highly informative presentation worked to prove the CCJ's adherence to modern conceptualizations of a high-quality court. The Court, evidently, delivered a "particular level of justice" in these cases.

Although the president's speech was dry, detailed, detached, and lacking any notable Caribbean color, it would be inaccurate to find this presentation devoid of Caribbeanness. The speech was delivered, after all, from the mouth of a Caribbean judge representing a Caribbean court who had made decisions that affected Caribbean people involved in Caribbean disputes. Caribbeanness, in short, can in no way be distinguished from the modern, high-quality words that were spoken. This speech by the president, like blue robes paired with waistcoats and Caribbean-made jewelry produced with fine metals, exemplifies the Court's branding strategy and performs the very values that it promotes: a Caribbeanness that coexists indistinguishably from high-quality modern law. Excellence comes from the mouths, minds, and pens of Caribbean people, making Caribbean jurisprudence thinkable, speakable, and realizable.

A Caribbean Gift

A number of years after I learned about the existence of the Caribbean-made jewelry stowed away in the recesses of Serena's mail room office, I encountered the jewelry again. In 2019, I had been invited to Belize as a speaker at the Sixth Biennial Conference for CAJO, an organization chaired by a CCJ judge and a conference that required a good deal of CCJ staff labor. I had attended a CAJO conference before, in 2013, while I was conducting the bulk of my field research and serving as a legal intern at the Court, and had thus been a provider of much of that labor in the past. This time, however, I was an invited guest, a role that I inhabited awkwardly, as I found myself drawn to pitching in to help my old friends, including Serena, who had by this point risen through the ranks of the CCJ. As the conference unfolded, the number of tasks never seemed to diminish, and I asked Serena for direction on how I could assist. She sent me to a table in the designated Secretariat's office where a group of familiar CCJ staff were frantically assembling thank-you bags for members of the local organizing committee that had been instrumental in making the conference a success. I was provided a pair of scissors, brilliant blue ribbon, and a number of small brown cardboard boxes containing none other than the Caribbean-made CCJ jewelry constructed from high-quality metal that had been hidden away, but apparently not forgotten, for many years now. My job was to tie bows and curl ribbons and include these boxes in the gift bags. What were once quite expensive souvenirs sold at the Court's gift shop were now being given away.

Though this could be read as a disappointing ending for these precious objects—that they had to be *given* away—their transformation from branded commodity to gift, I suggest, enhanced their value, not only in a Maussian sense of creating a chain of valuable obligations and relationships that could link the Caribbean together but also in the way that gift giving accords far more readily with the Court's sense of what it means to be of high quality.[34] As Serena and I had intuited back in her mail room office years before, there was always something awkward about the idea of selling the CCJ on a brooch, no matter what metal was used or what gem was featured. The proximity of a salable commodity to the administration of justice veered too closely to the commodification of the Court itself, a quality that would drag the CCJ down rather than raise it up. A quality that was associated, nonetheless, with the *old* Caribbean brand in which justice could be corrupted and judges could be bribed—in which law, in other words, might actually be for sale. In a rebranded Caribbean, modern, high-quality justice could not be bought or sold. Giving the jewelry as a gift, therefore, shed the taint of commodification, while it retained the high value and Caribbeanness of the artwork itself. Giving the jewelry as a gift, moreover, cast the Court as rife with resources and replete with thoughtful, tasteful, and impressive generosity—indications, in the Court's estimate, of a modern, high-quality institution. Indeed, while Serena and I had chuckled at the thought of selling this jewelry at the Court's gift shop, no one laughed at the idea of presenting it as a gift as we hurriedly cut, tied, and curled the Caribbean-colored ribbons that would decorate the boxes.

What I learned through my reacquaintance with the CCJ jewelry is that the Court had fine-tuned its branding strategy by teasing it apart from commodities and focusing more closely on performing the qualities and values its seeks to suture to the region itself. Still hampered by the notion that a modern, high-quality court cannot promote or persuade the public of its high-qualityness, the CCJ has implemented new strategies, which still cleverly integrate branding, to showcase and inform the public of its modern, top-notch Caribbeanness. It travels far more regularly as a Court, a feat (as described in chapter 3) that requires a good deal of resources and organization; it maintains a YouTube channel on which it livestreams all hearings and judgments, an innovation that shows off its technical prowess, modernity, and transparency; and it regularly updates its Facebook and Twitter accounts to notify the (Caribbean) public of each hearing, each judgment, and other news from the Court and around the Caribbean. Through these avenues of what can be seen as brand outreach, the CCJ displays exactly how the Caribbean does justice: sleek, professional, transparent, modern, and excellent, showcasing a new brand of Caribbean (of the CCJ's making) that appears far more capable than the one it seeks to replace.

7

A Region

In March 2022, a two-minute video circulated throughout Caribbean social media networks. In it, Hugh Small, a Jamaican attorney and former judge in the Bahamas who has obtained the esteemed rank of Queen's Counsel, which gives him sufficient status to appear before the Privy Council, can be heard narrating a rather strange scene. The scene opens to a jaunty camera and distracting swooshes of wind, focusing narrowly on a black metal canister. The canister belongs to Small, as is made obvious by not only the all-capital, gold painted lettering stating his name, "HUGH SMALL ESQ," but also Small's explanation as he opens and empties it. As his hand reaches into the frame to untie the short bit of twine that secures the canister's lid, he tells the viewing public that when he was called to the bar, barristers still had to wear wigs in court. And here, we now see, this canister—known informally as a "biscuit tin"—contains a pile of such dusty white, yellowing, and wiry horsehair wigs. The first wig to make it out of the biscuit tin belonged to his late father, Senior Puisne Judge Ronald Small, who acquired it when he was called to the bar in England in 1934. Clutching the wig by its curls, Small sets this wig aside on the cement wall upon which the canister sits. The next wig belonged to himself, he tells us. It is from 1963. And a final wig, he explains to the audience nonchalantly, "I'm not sure about this one, but I have it." With the biscuit tin finally empty, Mr. Small fills it anew, restacking the wigs with some care, one atop the other. When this is done, he steps away from the centerpiece on which the camera continues to focus.

"We need to stand on our own and get out of the Privy Council," he announces before beckoning over a young man holding a jug. "Pour some gas on that," he directs his assistant, who promptly begins pouring a light blue fluid over the wigs. "I want enough so that all of it will burn up," Small com-

PLATE 1. Full bench of the CCJ, in ceremonial court attire, during 2012–2013. *Standing, left to right*: the Honourable Mr. Justice Jacob Wit, the Honourable Mr. Justice Winston Anderson, the Honourable Mme. Justice Désirée Bernard, and the Honourable Mr. Justice David Hayton. *Seated, left to right*: the Honourable Mr. Justice Rolston Nelson, the Right Honourable Sir Dennis Byron, president of the Caribbean Court of Justice, and the Honourable Mr. Justice Adrian Saunders. Photograph courtesy of Caribbean Court of Justice.

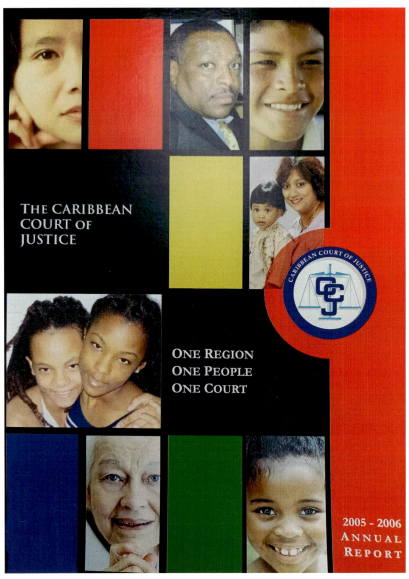

PLATES 2 AND 3. Covers of the inaugural annual report for the Caribbean Court of Justice, for 2005–2006 (*this page*) and the second annual report, for 2006–2007 (*next page*). Both cover images display a mix of races, ethnicities, ages, and genders in an effort to depict the "whole Caribbean." Each cover also includes the same tagline included on the CCJ's website: "One Region. One People. One Court."

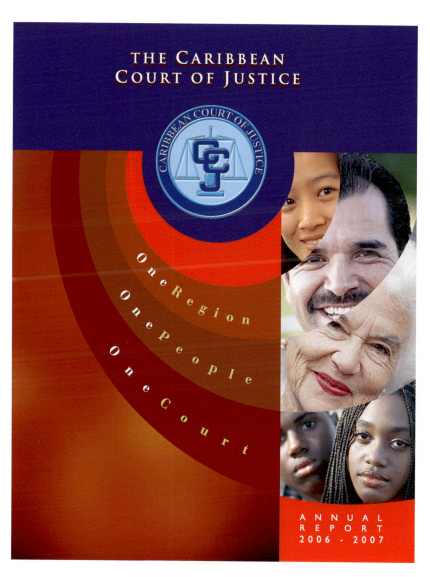

 PLATE 4. The seal of the Caribbean Court of Justice, featuring the Court's signature blue color and overlapping letters *C-C-J*. Permission to use this seal includes a guideline that it "may be used in a similar fashion as a logo or brand identity to represent the CCJ." Permission granted by Caribbean Court of Justice.

PLATE 5. The interior of the Caribbean Court of Justice painted in pastel "Caribbean" colors. *Counterclockwise from top left*: Public library on the ground floor, Office of the Registry and its lobby on the ground floor, Courtroom 1 on the first floor, and a judge's secretary's workstation on the third floor. Photographs by author.

mands. After a pause during which the viewer watches the blue tint of the flammable liquid staining the old white wigs, Small speaks again: "On behalf of the Jamaican people, I'd like to light a fire to indicate: time to leave the Privy Council and stand on our own." The young man senses his cue and strikes a match, placing it atop the wigs piled in the biscuit tin. With a crackle, singe, and substantial smoke and flames, the video ends as the wigs burn. On its own, this gesture is deeply symbolic. It is an unmistakable critique of the region's uncomfortably deep and continued connection to Britain and a powerful assertion, made by a very well-respected attorney and public figure, that Jamaican people are ready for a more complete form of independence.

Perhaps surprisingly for such a stunt, Small had not intended for this video to be distributed beyond his family, as he explained in a later interview.[1] But both social media and local news media picked up his story, covering it in several news outlets and supplementing the limited narration of the video with brief interviews with the attorney himself.[2] It is in these venues that Small explains his actions more thoroughly. The discovery of the wigs while packing up the belongings in his house for a move prompted Small to reflect on their meaning, which led, ultimately, to their burning. As he elaborated to the host of *Radio Jamaica*,

> I have been feeling for some time that we shouldn't allow the 60th anniversary [of Jamaica's independence] to come and still be in the position in which they were in the year that I was called to the bar. I was actually called to the bar about 5 weeks, 4 weeks before the 1st anniversary of independence in July of 1963. And I keep saying to myself, "Imagine that they *still* have the monarch as the head of state and that they *still* have not moved to the CCJ."[3]

Small continued to vent his frustration by noting that he was on the task force charged with putting together the 2007 Jamaican Justice Reform Report and that the report, released fifteen years earlier, recommended that Jamaica take the necessary steps to accede to the appellate jurisdiction of the CCJ and delink from the Privy Council. The task force's recommendation came after Jamaica had already attempted once to join the CCJ's appellate jurisdiction. That attempt, made in 2005, was overturned by the Privy Council in a case brought against the Jamaican government. The Privy Council determined that according to the Jamaican Constitution, the government had *not* followed the correct procedure for acceding to the appellate jurisdiction of the CCJ; it had only secured the approval of a simple majority of the Jamaican Parliament, not the constitutionally mandated two-thirds majority.[4] Small did not bring up the 2005 snafu, but the fact that nothing had been done despite the recommendation of the task force in 2007 was enough to upset him.

Even more infuriatingly to Small, all signs suggest that the Jamaican government has "no serious intention of tackling these important matters of state identity" anytime in the near future. To underscore the magnitude of this problem, Small noted that the sitting prime minister of Jamaica, Andrew Holness—Jamaica's first prime minister to be born after independence—recently accepted an appointment as a member of the Privy Council, when two prior prime ministers, Michael Manley and Bruce Golding, had refused. And equally disturbing to Small was the fact that the newspaper headlines on the day of his interview with *Radio Jamaica* all celebratorily announced the upcoming visit of Britain's Prince William and his wife, Kate. The interviewer commented that this was "ironic." No, Small corrected, "it is painful."[5]

As the life spans of such news items often are, Small's short video and the excitement that it ignited was rather short lived. For about a week, perhaps, did media continue to comment on it. The debate over the CCJ, though, never went away. Only six weeks later, another highly ranked Jamaican attorney published a column in the *Jamaica Observer* that, in erudite detail, proffered the opposing argument. She made a case for staying with the Privy Council.[6] Valerie Neita-Robertson, also Queen's Counsel, had recently won an appeal for her client at the Privy Council, and on the heels of that success, she was quick to break with her party's position on the CCJ versus Privy Council question and state her support of the Privy Council and her deep reservations about Caribbean justice.[7] Neita-Robertson then took a moment to shore up her argument before publishing her column in which she rehearses what are, by now, timeworn arguments against the CCJ. "We need to be confident that our political disputes are not going to be adjudicated within our region by people who are influenced by the cultural peculiarities and social and class biases which so affect us in our small space as those are not considerations which should affect or even determine justice," she wrote.[8] A Caribbean court with Caribbean judges, in other words, cannot be trusted to carry out true (which I read as "British") justice. She then makes a rather odd move of providing the details of a half dozen Jamaican and Eastern Caribbean cases that were ultimately overturned by the Privy Council, arguing that the local judges responsible for these miscarriages of justice—which were only corrected by the Privy Council—are the very judges who could be tapped to serve on the CCJ one day. Perhaps someday, she speculates at the end of her article, "our confidence and trust in the CCJ will be so demonstrably obvious that we can, with one voice, leave the Privy Council behind as we are sufficiently satisfied that justice will be done."[9] As of now, however, she cannot support such a move.

The Ongoing Region

I have opened the final chapter of this book with this particularly "painful," to borrow a word from Small, pairing of highly esteemed Jamaican attorneys pronouncing their differing views in different ways on the desired future of their legal system because it highlights the agonizing ongoingness of region making. To be sure, I offer Small's and Neita-Robertson's contributions as representative statements rather than anomalous fumings. The debate over the CCJ and all the social, cultural, colonial, and racial complexities it entails has never subsided in the years since the CCJ's advent. Every couple of years, one state or another led by one political party or another makes an attempt to accede to the Court's appellate jurisdiction. Some fail, such as those attempts in Saint Vincent and the Grenadines in 2009, in Grenada in 2016 and 2018, and in Antigua and Barbuda also in 2018, while some succeed, such as the attempts by Belize in 2010 and Dominica in 2014. Inevitably, the debates surrounding these attempts invite a flood of revisited arguments for and against the Court. Less frequently, a historic case passes through the CCJ that brings to the fore, once again, many of the same critiques, concerns, and voices of praise. In 2020, most notably, a high-profile elections case arrived at the CCJ from Guyana. This case challenged the validity of an election recount, which the CCJ ultimately decided in favor of the opposition party, which is, incidentally, traditionally supported by Guyana's Indo-Guyanese citizens. Still working its way up and down the local and regional court system, this case and its spin-off appeals provide a good deal of fodder for the CCJ debate. Well-worn questions about the racial and national makeup of the CCJ's bench, the Court's authority, and the legitimacy of a non-Guyanese court meddling so intimately in Guyanese politics peppered local and regional news media outlets and social media discussions. The outgoing and incoming CARICOM chairpersons both felt compelled to release public statements in support of the CCJ and its judgment and pledged the sustained commitment of the region to Guyanese people, to the rule of law, and to the transparency of elections throughout CARICOM.[10] In short, ambivalences and anxieties over the Caribbean-inflected, non-sovereign jurisprudence offered by the CCJ alongside the unrelenting sovereign aspirations of many states within the region have not subsided.

Given these endless debates, those who work at the CCJ could hardly be blamed for harboring any frustrations, which they do occasionally, sensitively voice.[11] What is less expected, though, is that they far more often present a measured but upbeat outlook. In early 2021, for example, in the midst of the COVID-19 pandemic that disrupted life around the world, I corresponded with Justice Matthews through email, as I had done throughout the years since returning from my long-term fieldwork at the CCJ. He shared his opinions on a recent article I had published, and I shared my congratulations on the CCJ's recent efforts to livestream all of its hearings. After reflecting on the COVID-19–related tragedies of the past year, he ended on a high note. "With Covid-19 the relatively small volume of our [cases] has decreased. But I've been using the time to get our systems and procedures in sync with best practices on our strategic planning agenda. So, the place is a hive of activity," he wrote. I was impressed, but by now I had come to expect the cautious optimism and unthwarted perseverance that worked its way into an otherwise depressing situation. Such hope is possible, I suggest, because the Court has come to appreciate the ongoingness of the regional project in which it is so devotedly engaged.

Undoubtedly, the regional project has not yet succeeded, but just as important, it has not failed. That is, there is a realization that the region is not yet, nor will it ever be, fully formed. It is always a project-in-the-making, much as the state might be understood as a "*state*ment, an ongoing claim" that is ever being constituted.[12] As chatter picks up across the Caribbean, as it did in May 2022, about Saint Lucia's possible accession to the CCJ's appellate jurisdiction or even Trinidad and Tobago's (a much larger fish, as I have discussed in the book), Justice Matthews keeps his "fingers crossed," as he wrote to me in 2022. He can hope, he seemed to say, that these events would transpire, but the Court has been down this road before, with some states joining and some states failing to join the appellate jurisdiction. With seventeen years now under its belt, the CCJ has learned these ups and downs of region making. There are people like Small and Neita-Robertson at every step along the way, and as much reason as there is to grow frustrated, there is reason to remain hopeful because the region will never be a mission accomplished.

And this is crucial to remember: *both* regionhood and sovereignty remain imagined futures in this part of the world, yet these futures differ dramatically. One, through work like the CCJ's, is envisioned as a means to foster an independent Caribbean, while the other, through the work of colonialism, is linked to a project that made the Caribbean dependent. One creates the possibility of an even playing field, while the other perpetuates the fiction of equality. One, the CCJ wholeheartedly believes, might be accomplished, while the other, many have observed, will likely remain an impossible aspiration.[13] This is why the CCJ keeps doing what it is doing and saying what is saying, and why, despite the slow accession of states, the setbacks of COVID-19, and the persuasive arguments of Neita-Robertson and others, Justice Matthews can sign off with an upbeat outlook. While a regional future may not be just around the corner, it is a far more hopeful one than a sovereign horizon never meant to arrive.

And this is also important to keep in mind: while the region is unfinished business, so too is, always, the nation-state, even for those nation-states that seem fully formed and fully functional. As others have noted, there is little reality to a state beyond its own "ongoing assertion;" its ongoing narration, enaction, and insistence of its ever-important presence.[14] And there is even more work involved in shaping the nation, suturing it to the state, and presenting the resulting package—"the nation-state"—as a natural, ahistorical creation.[15] The best we can do, as academics interested in the nation-state, therefore, is study something akin to the "state-idea" (instead of the state as an entity) and the "imagined community" (instead of a national body).[16] It is by studying these ongoing nation-state processes and projects, ideas and imaginaries that we are, in fact, studying the nation-state itself, as real as it ever can be. My point in bringing this up is to make the argument that this book's focus on the project of region making—the assertions behind it, the imagined future that sustains it, and the activities that define it—*is* a study of the region itself.

Acknowledgments

When it comes to the publication of this book, my debts of gratitude are not small. They span coasts and countries and have accumulated (and continue to accumulate) over the course of more than a decade. It is a daunting process to attempt to take account of these debts now because it is almost certain that this list will continue to grow and that I will unintentionally neglect to include some of those who are well deserving of recognition and repayment. Nevertheless and with great trepidation, here I try.

My greatest debt, without question, is to the wonderful and welcoming people of the Caribbean Court of Justice. To the president, judges, managers, secretaries, administrative staff, drivers, security personnel, and custodians—each of you helped make my time in Trinidad one of my life's most treasured experiences. I loved it. Every bit of it. You taught me so much, opened your hearts to me, shared your opinions and ideas with me, became my friends and thought partners, and helped me see the world through different eyes. I cannot begin to thank you for such generosity, and I only hope that you see this book—in which so many of you and your thoughts are reflected—as doing some justice to all that you have given me. I have thought deeply (and for a long time!) about what I have written, and I want for you all to be proud of what I have produced and know that I have done my best. I will always have the utmost respect for each of you and your vision. Although it is not possible to name all of those at the CCJ who impacted my research, I would be remiss if I failed to recognize the unflagging support that the Honourable Mr. Justice Adrian Saunders, president of the CCJ, has shown for this project. Thank you.

Beyond the walls of the courthouse, I benefited from wide and varied support and friendship across Trinidad and the region. Thank you to Averil and

Patrick Potter and their family for providing me with my home away from home and to Michael Johns for my trusty car and the always welcome bags of freshly picked mangoes and papaya. The Trinidad and Tobago Society for the Prevention of Cruelty to Animals, the Animal Welfare Network, and June Tompack: thank you for allowing me to care for so many adorable and adoptable dogs and cats. Rex, my own Trini pothound, brought me years of joy and snuggles. Many thanks to those members of the judiciary, the bar, and the University of the West Indies (UWI) faculty in Trinidad, Barbados, and Jamaica who were willing to answer my questions and converse with me over the course of this project—especially to Tracy Robinson, who has remained an incredibly supportive and unfailingly brilliant mentor. Maarit Forde, Alex Rocklin, and Brent Crosson, thank you for providing mid-fieldwork sounding boards. Heather Bracken and the Brown Sugar Dinner Club, thank you for helping me eat my way through Trinidad and Tobago. And, then, there are those at the CCJ with whom I developed friendships that well exceeded the bounds of the courthouse and the longevity of this research: Semone Moore, LeShaun Salandy, Paul Aqui, Sue Lan Chin, Kerine Dobson, and many others with whom I remain in touch today.

I am incredibly grateful for the academic communities that have held me up throughout this process. Enormous thanks are due to Kamari Clarke, Kevin Yelvington, Mindie Lazarus-Black, Aisha Khan, Marisa Wilson, and Toni Blackman, who were each instrumental in helping me make critical connections in Trinidad. As well to Deborah Thomas, Kwai Ng, and Heath Cabot, who have been generous with their time, thoughts, and support following my fieldwork. At the University of Chicago, Stephan Palmié, John Comaroff, Susan Gal, and Justin Richland guided me from my Cuban origins through my Anglo turn with unfaltering support and steady enthusiasm. You have shaped me into the scholar I am today. I also had the good fortune of crossing paths with many other spectacular people at Chicago. Within the Department of Anthropology, I benefited from conversations and courses I had with Joe Masco, Shannon Dawdy, Hussein Agrama, Jean Comaroff, Kesha Fikes, Francois Richard, Costas Nakassis, Michael Silverstein, and the inestimable Anne Ch'ien, who played an instrumental role in any successes I enjoyed and has smoothed any bumps I encountered. Thank you all. I must also thank the Center for Latin American Studies. Josh Beck and Jamie Gentry provided critical support as I navigated the challenges associated with research in the Caribbean. Agnes Lugo-Ortiz similarly deserves thanks for her advice and support. I am thankful as well to the Workshop for Latin American and Caribbean studies for letting me share the various seasons of my research and for the insightful comments Alejandra Azuero Quijano provided on an early

ACKNOWLEDGMENTS

chapter. To the wonderfully supportive group of students in Susan Gal's Ethnographic Writing seminar, thank you, as well.

There are, too, many friends and colleagues to whom I owe a great debt of gratitude. Sarah Adcock, Adam Baim, Elle Bush, Ella Butler, Hannah Chazin, Molly Cunningham, Angelica Felice, Kristin Hickman, Bryce Lowry, Ayesha Mulla, Mary Robertson, Anna Weichselbraun, and Kaya Williams, thank you for providing such an intellectually stimulating entrée to anthropology. I also gained immeasurably from the friendship, support, and intellectual prowess of many others. Rob Blunt is at the top of a long list that also includes Deepa Das Acevedo, Beth Brummel, Natalja Czarecki, Zeb Dingley, Karma Frierson, Genevieve Godbout, Kathryn Goldfarb, João Gonsalves, Colin Halverson, Elina Hartikainen, Yaqub Hilal, Eric Hirsch, Laura-Zoe Humphreys, Britta Ingebretson, Anna Jabloner, Jeff Kahn, Matthew Knisley, Duff Morton, Victoria Nguyen, Adam Sargent, Chris Sheklian, Jay Sosa, LaShandra Sullivan, Gabe Tusinski, Joey Weiss, Xiao-bo Yuan, and many others. To those of you who are scholar-parents: thank you for showing me how it's done and that it *can* be done. None of this would have been possible without my writing group, which has gone through numerous iterations over the years but has always had one constant; it has always been a powerhouse of fantastically talented and unbelievably supportive scholars who also happen to be really great people: Erin Moore, Hanna Garth, Mrinalini Tankha, Saiba Varma, Jessica Lopez-Espino, Amy McLachlan, Meghan Morris, Kate McHarry, Angela Fillingim, and Taylor Nelms. If only everyone could be so lucky to be supported by such a community of scholars.

During my time at the University of California, Irvine (UCI), I have continued to find the steady and wise footing I needed to finish this book. The UCI Chancellor's ADVANCE Postdoctoral Fellowship Program provided an extraordinary opportunity for me to begin my academic career. And the Departments of Criminology, Law and Society, Anthropology, and Global and International Studies have been wonderful guides in my further development. In particular, Mona Lynch, Susan Coutin, Eve Darian-Smith, Sora Han, Keramet Reiter, Hillary Berk, Emily Owens, Brandon Golob, Swettha Ballakrishnen, Kaaryn Gustafson, Bill Maurer, and Justin Richland have provided an enviable bank of good advice and big brains, and I look forward to many more years of conversation. Mitchell Coe, what can I say, your unfaltering support and unparalleled good humor as I crossed the finish line has been wonderfully unexpected, deeply appreciated, and truly irreplaceable; I cannot wait for the further laughter and conversation in the years ahead.

I must also thank the Andrew W. Mellon Foundation, the Wenner-Gren Foundation for Anthropological Research, and the Law & Social Sciences and Cultural Anthropology Programs of the National Science Foundation for funding major portions of this research and writing. Without these critical resources, I would not have been able to complete this project. I similarly benefited from a Nicholson Center for British Studies Graduate Student Fellowship, a Doolittle-Harrison Fellowship, a Leiffer Pre-Field Research Fellowship, and a Field Research Grant from the Center for Latin American Studies at the University of Chicago. I feel fortunate indeed to have been supported by such institutions. Thank you.

In the final phases of writing this book, I had the privilege of benefiting from the wisdom of a truly remarkable panel of academics who graciously read and commented on an earlier version of the manuscript. Jessica Cattelino, Bill Maurer, Renisa Mawani, and Justin Richland, I have tried my best to revise this book in a way that reflects your thoughtful comments and suggestions. Endless thanks for taking the time to share these with me. Your careful work has, without a doubt, vastly improved this book.

I also could not be more grateful for the guiding hand, wisdom, faith, kindness, and patience of my editor Mary Al-Sayed, editorial associate Fabiola Enríquez, and the team of experts at the University of Chicago Press. Mary, the breathtaking speed at which you respond to my emails continues to astound me. You have made this process as smooth and efficient as possible, and I feel truly honored to be able to work with you.

Finally, there is my family. Mom, Dad, Gary, and Kent: you've had to hear a lot about ecology, law, and anthropology through years with me as your daughter and sister, and I can't believe how tolerant you have been. I'm not easy. I know that. Leif, my dear, thank you for being you and here, happy, humorous, whip-smart, and perfect. Hesper, my love, you are small, mighty, zesty, and everything good about the world. I love you both to pieces. Without you two, my days would be far less bright and inspired. This book is for you.

An earlier draft of some sections of chapter 1 and chapter 5 was previously published in "Law, Language and a Non-Sovereign Caribbean," *American Anthropologist* 122, no. 4 (2020): 721–32. An earlier exploration of some of the issues raised in chapter 2 was previously published in "Time and Transcendence: Narrating Higher Authority at the Caribbean Court of Justice," *Law & Society Review* 50, no. 3 (2016): 674–702. And some of the ethnographic data presented in chapter 6 were previously analyzed and published in "'Yes, [We Bow,] but Not a Deep Bow': Qualia and the Thinkability of Caribbean Jurisprudence," *Law, Culture, and the Humanities* 18, no. 2 (2022): 462–81.

Appendix: Methods and Positionality

My success in gaining entrée to and conducting research at the CCJ was made possible through the gracious generosity of several relative strangers—a generosity I strive to replicate in my own career. I had no personal connections to the CCJ and no clue how to approach the Court other than a "cold email" and a request for a tour made through the CCJ's website—which is exactly what I did. The response I received was warm and welcoming, but I knew it would take something more for me to connect with those at the CCJ who held decision-making power: the judges. For this, my advisor helped put me in touch with a senior legal anthropologist who had recently conducted several interviews at the Court; she offered to e-introduce me to one of the judges there, Justice Matthews. Through this introduction, I was able to arrange a meeting with Justice Matthews during my first visit to the Court, which I describe in chapter 1. As the senior scholar predicted, Matthews was open and excited about the possibility of hosting a sociocultural anthropology doctoral student at the CCJ for a year, but even he was not the one who could extend this invitation or grant the necessary permission—that would be the president of the Court, an open-minded but less gregariously inviting person. The president, or "Chief," as he was colloquially called, was, rightfully, far more concerned with fostering the development of a new court than with hosting an American anthropologist. Like Matthews, he viewed my proposed research as a possible avenue to bring welcome attention to the still-new Court, but, as its president, he also appreciated how it would add a further, unnecessary burden to his already crowded list of responsibilities. Specifically, as an early acquaintance at the Court relayed to me, the Chief understood that I "wanted to see them naked," to put it in slightly vulgar metaphorical terms, but he could not be sure whether I wanted to write about "the warts and the ugly parts, or about the good parts." Yet, the president and others also understood that they could not ask a researcher to only write what the Court deemed acceptable. Justice Matthews, therefore, played an important role in guiding me as I prepared a written proposal for the president to consider. The proposal had to allay the president's concerns to the extent possible and detail the research that I wanted to conduct. It also, as Matthews suggested, should emphasize my willingness to volunteer at the Court.

I followed this advice as best I could. I presented an honest research question that highlighted my search for knowledge and my desire for greater understanding (rather than, say, a hunt for juicy bits of gossip that could fuel a sensationalist critique), and I offered, eagerly, to work at the Court for the duration of my research, explaining that, as an anthropologist engaged in participant-observation, this could be a mutually beneficial arrangement. Specifically, as a former litigator in the United States, I suggested that I might serve as a voluntary legal intern, with the caveat that, although I was trained in the common law, my experience was both rusty and very American. The proposal worked, and I was able to leave Trinidad after that initial visit with a letter from the president of the CCJ agreeing to my extended presence as a researcher at the Court. And the Court, in turn, facilitated my extended presence in Trinidad.

When I returned to Port of Spain several months later, I was able to begin my long-term research immediately. I had been organizationally slotted into the Court as part of the Internship Programme and was provided a desk and computer in the publicly accessible library of the Court located on the ground floor. Initially, I was concerned that this location would keep me far from the action, as the judges' chambers were located three stories above me. Shouldn't a legal anthropologist, after all, be studying the legal actors? It turned out, as I hope the book has shown, that I was wrong. The "work" of the Court had as much to do with what happened on the third floor than with what occurred throughout the courthouse as an institution, and the library was one of the locations in the courthouse—below most of the managerial offices and well below the judges' chambers—where many of the CCJ staff felt comfortable gathering and talking freely. So, while my initial inclination was to focus on the law and the legal work of the Court, preliminarily prescribing it the utmost importance, I learned, through my location in the library, to broaden my ethnographic vision and to alternately surface and study the many other aspects of the CCJ's work. Specifically, I adjusted my approach to look more closely at the edges of the CCJ's work, rather than at the center. I did observe many Court hearings and often queried judicial thinking, but I spent far more time concentrating on the conversations I heard about the CCJ, the debates over it, the laughter within it, the tangles of cords and mountains of files produced by it, and the colors, badges, faces, and accents that defined it. In these minutiae, I found, the tools and techniques of sovereign nation-state-making are tweaked and tamed to another end, and in these details, I could appreciate how law has become implicated in the project of constructing the Caribbean not merely through the production of a regional jurisprudence and the exercise of a regional jurisdiction but also—and perhaps more so—through the symbolic weight and constitutive power of having a court of *almost* one's own. It was through this oblique approach, in which I peered around the glaring light of the law, that I formulated my arguments.

The research methods I used to collect the data I draw from in this book, as I had detailed them in the proposal for the president, are broadly ethnographic and include participant-observation, interviews, document review, website analysis, and archival research and took place within the Court, around Trinidad and Tobago, at the University of the West Indies at Cave Hill and Saint Augustine, and in Jamaica, Barbados, and Belize, as the CCJ traveled to each of these states over the course of my research. I listened to and observed the words and activities of the legally inclined, as well as those of people who are not. In all, I spent approximately sixteen months in the Caribbean conducting anthropological fieldwork in and about the Caribbean Court of Justice. The majority of this research took place in 2012–13, when I lived in Port of Spain and worked in the courthouse, but I also made return trips in 2018 and 2019—to Trinidad and elsewhere—where I continued to study the region-making work of the CCJ.

My role as an intern proved to be very helpful in integrating into the CCJ's activities; I was expected to—and gladly did—attend each court hearing, remain up-to-date on case matters, attend staff meetings, serve on committees, assist with the organization of conferences, and participate in office social events. I also found that I was regularly requested to assist with the preparation of various speeches and presentations that some of the judges gave during my stay at the Court. The breadth of these experiences, during which I was actively participating and observing, exposed me to the variety of the CCJ's work and helped me understand what was seen as a priority from the Court's perspective. Meeting with judges to discuss what they wanted to emphasize in their speeches, for instance, provided insight into how the judges sought to position the CCJ vis-à-vis the Caribbean region and the world.

In addition to the tasks I completed as an intern, I also requested access to particular events and activities arranged by the Court, which allowed me to accompany nearly every tour that was given of the courthouse, sit in on question-and-answer sessions offered by the judges to members of the public, and join the Court on its public education visits to Trinidad schools, which began during the last several weeks of my fieldwork. I also traveled with the Court as it heard testimony in Barbados and Jamaica for the *Myrie v. Barbados* trial, and I participated in or helped facilitate three conferences organized by the CCJ on behalf of its various affiliated organizations. Through this work, I gained a substantial familiarity with the Court and the people who populate it. I learned the courtroom procedures, the daily routines, the seasonal patterns, the yearly ebb and flow, and what counts as an extraordinary event and what does not. I enjoyed regular conversations with all seven of the CCJ judges, as well as nearly all the staff members, and I became familiar with many of the Court's various ephemera and artifacts, such as its website, brochures, pamphlets, announcements, and other CCJ publications. While participating in these activities and conversations, I recorded detailed field notes in a small spiral notebook that traveled with me everywhere and could be tucked discreetly in my front pocket. I also maintained a separate yellow legal notepad in which I took notes pertaining to my job as an intern. Depending on which notebook I was writing in, my interlocutors could detect which "hat"—anthropologist or intern—I had on at any given time.

My participation and observation at the Court were complemented by interviews and archival research. Specifically, I conducted interviews with each of the CCJ judges; numerous CCJ staff members; judges and attorneys from Trinidad, Barbados, and Jamaica; and various "regionalist" academics teaching at the University of the West Indies. These recorded interviews were informal, open-ended, and lasted one to one-and-a-half hours. They covered a broad range of topics, including regionalism, the Court and its work, the meaning of terms such as "Caribbean jurisprudence," and the Privy Council and other persistent reminders of colonialism. My archival work took place in Trinidad and Tobago's National Archives, Supreme Court Library, and Parliament Library, as well as the British National Archives in Kew, England. To gain a better understanding of the place of the Privy Council in the English-speaking Caribbean, I used Trinidad and Tobago—which, like most of the region, has not yet acceded to the appellate jurisdiction of the CCJ—as a case study. I asked of the archives whether, how, when, and in what ways the people of Trinidad and Tobago contemplated leaving or retaining the Privy Council as a final court of appeal. I focused specifically on four critical time periods in Trinidad and Tobago's history: the formation of the West Indies Federation in 1958, the achievement of independence in 1962, the transformation into a republic in 1976, and the opening of the Caribbean Court of Justice in 2005. I tracked parliamentary debates, public and political commentary on constitutional reform efforts, drafts of constitutions, commission of enquiry reports, meeting memoranda, and Colonial Office and House of Lords correspondence and reports for each of these periods.

Finally, my fieldwork necessarily included my interactions with the Caribbean people I encountered while living in Trinidad and Tobago for more than a year and traveling on Court business in Jamaica and Barbados. In Trinidad, I actively sought such encounters through weekly volunteer work and organized social events. I made a point of asking those with whom I interacted—who were often quite curious as to why I was living there—about their thoughts on the CCJ. I also tracked the three major newspapers in Trinidad and watched the local news nightly. It is from the breadth and depth of all these sources that I was able to gather a broad perspective on the Court, the region, the nation-state, and the omnipresence of the Privy Council, and it is from this research that this book took shape.

Positionality and Responsibility

During my time at the CCJ, I developed close friendships with many of those at the Court, allowing the intrusiveness of my role as researcher—even with the switching notebooks—to often fade into the background. With the president of the CCJ, this was not the case; I was always a researcher in his eyes. And not just any researcher, but one from the Global North. This was something that rankled him, as he once explained with a frankness that typified him.

Midway through my research, I attended a dinner reception at the president's house in honor of a visiting official from the International Criminal Tribunal for Rwanda (ICTR), who was a guest of the CCJ. It was an elegant affair, despite the invitation's indicated dress code of "casual," and the guest list included judges, lawyers, former employees of the ICTR, the ambassador from Nigeria, and several CCJ staff. After much time for dinner, conversation, and numerous speeches, a fellow legal intern and I began to make our rounds to thank the hosts and bid farewell. We reached the president as he was conversing with the guest of honor, to whom he introduced me. As part of his introduction, he explained to the visitor that "there is something about her [meaning, me] that I'm pissed about." As the blood drained from my face, he qualified this: "Well, it's not about her particularly, but it pisses me off that it took an American anthropologist to have the vision to come to the CCJ, volunteer as an intern, and create this project." It was a brilliant plan, he thought, but what "pissed him off" was that a Caribbean student had not thought of it. I feebly interjected, offering several reasons why this might be so and suggested that perhaps a Caribbean student would be well placed to conduct a similar study in the United States. To this suggestion, the president responded with a look and a flatly delivered truth: the fact is, there is no Caribbean student at the Supreme Court of the United States that is doing what I was doing at the CCJ. He did not need to add the obvious, which was that it was highly unlikely that a Caribbean student studying the Supreme Court would ever be allowed the level of access the CCJ had given me. Indeed, it is doubtful whether the Supreme Court would permit this level of access to anyone. I can extract from this awkward exchange with the president both a compliment and a call to attention. He respected my research, but as he had made clear, I inhabited an extraordinarily privileged position as an American (with slightly brown skin and an often unplaceable ethnicity—often read, inaccurately, as "chinee" by Trinidadians—but American nonetheless) in the Caribbean that opened doors for me. I was reaping the rewards of the very colonial inequities that I sought to critique. Yet, the president trusted me to do right by this privilege afforded to me. So, too, did the others who spoke to me and shared their time and wisdom with me, some of whom, like the president, forced me to acknowledge the racial, social, and historical dynamics of the research I was conducting.

The president's comments have stayed with me in the years that have followed, providing an ever-present, well-deserved, and highly productive unease. They have forced me to consider how I think and write about the CCJ, what power I wield as an American anthropologist, what it means to do right by my interlocutors, and how, at the same time, I can honor the rigors of social science. This is how I arrived at a primary frame for this book: possibility. It is simply not my place to take a side in the debate, which often dominated public discussions during my time in Trinidad, about the CCJ's success or failure, its efficacy or inadvisability, its remarkable potential or farcical nature, or its ability to measure up to the Privy Council and its law lords. I could not and would not expose the Court's "naked body" in a way that opened it to more surface-level critiques. I could, on the other hand, provide a deeper understanding of the CCJ's work, its motivations, and the complex challenges it faced as it established itself as a new regional institution and continues to face today. Indeed, as much as this book is built on a framework of possibility, it is also my job as an anthropologist and it is also my duty to the president and all others, to show how this possibility exists alongside a history of unsuccessful regional attempts, amid a population that has long grown wary and weary, and within a world structured by conditions created through colonialism. It is within this fraught landscape that the CCJ strives. I have, therefore, approached this book and the Court's work as a genuine invitation to rethink the way the world could be organized differently, even in the face of what often seems to be impossible odds. The CCJ offers this possibility.

Notes

Orientation

1. James Ferguson, "Declarations of Dependence: Labour, Personhood, and Welfare in Southern Africa," *Journal of the Royal Anthropological Institute* 19 (2013): 224.
2. According to the Agreement, article 3, section 3, "The Seat of the Court shall be in the territory of a Contracting Party as determined by a qualified majority of the Contracting Parties but, as circumstances warrant, the Court may sit in the territory of any other Contracting Party." Agreement Establishing the Caribbean Court of Justice (Georgetown, Guyana: Caribbean Community [CARICOM] Secretariat, 2001).
3. Agreement, art. 3, sec. 4.
4. See, e.g., *Daily Express* (Trinidad and Tobago), "Mark: No CCJ Support; Call Us Colonialists if You Want," May 26, 2022; Edward Seage, "CCJ Can Still be Manipulated," *Gleaner* (Jamaica), December 14, 2014, http://jamaica-gleaner.com/gleaner/20141214/focus/focus2.html; *Trinidad Express*, "AG: Govts Not in Selection of CCJ Judges," May 5, 2012.
5. See Kamari Clarke, "Assemblages of Experts: The Caribbean Court of Justice and the Modernity of Caribbean Postcoloniality," *Small Axe* 17, no. 2 (July 2013): 88–107, for additional discussion of the CCJ's bench.
6. Caribbean Court of Justice (CCJ), "CCJ Trust Fund: Financing the Court," accessed August 10, 2022, https://ccj.org/about-the-ccj/ccj-trust-fund/.
7. Revised Agreement Establishing the CCJ Trust Fund (Georgetown, Guyana: Caribbean Community [CARICOM] Secretariat, 2004), article 3.
8. Duke E. Pollard, *The Caribbean Court of Justice: Closing the Circle of Independence* (Kingston, Jamaica: Caribbean Law Publishing, 2004), 235.

Chapter One

1. Although all names are pseudonyms, the book follows the naming practices of the Court, wherein judges and senior administrators are more formally addressed with their title and surname, such as "Justice Matthews" or "Ms. Carl," and junior staff members are typically called by their first names, such as "Serena" or "Peter."
2. See, e.g., United Nations Office on Drugs and Crime, accessed May 25, 2020, https://dataunodc.un.org.

3. See, e.g., Naor H. Ben-Yehoyada, *The Mediterranean Incarnate: Transnational Region Formation between Sicily and Tunisia since World War II* (Chicago: University of Chicago Press, 2017); Gustav Peebles, *The Euro and Its Rivals: Currency and the Construction of a Transnational City* (Bloomington: Indiana University Press, 2011); Cris Shore, *Building Europe: The Cultural Politics of European Integration* (London: Routledge, 2000). A "Hot Spots" Forum in *Cultural Anthropology* also offers reflections on the wide range of challenges that the European Union faces against a backdrop of heightened nationalism; see Kelly Alexander, "Europe in the Balance," *Fieldsights*, October 22, 2019, https://culanth.org/fieldsights/series/europe-in-the-balance.

4. In a speech to the United Nations General Assembly on September 19, 2017, for example, President Trump spoke of "sovereignty" and "sovereign" nations twenty-one times. Only three months earlier, his administration announced that the United States would be pulling out of the Paris Agreement on climate change mitigation, and only three weeks later, he announced that he would decertify the Iran Nuclear Deal.

5. Yarimar Bonilla also writes on sovereignty as a problem; see Yarimar Bonilla, *Non-Sovereign Futures: French Caribbean Politics in the Wake of Disenchantment* (Chicago: University of Chicago Press, 2015), 12. Drawing on the work of Thomas Holt, Bonilla sees the problem of sovereignty as somewhat analogous to, even intertwined with, the problem of freedom described by Holt. See Thomas Holt, *The Problem of Freedom: Race, Labor, and Politics in Jamaica and Britain, 1832–1938* (Baltimore: Johns Hopkins University Press, 1992).

6. See Adom Getachew, *Worldmaking after Empire: The Rise and Fall of Self-Determination* (Princeton, NJ: Princeton University Press, 2019).

7. It is worth noting that postcolonial literature and academic texts are replete with observations on and discussions of the presence of mimicry in postcolonial settings, offering distinct takes on the effects and possibilities of mimicry but always remaining within the realm of mimesis. Frantz Fanon, for example, understands "sickening mimicry" as the exercise of unrepentant and impenetrable colonial power over a population and thus urges a radical break from the colonizer and the colonized past; see Frantz Fanon, *The Wretched of the Earth*, trans. Richard Philox (New York: Grove Press, 2004). V. S. Naipaul offers a similarly scathing view of mimicry and "mimic men," who copy their British colonizers to the point of loss of self; see V. S. Naipaul, *The Mimic Men* (New York: Vintage International, 2001). Unlike Fanon, Naipaul does not suggest the possibility of a revolutionary escape. Homi Bhabha also does not see the possibility of escaping mimicry, which he calls "one of the most elusive and effective strategies of colonial power and knowledge," but suggests that within mimicry itself there is the potential for an eventual disruption of colonial power; see Homi Bhabha, *The Location of Culture* (New York: Routledge, 1994), 122. Anthropologists, James Ferguson notes, have increasingly dealt with the "embarrassment of [ ] mimicry"—embarrassing because mimicry seemed "to confirm the claim of the racist colonizer" that European ways were superior—by insisting that imitation was "in fact a gesture of resistance to colonialism"; see James Ferguson, "Of Mimicry and Membership: Africans and the 'New World Society,'" *Cultural Anthropology* 17, no. 4 (2002): 553–54. Ferguson, stepping aside from the language of resistance, argues that mimicry might be best understood as a claim to membership within "the new world society" ("Of Mimicry"). Here, while acknowledging that mimicry has certainly found its place within Caribbean societies, I argue that it would not be an accurate characterization of the CCJ's region-making work.

8. Constantine V. Nakassis, "Brand, Citationality, Performativity," *American Anthropologist* 114, no. 4 (2012): 627, 626.

9. Nakassis, "Brand, Citationality, Performativity."

10. Michel-Rolph Trouillot, "North Atlantic Universals: Analytical Fictions, 1492–1945," *South Atlantic Quarterly* 101, no. 4 (2002): 847–48.

11. Linden Lewis, "The Dissolution of the Myth of Sovereignty in the Caribbean," in *Caribbean Sovereignty, Development and Democracy in an Age of Globalization*, ed. by Linden Lewis (New York: Routledge, 2013), 68–87.

12. Linden Lewis, "Introduction: Sovereignty, Heterodoxy, and the Last Desperate Shibboleth of Caribbean Nationalism," in *Caribbean Sovereignty, Development and Democracy in an Age of Globalization*, edited by Linden Lewis, (New York: Routledge, 2013), 1–16.

13. Thomas Blom Hansen and Finn Stepputat, "Sovereignty Revisited," *Annual Review of Anthropology* 35 (2006): 295–315.

14. Ann Laura Stoler, ed., *Imperial Debris: On Ruins and Ruination* (Durham, NC: Duke University Press, 2013).

15. Clarke, "Assemblages of Experts."

16. Lewis, "Introduction"; Getachew, *Worldmaking after Empire*; Begoña Aretxaga, "Maddening States," *Annual Review of Anthropology* 32 (2003): 393–410.

17. Bonilla, *Non-Sovereign Futures*; Trouillot, "North Atlantic Universals."

18. I return to the region's lack of felt presence in chapter 3.

19. Michael Anthony Lilla, *Promoting the Caribbean Court of Justice as the Final Court of Appeal for States of the Caribbean Community* (Williamsburg, VA: National Center for State Courts, 2008).

20. Lilla, *Promoting the Caribbean Court of Justice*, 2.

21. See Getachew, *Worldmaking after Empire*.

22. *The Eighteenth Brumaire of Louis Napoleon* (original German title *Der 18te Brumaire des Louis Napoleon*) is an essay written by Karl Marx between December 1851 and March 1852, first published in 1852.

23. Mindie Lazarus-Black, "The (Heterosexual) Regendering of a Modern State: Criminalizing and Implementing Domestic Violence Law in Trinidad," *Law & Social Inquiry* 28, no. 4 (2003): 979–1008.

24. Quoting Jacqueline Rose (*States of Fantasy* [Oxford: Clarendon Press, 1996], 4) and citing Giorgio Agamben (*Homo Sacer: Sovereign Power and Bare Life* [Stanford, CA: Stanford University Press, 1998]), Aretxaga remarks, "The state can be considered then as 'a privileged setting for the staging of political fantasy in the modern world'" ("Maddening States," 403). With regard to the nation, Hobsbawm notes, "The basic characteristic of the modern nation and everything connected with it is its modernity"; E. J. Hobsbawm, *Nations and Nationalism since 1780: Programme, Myth, Reality* (New York: Cambridge University Press, 1990), 14. Linking the nation to the state and drawing, as well, from Agamben (*Homo Sacer*), Hansen and Stepputat understand "the nation-state as the main vehicle of sovereign power" and suggest that "most modern states claim effective legal sovereignty over a territory and its population in the name of the nation and the popular will" ("Sovereignty Revisited," 297). See also Lewis, "Introduction"; Lewis, "Dissolution of Myth."

25. See, e.g., Yarimar Bonilla, "Unsettling Sovereignty," *Cultural Anthropology* 32, no. 3 (2017): 330–39; Lewis 2013; Hansen and Stepputat, "Sovereignty Revisited"; Aretxaga, "Maddening States." This understanding of sovereignty, in which it is hitched to the nation-state, in no way purports to describe the multifaceted ways in which sovereignty can be understood and experienced. To acknowledge but one example, Native American political sovereignty is not dependent on and knit to the existence of an independent indigenous state; see, e.g., Jessica Cattelino, *High Stakes: Florida Seminole Gaming and Sovereignty* (Durham, NC: Duke University Press, 2008);

Audra Simpson, *Mohawk Interruptus: Political Life Across the Borders of Settler States* (Durham, NC: Duke University Press, 2014); Justin B. Richland, *Cooperation without Submission: Indigenous Jurisdictions in Native Nation—US Engagements* (Chicago: University of Chicago Press, 2021).

26. See e.g., Hansen and Stepputat, "Sovereignty Revisited"; Aretxaga, "Maddening States."

27. Lewis, "Dissolution of Myth", 68.

28. Arjun Appadurai, "Sovereignty without Territoriality," In *The Anthropology of Space and Place: Locating Culture*, ed. S. E. Low and D. Lawrence-Zúñiga (1996; repr., Malden, MA: Blackwell 2003), 338.

29. Benedict Anderson, *Imagined Communities: Reflections on the Origin and Spread of Nationalism* (1983; repr., New York: Verso, 2006); Hobsbawm, *Nations and Nationalism since 1780*.

30. Richard Bauman and Charles L. Briggs, *Voices of Modernity: Language Ideologies and the Politics of Modernity* (Cambridge: Cambridge University Press, 2003); Anderson, *Imagined Communities*; Judith Irvine and Susan Gal, "Language Ideology and Linguistic Differentiation," in *Regimes of Language*, ed. P. Kroskrity (Santa Fe, NM: School of American Research Press, 2000), 35–84.

31. Appadurai, "Sovereignty without Territoriality"; Lewis, "Dissolution of Myth."

32. Louis Althusser, "Ideology and Ideological State Apparatuses: Notes Towards an Investigation," in *Lenin and Philosophy and Other Essays*, trans. Ben Brewster (1971; repr., New York: Monthly Review Press, 2001), 85–126.

33. Andrew Graan, "The Nation Brand Regime: Nation Branding and the Semiotic Regimentation of Public Communication in Contemporary Macedonia." *Signs and Society* 4, no. S1 (2016): S70–S105, https://doi.org/10.1086/684613.

34. Sally Merry, *Colonizing Hawai'i: The Cultural Power of Law* (Princeton, NJ: Princeton University Press, 2000); Bill Maurer, *Recharting the Caribbean: Land, Law, and Citizenship in the British Virgin Islands* (Ann Arbor: University of Michigan Press, 1997).

35. Bonilla, "Unsettling Sovereignty," 331.

36. Bonilla, *Non-Sovereign Futures*, Bonilla, "Unsettling Sovereignty"; Trouillot, "North Atlantic Universals"; Michel-Rolph Trouillot, *Silencing the Past: Power and the Production of History* (Boston: Beacon Press, 1995); Lewis, "Introduction"; Lewis, "Dissolution of Myth."

37. In addition to work done by Bonilla (*Non-Sovereign Futures*) and Trouillot (*Silencing the Past*), Sally Merry (*Colonizing Hawai'i*) provides an account of the way in which "sovereignty" provided the legal justification for the ultimate colonization of Hawai'i.

38. Martin Chanock described law as the "cutting edge of colonialism" in his *Law, Custom, and Social Order: The Colonial Experience in Malawi and Zambia* (New York: Cambridge University Press, 1985), 4. It should be recognized that this law was exercised as a privilege of the sovereign and imperial state.

39. See, e.g., Chanock, *Law, Custom, and Social Order*.

40. See, e.g., Chanock, *Law, Custom, and Social Order*; John L. Comaroff, "Reflection on the Colonial State in South Africa and Elsewhere: Factions, Fragments, Facts and Fictions," *Social Identities* 4, no. 3 (1998): 321–61.

41. Stoler, *Imperial Debris*; Ann Laura Stoler, *Duress: Imperial Durabilities in Our Times* (Durham, NC: Duke University Press, 2016).

42. See Merry, *Colonizing Hawai'i*; Trouillot, *Silencing the Past*; Lewis, "Introduction."

43. Trouillot, "North Atlantic Universals." See also Yarimar Bonilla, "Ordinary Sovereignty," *Small Axe: A Caribbean Journal of Criticism* 42 (2013): 152–65; Bonilla, *Non-Sovereign Futures*.

44. Lewis, "Introduction."

NOTES TO PAGES 22-28

45. Deborah A. Thomas, *Exceptional Violence: Embodied Citizenship in Transnational Jamaica* (Durham, NC: Duke University Press, 2011); Deborah A. Thomas, *Political Life in the Wake of the Plantation: Sovereignty, Witnessing, Repair* (Durham, NC: Duke University Press, 2019).

46. Bonilla, *Non-Sovereign Futures*.

47. Bonilla, *Non-Sovereign Futures*.

48. Bonilla, *Non-Sovereign Futures*, xiv.

49. Bonilla, *Non-Sovereign Futures*, xiii.

50. Simpson, *Mohawk Interruptus*.

51. Bonilla, *Non-Sovereign Futures*, 151.

52. Bonilla, *Non-Sovereign Futures*, 15.

53. The CCJ's Mission and Vision statements have since been updated, but from the Court's inception and through the time of my field research there, the Court's Vision statement read: "To provide for the Caribbean Community an accessible, fair, efficient, innovative and impartial justice system built on a jurisprudence *reflective of our history, values and traditions* while maintaining an inspirational, independent institution worthy of emulation by the courts of the region and the trust and confidence of its people." Caribbean Court of Justice, *Annual Report 2005–2006* (Port of Spain, Trinidad and Tobago: CCJ, 2006), 2, emphasis added.

54. Max Weber, *The Protestant Ethic and the Spirit of Capitalism* (New York: Charles Scribner's Sons, 1958).

55. Getachew, *Worldmaking after Empire*.

56. Bonilla, *Non-Sovereign Futures*.

57. Ben-Yehoyada, *Mediterranean Incarnate*.

58. See, e.g., Caricom 2017; Revised Treaty of Chaguaramas Establishing the Caribbean Community Including the CARICOM Single Market and Economy (Georgetown, Guyana: Caribbean Community [CARICOM] Secretariat, 2001).

59. Shore, *Building Europe*; see also Peebles, *Euro and Its Rivals*.

60. Peebles, *Euro and Its Rivals*.

61. CARICOM, "Our Work," accessed July 25, 2022, https://caricom.org/our-work/.

62. Ben-Yehoyada, *Mediterranean Incarnate*, 24, emphasis in original.

63. See e.g., Stephan Palmié and Francisco A. Scarano, eds., *The Caribbean: A History of the Region and its Peoples* (Chicago: University of Chicago Press, 2011); Michel-Rolph Trouillot, "North Atlantic Universals"; Michel-Rolph Trouillot, "The Caribbean Region: An Open Frontier in Anthropological Theory," *Annual Review of Anthropology* 21 (1992): 19–42; Sidney W. Mintz, "The Caribbean as a Socio-Cultural Area," in *Peoples and Cultures of the Caribbean: An Anthropological Reader*, edited by M. M. Horowitz (Garden City, NY: American Museum of Natural History Press, 1971), 17–46; Sidney W. Mintz, "The Caribbean Region," *Daedalus* 103, no. 2 (1974): 45–71.

64. The phrase "transnational constellations" comes from Ben-Yehoyada, *Mediterranean Incarnate*.

65. See, e.g., Giorgio Agamben, *State of Exception* (Chicago: University of Chicago Press, 2005), Carl Schmitt, *Political Theology* (Chicago: University of Chicago Press, 2006); Thomas Hobbes, *Leviathan* (Baltimore: Penguin Books, 1968).

66. See, e.g., Bradin Cormack, *A Power to Do Justice: Jurisdiction, English Literature, and the Rise of Common Law, 1509–1625* (Chicago: University of Chicago Press, 2007); Robert T. Ford, "Law's Territory (A History of Jurisdiction)," *Michigan Law Review* 97, no. 4 (1999): 843–930; Shaun McVeigh, ed., *Jurisprudence of Jurisdiction* (New York: Routledge Cavendish Press, 2007); Bill Maurer, "Jurisdiction in Dialect: Sovereignty Games in the British Virgin Islands," in

European Integration and Postcolonial Sovereignty Games: The EU Overseas Countries and Territories, ed. R. Adler-Nissen and U. P. Gad (New York: Routledge, 2013), 130–44; Justin B. Richland, "Hopi Tradition as Jurisdiction: On the Potentializing Limits of Hopi Sovereignty," *Law & Social Inquiry* 36, no. 1 (2011): 201–34; Justin B. Richland, "Perpetuity as (and against) Rule: Law, Tradition, Juris-diction," paper presented at the American Bar Foundation, Chicago, October 17, 2012; Justin B. Richland, "Jurisdiction: Grounding Law in Language," *Annual Review of Anthropology* 42 (2013): 209–26. I flag this definition because it has been particularly instructive in the shaping of my argument; exactly how and when the CCJ speaks the law offers a window of understanding into its relationship to sovereignty. This is a topic I return to in chapter 5.

67. Merry, *Colonizing Hawai'i*.

68. Lazarus-Black, "(Heterosexual) Regendering," 979.

69. Lauren Benton, *Law and Colonial Cultures: Legal Regimes in World History, 1400–1900* (Cambridge: Cambridge University Press, 2002), 6. I note that Benton crafts a powerful argument showing how a particular state-centered idea of law has come to be associated with "modern." She, however, pushes against the notion that this legal ordering has come primarily (and certainly not exclusively) from any particular location. While I agree with this in principle, it seems clear that within the Anglophone Caribbean, the influence of British law and order dominates and shapes much of the legal sphere in which the CCJ operates.

70. Benton, *Law and Colonial Cultures*, 6.

71. Sally Falk Moore, *Social Facts and Fabrications: "Customary" Law on Kilimanjaro, 1880–1980* (London: Cambridge University Press, 1986). See also Chanock, *Law, Custom, and Social Order*. I refer to "customs" and "customary law" using scare quotes to highlight the fact, as Moore has persuasively shown, that these "customs" and laws have been necessarily reworked, re-created, and invented anew given massively changed social environments. The CCJ, I suggest, has also created "customs" and invented "traditions" that draw on preexisting practices but are reframed in ways that can lend legitimacy and authority to the Court's region-making project. This is something I touch on in chapter 5. See also E. J. Hobsbawm and T. O. Ranger, *The Invention of Tradition*. (Cambridge: Cambridge University Press, 1983).

72. Sally Falk Moore, *Law as Process: An Anthropological Approach* (London: Routledge and Kegan Paul, 1978).

73. The idea of the Caribbean and colonies more generally as places of legal experimentation is not new. As John Comaroff observes, "European overseas 'possessions' were often laboratories for experimentation with, even for the production of, legal instruments, institutions, principles, procedures; also modes of regulation." John L. Comaroff, "Colonialism, Culture, and the Law: A Foreword." *Law and Social Inquiry* 26, no. 2 (2001): 310.

74. Althusser, "Ideology and Ideological State Apparatuses."

75. On "juris-diction," see, e.g., Cormack, *A Power to Do Justice*; Ford, "Law's Territory"; McVeigh, *Jurisprudence of Jurisdiction*; Maurer, "Jurisdiction in Dialect"; Richland, "Hopi Tradition as Jurisdiction"; Richland, "Perpetuity as (and against) Rule," 20.

76. Graan has observed the branding of Macedonian history; Comaroff and Comaroff have written about the commodification of ethnicity in South Africa and elsewhere; van Ham describes the marketization of democracy in European states; and Maurer points to the market advantages that tax-free offshore incorporation has provided to the British Virgin Island "nation." See Andrew Graan, "Counterfeiting the Nation? Skopje 2014 and the Politics of Nation Branding in Macedonia," *Cultural Anthropology* 28, no. 1 (2013): 161–79; Graan, "Nation Brand Regime"; John L. Comaroff and Jean Comaroff, *Ethnicity, Inc.* (Chicago: University of Chicago Press, 2009); Peter van

Ham, "Place Branding: The State of the Art," *Annals of the American Academy of Political and Social Science* 616, no. 1 (March 2008): 126–49; Maurer, *Recharting the Caribbean*.

Chapter Two

1. Getachew, *Worldmaking after Empire*.
2. C.f. David Scott, *Conscripts of Modernity: The Tragedy of Colonial Enlightenment* (Durham, NC: Duke University Press, 2004).
3. Anderson, *Imagined Communities*.
4. Anderson, *Imagined Communities*, 11–12. Page numbers are from the 2006 edition.
5. Ernest Renan, *What Is a Nation?* (1882; repr., Toronto, Tapir Press, 1996). Page numbers are from the 1996 edition.
6. Renan, *What Is a Nation?* 45.
7. See Renan, *What Is a Nation?*
8. See E. Gellner, *Nations and Nationalism* (Ithaca, NY: Cornell University Press, 1983), 47, cited in Hobsbawm, *Nations and Nationalism since 1780*, 10. See also Geoff Eley and Ronald Grigor Suny, "Introduction: From the Moment of Social History to the Work of Cultural Representation," in *Becoming National: A Reader*, ed. Geoff Eley and Ronald Grigor Suny (New York: Oxford University Press, 1996), 24.
9. Eley and Suny, "Introduction," 24.
10. Liisa Malkki, *Purity and Exile: Violence, Memory, and National Cosmology among Hutu Refugees in Tanzania* (Chicago: University of Chicago Press, 1995), 55.
11. Bridget Brereton, *An Introduction to the History of Trinidad and Tobago* (Oxford: Heinemann Educational Publishers, 1996), 55.
12. See, e.g., Thomas, *Political Life in the Wake of the Plantation*; Thomas, *Exceptional Violence*.
13. Getachew, *Worldmaking after Empire*, 25.
14. Getachew, *Worldmaking after Empire*, 23–25.
15. Getachew, *Worldmaking after Empire*, 24.
16. Norman Girvan, "Reinventing the CSME," speech delivered at the third biennial Caribbean Association of Judicial Officers Conference, Accra Beach Hotel, Bridgetown, Barbados, September 27, 2013, 7.
17. See also Patrick Antoine, "An Assessment of the Original Jurisdiction," in *The Caribbean Court of Justice: The First 10 Years* (London: LexisNexis, 2016).
18. Dominions Office, West Indies Department, United Kingdom, *Trinidad & Tobago Independence Constitution: Statement by the Secretary of State for the Colonies*, June 5, 1962, 1.
19. At the regional level, the Committee of the Organisation of Commonwealth Caribbean Bar Associations (OCCBA) prepared a report in 1972 that called for a Regional Court of Appeal to "replac[e] and assum[e] the jurisdiction of the Judicial Committee" and, representing the first apparent proposal of this nature, also suggested that "an original jurisdiction be vested in the court in respect of matters referred to it by agreement between Caribbean States . . . on such matters as interpretation of the [Caribbean Free Trade] Agreement" (as cited on CCJ Website, accessed April 29, 2015). At the state level, similar suggestions were proffered. To use Trinidad and Tobago as an example once again, a Commission on Constitutional Reform chaired by the well-respected Trinidadian lawyer Sir Hugh Wooding prepared an extensively researched and thorough report, published in 1974. It also recommended the abolition of appeals to the

Privy Council; see Constitution Commission of Trinidad and Tobago, *Report of the Constitution Commission* (Port of Spain, Trinidad and Tobago, 1974), 122. The Wooding Commission Report was not alone in making this recommendation. Duke Pollard notes that "every constitutional Commission appointed in any Commonwealth Caribbean country since 1974 has recommended severance of ties with the Privy Council" (*Closing the Circle of Independence*, 197).

What is particularly interesting about the Wooding Commission Report, as well as Pollard's carefully worded observation is that the recommendation is *not* to create a Caribbean Court of Appeal but only to sever ties with the Privy Council. In Trinidad, this would have left Trinidad's own Court of Appeal to serve as the final court of appeal for that state. Nevertheless, the Wooding Commission Report (and those similar reports that followed its lead) is regularly offered in Trinidad and across the Caribbean as an important document in furthering the development of a regional court. See, e.g., Cheryl Thompson-Barrow, *Bringing Justice Home: The Road to Final Appellate and Regional Court* (London: Commonwealth Secretariat, 2008); Pollard, *Closing the Circle of Independence*; Hugh Rawlins, *The Caribbean Court of Justice: The History and Analysis of the Debate* (Georgetown, Guyana: CARICOM Secretariat, 2000).

The report is also remarkable in that its recommendation to cease appeals to the Privy Council follows six and a half pages that detail the overwhelming preference of the public, including lawyers, to *retain* appeals to the Privy Council. In the end, as the British High Commissioner to Trinidad and Tobago stated in his annual report for 1974, the "far-reaching recommendations on constitutional reform" presented by Wooding "were later thrown more or less to the winds"; see Foreign and Commonwealth Office, United Kingdom, *Trinidad & Tobago: Annual Review for 1974*, Diplomatic Report No. 56/75, 3. While the issue was debated in Trinidad and Tobago's Senate and put before the House of Representatives, the arguments *against* delinking from the Privy Council carried the day. That, and a concern that the inclusion of such a controversial provision would cause the entire proposed Draft Constitution for a new Republic of Trinidad and Tobago to fail. Indeed, there was much at stake beyond a continued link to the Privy Council, and those matters—such as the establishment of a republic—frequently eclipsed the question of replacing a court system that was functioning smoothly. If it ain't broke, why fix it?

20. Shridath Ramphal and the West Indian Commission, *Report of the West Indian Commission: Time for Action*, 2nd ed. (Kingston, Jamaica: The Press—University of the West Indies, 1993), 498.

21. Ramphal and West Indian Commission, *Time for Action*, 498–501.

22. Caribbean Court of Justice, website, accessed August 19, 2022, https://ccj.org.

23. To accede to the CCJ's appellate jurisdiction, each state must follow its own statutory and constitutional requirements, which can be rather complex. This caused a significant issue when Jamaica attempted to join the Court's appellate jurisdiction in 2005, as I note later in the chapter.

24. Antoine, *Caribbean Court of Justice: The First Ten Years*.

25. Ingo Venzke, "Understanding the Authority of International Courts and Tribunals: On Delegation and Discursive Construction," *Theoretical Inquiries in Law* 14 (November 2013): 399–400.

26. Walter Benjamin, "Critique of Violence," in *Reflections: Essays, Aphorisms, Autobiographical Writings*, trans. Edmund Jephcott (New York: Harcourt Brace Jovanovich, 1978), 277–300; Bruno Latour, *The Making of Law: An Ethnography of the Conseil d'État*, trans. Marina Brilman and Alain Pottage (Cambridge: Polity Press, 2010).

27. Notably, in 2006, Satnarine Sharma, the chief justice of Trinidad and Tobago from 2002 to 2008, was arrested and charged with corruption for attempting to influence the trial of a former prime minister. The charges were eventually dropped.

28. Jacques Derrida, "The Force of Law: The Mystical Foundation of Authority," in *Acts of Religion*, ed. Gil Anidjar, trans. Mary Quaintance (New York: Routledge, 2002), 239–40.

29. See, e.g., John Comaroff, "Reflections on the Rise of Legal Theology: Law and Religion in the Twenty-First Century," *Social Analysis* 53, no. 1 (2009): 193–216; Peter Goodrich, "Specters of Law: Why the History of the Legal Spectacle Has Not Been Written," *UC Irvine Law Review* 1, no. 3 (2011): 773–812; Paul W. Kahn, *The Reign of Law: Marbury v Madison and the Construction of America* (New Haven, CT: Yale University Press, 1997); Derrida, "Force of Law."

30. Benjamin, "Critique of Violence."

31. In this chapter, I use the term "time-space" because it emphasizes time and temporality, which relate most closely to the Court's mythmaking activities. In chapter 3, however, I analyze the CCJ's work in crafting a regional space and thus refer to "space-time."

32. Kahn, *Reign of Law*.

33. According to the Privy Council's website, "The jurisdiction of the Privy Council originates from Norman times but the present constitution of the JCPC is based on the Judicial Committee Act 1833." Judicial Committee of the Privy Council, "FAQs: When Was the JCPC Established?" accessed July 26, 2022, https://www.jcpc.uk/faqs.html#1b. The Normans ruled England from 1066 to 1154, making the Privy Council roughly one thousand years old. See also Lloyd Barnett, "An Assessment of the Appellate Jurisdiction: Ten Years of Adjudication in the Caribbean Court of Justice and Reflections on a Decade of Caribbean Jurisprudence," in Antoine, *Caribbean Court of Justice: The First 10 Years*, 29, which covers the more than four centuries of the Privy Council's involvement in Caribbean affairs.

34. Jones Bahamas, "Privy Council Has Fourth Sitting in The Bahamas," *Bahama Journal*, February 21, 2017, http://jonesbahamas.com/privy-council-has-fourth-sitting-in-the-bahamas/.

35. See Deborah A. Thomas, "Time and the Otherwise: Plantations, Garrisons, and Being Human in the Caribbean." *Anthropological Theory* 16, no. 2–3 (2016): 177–200.

36. Jacques Derrida, "Declarations of Independence," *New Political Science* 15 (1986): 9.

37. Articles 211–24 in the Revised Treaty of Chaguaramas.

38. See Girvan, "Reinventing the CSME."

39. CARICOM, *What It Is, What It Does*, rev. ed. (Georgetown, Guyana: CARICOM Secretariat, 2003); CARICOM, *Your Questions Answered*, rev. ed. (Georgetown, Guyana: CARICOM Secretariat, 2003).

40. Carol J. Greenhouse, "Just in Time: Temporality and the Cultural Legitimation of Law," *Yale Law Journal* 98, no. 8 (1989): 1631–51.

41. I draw here from Maurer (*Recharting the Caribbean*), in which he describes how the authoring of the International Business Companies Ordinance of 1984 by British Virgin Islanders contributed to the "authorization" of the BVI nation. The BVI nation, in turn, as its residents believed, required autochthonous laws such as the IBC, which could reflect the BVI culture.

42. Getachew, *Worldmaking after Empire*.

43. Cf. Scott, *Conscripts of Modernity*.

Chapter Three

1. Shanique Myrie and the State of Jamaica v. the State of Barbados [2013] CCJ 3 (OJ), para. 1.

2. I write the facts of this case as they are alleged in Myrie's court filings, rather than as the "truth" of what happened. This is because the CCJ, as I describe later in the chapter, found that

while the majority of Myrie's allegation had been sufficiently proven to be true through the evidence adduced at trial, there remained several allegations that did not meet that threshold.

3. Ronald Mason, "Kick CARICOM to the Kerb," *Gleaner* (Jamaica), May 5, 2013, http://jamaica-gleaner.com/gleaner/20130505/cleisure/cleisure5.html. I discuss this article in greater detail in chapter 4.

4. This hierarchy of states is addressed in more detail in chapter 4.

5. Myrie and Jamaica v. Barbados, para. 52.

6. Myrie and Jamaica v. Barbados, para. 10. Interestingly, this paragraph continues, "It should be noted, however, that the Court is an international court authorized to apply 'such rules of international law as may be applicable' (citing Article 217 of the Revised Treaty of Chaguaramas) of which human rights law is an inextricable part. It stands to reason therefore that, in the resolution of a claim properly brought in its original jurisdiction, the Court can and must take into account principles of international human rights law when seeking to shape and develop relevant Community law." I interpret this statement of the Court's to mean that although it does not have jurisdiction to adjudicate violations of international human rights treaties, it does have an obligation to consider the principles of human rights law when determining regional matters. In threading the needle thus, the CCJ locates the region within the international, assuring the public that neither the region nor the Court are going it alone.

7. Myrie and Jamaica v. Barbados, para. 100.

8. 7 News Belize, "What CARICOM Citizenship Means," October 4, 2013, http://www.7newsbelize.com/sstory.php?nid=26712.

9. Ronald Sanders, "Caribbean Court of Justice Delivers for the Caribbean People," *Sir Ronald Sanders* (blog), October 10, 2013, http://www.sirronaldsanders.com/viewarticle.aspx?ID=400.

10. Myrie and Jamaica v. Barbados, para. 63, quoting Ramphal, *Time for Action*.

11. See Appadurai, "Sovereignty without Territoriality," 338; Steffen Dalsgaard, "The Time of the State and the Temporality of the Gavman in Manus Province, Papua." *Social Analysis* 57, no. 1 (2013): 34–49; Justin Mueller, "Temporality, Sovereignty, and Imperialism: When Is Imperialism?" *Politics* 36, no. 4 (2016): 428–40; see also James Ferguson and Akhil Gupta, "Spatializing States: Toward an Ethnography of Neoliberal Governmentality." *American Ethnologist* 29, no. 4 (2002): 981–1002.

12. As I discuss in chapter 6, the CCJ, though it must confront the challenges posed by water, also works to posit the power of the Caribbean Sea another way; it presents the sea as a force that binds its member states together—a touchstone of commonality and identity.

13. There is, however, a subregional currency: the Eastern Caribbean dollar, which is used by most of the states belonging to the Organization of Eastern Caribbean States (OECS): Antigua and Barbuda, Dominica, Grenada, Saint Kitts and Nevis, Saint Lucia, and Saint Vincent and the Grenadines (all of which are also members of CARICOM). Anguilla and Monserrat, which are British Overseas Territories, also use the Eastern Caribbean dollar. Monserrat is a full member of OECS, while Anguilla is an associate member. To be sure, the presence of this subregion further complicates the CCJ's work.

14. Gertrude Stein, *Everybody's Autobiography* (1937; repr., New York: Cooper Square Publishers, 1971).

15. Myrie and Jamaica v. Barbados, para. 63.

16. Appadurai, "Sovereignty without Territoriality," 338.

17. Charles Tilly, "The Time of States," *Social Research* 61, no. 2 (1994): 275.

18. See e.g., Mueller, "Temporality, Sovereignty, and Imperialism"; Appadurai, "Sovereignty without Territoriality"; Dalsgaard, "Time of the State"; Tilly, "Time of States"; Ferguson and Gupta, "Spatializing States"; Mariana Valverde, "'Time Thickens, Takes on Flesh': Spatiotemporal Dynamics in Law," in *The Expanding Spaces of Law: A Timely Legal Geography* (Palo Alto, CA: Stanford University Press, 2014); Mariana Valverde, *Chronotopes of Law: Jurisdiction, Scale, and Governance* (New York: Routledge, 2015); See also Philip Abrams, "Notes on the Difficulty of Studying the State." *Journal of Historical Sociology* 1 (1988): 58–89.

19. Mueller, "Temporality, Sovereignty, and Imperialism," 431.

20. Abrams, "Notes on the Difficulty of Studying the State," 82.

21. Maurer, *Recharting the Caribbean*.

22. Before videoconferencing was fully enabled across the CCJ's member states, telephone conferences served to link distant parties and attorneys. These, too, suffered from some technological inconsistencies.

23. See Anderson, *Imagined Communities*.

24. Maurer, *Recharting the Caribbean*.

25. The reduced level of planning and exertion by the CCJ staff for the Barbados segment of the trial was a direct reflection of the differences in resources between the Jamaican judicial system and the Barbadian judicial system. And these disparate levels of resources between the two states were at the core of the *Myrie* case and the events that led to it.

26. For a detailed discussion of liming, see Thomas Hylland Eriksen, "Liming in Trinidad: The Art of Doing Nothing," *Folk* 32 (1990): 23–43.

27. Myrie and Jamaica v. Barbados, para. 10.

28. Karyl Walker, "Stay Out!—13 Jamaicans Turned Away from Trinidad: Action Violates Caricom Treaty," *Jamaica Observer*, November 21, 2013.

Chapter Four

1. See Maurer, *Recharting the Caribbean*, 129.

2. Caribbean Court of Justice, *Court Report 2011/2013* (Port of Spain, Trinidad and Tobago: CCJ, 2013), 7.

3. Caribbean Court of Justice, *Court Report 2011/2013*, 7.

4. See Lee Cabatingan, "Fashioning the Legal Subject: Popular Justice and Courtroom Attire in the Caribbean," *Political and Legal Anthropology Review* 42, no. S1 (2018): 69–84.

5. See Caribbean Court of Justice, website, May 2021. An earlier version of the home page also featured scrolling text that similarly stated, "Our people, our region, our court."

6. Caribbean Court of Justice, *Annual Report 2005–2006*; Caribbean Court of Justice, *Annual Report 2006–2007* (Port of Spain, Trinidad and Tobago: CCJ, 2007), https://ccj.org/wp-content/uploads/2021/03/2006-2007.pdf.

7. See, e.g., Lee Cabatingan, "'Yes, [We Bow,] But Not a Deep Bow': Qualia and the Thinkability of Caribbean Jurisprudence," *Law, Culture and the Humanities* 18, no. 2 (2022): 462–81.

8. Althusser, "Ideology and Ideological State Apparatuses."

9. Althusser, "Ideology and Ideological State Apparatuses," 118.

10. Michael Warner, "Publics and Counterpublics," *Public Culture* 14, no. 1 (2002): 58.

11. Warner, "Publics and Counterpublics," 59.

12. Warner, "Publics and Counterpublics," 61.

13. Charles L. Briggs, "Why Nation-States and Journalists Can't Teach People to Be Healthy: Power and Pragmatic Miscalculation in Public Discourses on Health," *Medical Anthropology Quarterly* 17, no. 3 (2003): 287–321; Judith Butler, *Psychic Life of Power: Theories in Subjection* (Stanford, CA: Stanford University Press, 1997).

14. Warner, "Publics and Counterpublics," 61.

15. Briggs, "Why Nation-States and Journalists Can't Teach," 291.

16. Briggs, "Why Nation-States and Journalists Can't Teach," 309.

17. Michael Herzfeld, *Cultural Intimacy: Social Poetics in the Nation-State* (New York: Routledge, 1996).

18. Sue-Ann K. Lowe, "The CCJ Offers Guidance on Appeals," *Guyana Times*, November 19, 2013, http://www.guyanatimesgy.com/2013/11/19/the-ccj-offers-guidance-on-appeals/, emphasis added.

19. Caribbean Court of Justice, *CCJ Corner* brochure (Port of Spain, Trinidad and Tobago: CCJ, 2013).

20. See, e.g., *Daily Express*, (Trinidad and Tobago), "Caught Red-Handed": Da Costa Handel Marshall v the Queen [2013] CCJ 11 (AJ)," May 31, 2014, https://trinidadexpress.com/news/local/caught-red-handed/article_110d3643-b33f-53ad-8afa-e89c416794e0.html.

21. In his seminal book *Imagined Communities*, Benedict Anderson posits how the newspaper played just such a role in the development of nationalism.

22. See, e.g., Oliver Jones and Chantal Ononaiwu, "Smoothing the Way: The Privy Council and Jamaica's Accession to the Caribbean Court of Appeal," *Caribbean Law Review* 16 (2010): 183–97.

23. Trinidad and Tobago Constitution Reform Commission, *National Consultation on Constitutional Reform: Report*, Ministry of Legal Affairs, December 27, 2013, 42–44.

24. Government of the Commonwealth of Dominica, "Dominica Accedes to CCJ," Government Information Service news release, March 9, 2015, http://www.news.gov.dm/news/2292-dominica-accedes-to-ccj.

25. Mason, "Kick CARICOM to the Kerb."

26. See, e.g., Derrick Nicholas, "Not a Caribbean Man?" *Caribarena Antigua*, May 21, 2013, http://www.caribantigua.com/antigua/; Ronald Sanders, "Not a Caribbean Man?" *Caribbean 360*, May 16, 2013, http://www.caribbean360.com/; Ronald Sanders, "Not a Caribbean Man?" *Freeport News* (Bahamas), June 3, 2013, http://freeport.nassauguardian.net/; Hillbourne Watson, "Beyond Ronald Mason's Diatribe," *Stabroek News* (Guyana), May 20, 2013, http://www.stabroeknews.com/2013/features/in-the-diaspora/05/20/beyond-ronald-masons-diatribe/.

27. Briggs, "Why Nation-States and Journalists Can't Teach," 2003.

28. See, e.g., Parsuram Maharaj, letter to the editor, *Indo-Caribbean World*, December 15, 2004, http://www.indocaribbeanworld.com/archives/december15/mainews3.html; Anna Ramdass, "No Indian Judges in CCJ," *Trinidad Express*, April 10, 2008, http://caribbeancourtofjustice.blogspot.com/2008/04/race-and-ccj.html.

29. The Right Honourable Sir Dennis Byron, "Considering Diversity: The Judicial Selection Process for the Caribbean Court of Justice and Beyond," speech delivered at the International Bar Association Conference, Boston, MA, October 7, 2013.

30. Heather-Lynn Evanson, "CCJ Rules in Myrie's Favour," *Nation News* (Barbados), October 5, 2013, http://www.nationnews.com/nationnews/news/16509/ccj-rules-myrie-favour. The quotation is from someone who posted in the Comments section following the article.

31. David, "Caribbean Court of Justice Shanique Myrie Decision," *Barbados Underground* (blog), October 3, 2013, https://barbadosunderground.wordpress.com/2013/10/03/caribbean

-court-of-justice-shanique-myrie-decision/. The comment was posted in the Comments section following David's blog post by someone using the handle "Bush Tea."

32. When, in 2010, Trinidad's prime minister Kamla Persad-Bissessar likened Trinidad and Tobago to an ATM for the rest of the region, many Trinidadians cringed at her arrogance but generally agreed with the overall message: Trinidad was rich and powerful. Many of my other interlocutors often added that Barbados also had the financial and social stability to comfortably reside at the top of the Caribbean hierarchical order.

33. The Organization of Eastern Caribbean States (OECS) includes Antigua and Barbuda, Dominica, Grenada, Montserrat, Saint Lucia, Saint Kitts and Nevis, and Saint Vincent and the Grenadines. Anguilla and the British Virgin Islands are associate members. All, except for Anguilla, the British Virgin Islands, and Montserrat, which remain British dependencies, are signatories of the Agreement Establishing the CCJ and are therefore included in the Court's original jurisdiction and can join the Court's appellate jurisdiction.

34. See also Maurer, *Recharting the Caribbean*.

35. Walter B. Alexander, letter to the editor, *Stabroek News* (Guyana), May 27, 2013. http://www.stabroeknews.com/2013/opinion/letters/05/27/we-still-have-a-nation-to-build/.

36. Kim Boodram, "Complaints about Caricom Produce at Macoya Market," *Trinidad Express*, May 7, 2013, http://www.trinidadexpress.com/news/Complaints-about-Caricom-produce-at-Macoya-market-206519781.html.

37. Notably, many of these same events and occurrences go a long way toward reinforcing the seeming spatiotemporal steadiness of the state, too, as discussed in chapter 3.

38. Herzfeld, *Cultural Intimacy*.

39. To be precise, the CCJ has three "official" languages—English, French, and Dutch—and signage at the Court is written in all three languages. However, all of its hearings are conducted in English, its judgments are written in English, its staff and judges speak English, and its public library contains books written in English. At the time of my research, one of the judges was a native speaker of Dutch, but the Court, as an institution, was essentially and nearly exclusively English-speaking. I revisit this topic in chapter 5.

Chapter Five

1. Relatedly, Master Jacobs was also behind the decision to feature the variety of smiling Caribbean faces on the cover of the first two annual reports for the CCJ, discussed in chapter 4 and as shown in plates 2 and 3 in the inset illustrations at the start of chapter 7.

2. E.g., Cormack, *A Power to Do Justice*; Ford, "Law's Territory"; McVeigh, *Jurisprudence of Jurisdiction*; Maurer, "Jurisdiction in Dialect"; Kwai Hang Ng, *The Common Law in Two Voices: Language, Law, and the Postcolonial Dilemma in Hong Kong* (Palo Alto, CA: Stanford University Press, 2009); Richland, "Hopi Tradition as Jurisdiction"; Richland, "Perpetuity as (and against) Rule"; Richland, "Jurisdiction: Grounding Law in Language."

3. Bonilla, *Non-Sovereign Futures*, xiv.

4. See, e.g., Bauman and Briggs, *Voices of Modernity*; Johann Gottfried von Herder, "Treatise on the Origin of Language" in *Philosophical Writings*, ed. and trans. Michael Forster (Cambridge: Cambridge University Press, 2002), 65–164; Gellner, *Nations and Nationalism*; Susan Gal, "Politics of Translation," *Annual Review of Anthropology* 44 (2015): 225–40.

5. E.g., Rogers Brubaker, *Ethnicity without Groups* (Cambridge, MA: Harvard University Press, 2004).

6. Gal, "Politics of Translation."

7. Richland, "Perpetuity as (and against) Rule," 8; see also Richland, "Hopi Tradition as Jurisdiction"; Richland, "Jurisdiction: Grounding Law in Language"; Cormack, *A Power to Do Justice*; McVeigh, *Jurisprudence of Jurisdiction*; Maurer, "Jurisdiction in Dialect"; Ford, "Law's Territory."

8. Hobbes, *Leviathan*; Agamben, *State of Exception*; Schmitt, *Political Theology*.

9. Cormack, *A Power to Do Justice*, 9.

10. Ford, "Law's Territory," 13.

11. In chapter 6, I discuss how the CCJ's Public Education and Communication team walks a fine line between education and persuasion. Whereas education was viewed as acceptable behavior for a court, persuasion was thought to be unseemly. Presenting to a group of schoolchildren at a place of education safely fell into the educational category, though there was clearly a persuasive element to the Court's motivations.

12. In the wake of the #MeToo movement, some readers might be surprised to find that the CCJ would have selected an example in which a woman's body was approached and touched without consent and that Serena's explanation—which I discuss further in the following paragraphs—does not call out this behavior as a failure to recognize a woman's right to her own body. While I cannot be sure, I think that the CCJ would now, post-#MeToo, select a different example to highlight the same points, given the Court's sensitivity to remaining at the forefront of modern cultures of legality. At the time of this school presentation, however, the organizers of this school visit did not consider the alternate messages that their example could generate, to wit, that the CCJ *might* come across as dismissive of this woman's concern. Rather, the organizers focused on the cultural specificity of "wining"; it is a both a word that comes from the Caribbean and a form of dance that is well understood by the youth of the Caribbean. See also Daniel Miller, "Absolute Freedom in Trinidad," *Man* 26, no. 2 (1991): 323–41.

13. Anderson, *Imagined Communities*; Bauman and Briggs, *Voices of Modernity*; Susan Gal, "Contradictions of Standard Language in Europe: Implications for the Study of Practices and Publics," *Social Anthropology* 14, no. 2 (2006): 163–81.

14. Gal, "Contradictions of Standard Language"; Irvine and Gal, "Language Ideology."

15. Deborah A. Thomas, *Modern Blackness: Nationalism, Globalization, and the Politics of Culture in Jamaica* (Durham, NC: Duke University Press, 2004); Thomas, *Exceptional Violence*.

16. Gal, "Contradictions of Standard Language."

17. Miller, "Absolute Freedom in Trinidad."

18. See Anderson, *Imagined Communities*; Bauman and Briggs, *Voices of Modernity*; Gal, "Contradictions of Standard Language."

19. Gal, "Contradictions of Standard Language."

20. Thomas, *Modern Blackness*; Thomas, *Exceptional Violence*.

21. Judith Irvine and Susan Gal (in "Language Ideology") have described *fractal recursivity* as "the projection of an opposition, salient at some level of a relationship, onto some other level," and this is precisely the way in which the difference between "Your Honour" and "My Lord" has been imbued with a more profound meaning by those at the CCJ.

22. Irvine and Gal, "Language Ideology."

23. Irvine and Gal, "Language Ideology."

24. Irvine and Gal, "Language Ideology"; see also Maurer, *Recharting the Caribbean*.

25. Jane E. Goodman, Matt Tomlinson, and Justin B. Richland, "Citational Practices: Knowledge, Personhood, and Subjectivity," *Annual Review of Anthropology* 43 (2014): 449–63; Justin B.

NOTES TO PAGES 113–123

Richland, "Pragmatic Paradoxes and Ironies of Indigeneity at the 'Edge' of Hopi Sovereignty," *American Ethnologist* 34, no. 3 (2007): 540–57; see also Ng, *Common Law in Two Voices*.

26. Pollard, *Closing the Circle of Independence*.

27. Maurer, *Recharting the Caribbean*.

28. Trouillot, "North Atlantic Universals"; see also Bonilla, "Ordinary Sovereignty"; Bonilla, *Non-Sovereign Futures*; Bonilla, "Unsettling Sovereignty."

29. Caribbean Court of Justice, *Annual Report 2005–2006*, 6.

30. Caribbean Court of Justice, *Annual Report 2005–2006*, 6. See also Hobsbawm and Ranger, *Invention of Tradition*.

31. Caribbean Court of Justice, *Annual Report 2005–2006*, 6, emphasis in original.

32. Richland, "Perpetuity as (and against) Rule," 8.

33. E.g., Cormack, *A Power to Do Justice*; Ford, "Law's Territory"; McVeigh, *Jurisprudence of Jurisdiction*; Maurer, "Jurisdiction in Dialect"; Richland, "Hopi Tradition as Jurisdiction"; Richland, "Perpetuity as (and against) Rule"; Richland, "Jurisdiction: Grounding Law in Language."

34. Simpson, *Mohawk Interruptus*.

35. Susan U. Philips, "Balancing the Scales of Justice in Tonga," in *Scale: Discourse and Dimensions in Social Life*, ed. E. Summerson Carr and Michael Lempert (Berkeley: University of California Press, 2016), 112–32.

36. Philips, "Balancing the Scales."

37. Mindie Lazarus-Black, *Everyday Harm: Domestic Violence, Court Rites, and Cultures of Reconciliation* (Urbana: University of Illinois Press, 2007), 99; see also Philips, "Balancing the Scales."

38. C.f. Agamben, *Homo Sacer*; Agamben, *State of Exception*; Schmitt, *Political Theology*.

39. C.f. Hobbes, *Leviathan*.

40. Cf. Cormack, *A Power to Do Justice*; Richland, "Hopi Tradition as Jurisdiction"; Richland, "Perpetuity as (and against) Rule"; Richland, "Jurisdiction: Grounding Law in Language."

41. Cf. Philips, "Balancing the Scales."

42. Bonilla, *Non-Sovereign Futures*.

Chapter Six

1. See, e.g., Comaroff and Comaroff, *Ethnicity, Inc.*; Graan, "Nation Brand Regime"; Graan, "Counterfeiting the Nation?"; van Ham, "Place Branding."

2. Van Ham, "Place Branding," 128–29. See also Melissa Aronczyk, *Branding the Nation: The Global Business of National Identity* (Oxford: Oxford University Press, 2013).

3. See e.g. Graan "Counterfeiting the Nation?"; Graan, "Nation Brand Regime"; van Ham, "Place Branding"; Comaroff and Comaroff, *Ethnicity, Inc.*

4. Graan, "Nation Brand Regime."

5. See van Ham, "Place Branding."

6. Graan, "Nation Brand Regime." While a more detailed understanding of how branding works can quickly lead down a semiotics rabbit hole, I have attempted here to avoid such a technical discussion, as it is not necessary for the argument of this chapter. For further reading, see Paul Manning, "The Semiotics of Brand," *Annual Review of Anthropology* 39 (2010): 33–49; Asif Agha, "The Tropes of Branding in Forms of Life," *Signs and Society* 3, no. S1 (2015): S174-S194; and Nakassis, "Brand, Citationality, Performativity."

7. Graan, "Nation Brand Regime," S80.

8. Graan, "Nation Brand Regime," S80.

9. Christine Schwöbel-Patel, "The Rule of Law as a Marketing Tool: The International Criminal Court and the Branding of Global Justice," in *Handbook on the Rule of Law*, ed. Christopher May and Adam Winchester (Cheltenham, UK: Edward Elgar Publishing, 2018), 434–51; Christine Schwöbel-Patel, "The Re-Branding of the International Criminal Court (and Why African States Are Not Falling for It)," Opinio Juris, October 28, 2016, https://opiniojuris.org/2016/10/28/the-re-branding-of-the-international-criminal-court-and-why-african-states-are-not-falling-for-it/.

10. Schwöbel-Patel, "Re-Branding of the International Criminal Court."

11. Schwöbel-Patel, "Rule of Law as a Marketing Tool."

12. Judicial Committee of the Privy Council, "The Supreme Court," accessed August 3, 2022, https://www.supremecourt.uk/visiting/accessible-tour.html.

13. Rickey Singh, "This Amusing Chase After CCJ," *Trinidad Express*, September 25, 2013.

14. Singh, "This Amusing Chase."

15. For longer discussions on the relationship between food and identity in the broader Caribbean, see Stephan Palmié, "Ackee and Saltfish vs. amalá con quimbombo? A Note on Sidney Mintz's Contribution to the Historical Anthropology of African American Cultures," *Journal de le société des américanistes* 91–92 (2005): 89–122; Hanna Garth, ed., *Food and Identity in the Caribbean* (New York: Bloomsbury Press, 2013).

16. Marvin Forbes, "Letter of the Day: CCJ A Loud Sounding Nothing," *Gleaner* (Jamaica), January 26, 2015, http://jamaica-gleaner.com/gleaner/20150126/letters/letters1.html.

17. See, e.g., Fanon, *Wretched of the Earth*; Naipaul, *Mimic Men*; Bhabha, *Location of Culture*; Ferguson, "Of Mimicry."

18. Nakassis, "Brand, Citationality, Performativity."

19. Although, as I described in chapter 5, a series of educational visits to local Trinidadian secondary schools began during the latter half of my fieldwork.

20. Caribbean Court of Justice website, accessed April 6, 2018, http://www.ccj.org/.

21. As I have noted earlier, two CCJ judges during my long-term fieldwork at the Court in 2012–2013 were not from the Caribbean. Moreover, they were white. The CCJ, however, always emphasized their strong ties to the Caribbean and, especially, their internationally recognized expertise in trust law and civil law. The inclusion of these two judges on the CCJ bench was interpreted by more than one of my interviewees as an effort to appease regional concerns. As one judge at a state court explained to me:

> I mean, I don't think anybody who is honest with you will not admit that that was done in a transitionary phase to try and bring an assurance to an insecure people, I mean regionally, that, "Okay, this is not completely regional. We have an Englishman who's also white." Not a woman, mind you. Has to be a man . . . And, "Okay, we can relax. We can trust a little bit more." . . . Which of course, from my point of view, is most tragic. But maybe pragmatically wise.

22. See Caribbean Court of Justice, "CCJ Trust Fund," accessed August 4, 2022, https://www.ccj.org/about-the-ccj-ccj-trust-fund.

23. As described, the policing of attire at the Court was very much a gendered practice, with women giving and receiving the great majority of reprimands. This observation accords with those made by Freeman in Barbados and Colleen Ballerino Cohen in the British Virgin Islands (BVI), both of whom noted the carefully selected and critically judged business attire worn by working women in those Anglophone Caribbean locales. See Carla Freeman, "Designing

Women: Corporate Discipline and Barbados's Off-Shore Pink-Collar Sector," *Cultural Anthropology* 8, no. 2 (1993): 169–86; Carla Freeman, *High Tech and High Heels in the Global Economy: Women, Work, and Pink-Collar Identities in the Caribbean* (Durham, NC: Duke University Press, 2000); Colleen Ballerino Cohen, "Contestants in a Contested Domain: Staging Identities in the British Virgin Islands," in *Beauty Queens on the Global Stage: Gender, Contests, and Power*, ed. C. B. Cohen, R. Wilk, and B. Stoeltje (New York: Routledge, 1996). Women, Cohen demonstrates, mark their professional success "by wearing pantyhose, pumps, and well-matched suits or separates" (135). Moreover, since these professional positions are largely occupied by BVI "Belongers," this same attire indexes their national status. Freeman similarly shows how the growing "pink-collar" workforce in Barbados contributes to an emerging sense of what it means to be a modern Caribbean woman who belongs to a modern Caribbean state (2000).

24. Maurer, "Jurisdiction in Dialect," 131.

25. The video is no longer available on the website.

26. Lazarus-Black, "(Heterosexual) Regendering," 985.

27. *Marjorie Knox v. Deane, et al.* CCJ Civil Appeal No. BBCV2020/002.

28. *Rambarran v. The Queen* CCJ Appeal No. BBC2015/002, para. 51.

29. Though, as discussed in chapter 5, the CCJ often erased these differences in furtherance of region building.

30. CCJ, *Annual Report 2005-2006*, 6.

31. Why Caribbean houses are often painted in this color scheme is another question without a clear answer. There are several hypotheses. One idea is that the color palette provides an enticing, cheery invitation for tourists. Another points to a Governor General of Curaçao from the 1800s who once blamed the stark white buildings for causing his migraines, thus ordering all buildings to be painted a color other than white. And another notes the heat-reflective qualities of light-colored paint. See "Caribbean Currents—Rhyme and Reason behind Region's Colors," *Philadelphia Tribune*, October 11, 2019. Indeed, none of these possibilities are mutually exclusive.

32. The Right Honourable Sir Dennis Byron, "The CCJ Developing Caribbean Jurists and Jurisprudence," speech at Organisation of Eastern Caribbean States (OECS) Bar Association's Eighth Regional Law Fair, Rex Halcyon Hotel, Antigua, September 16, 2011.

33. "CCJ Developing Caribbean Jurists," 8.

34. Marcel Mauss, *The Gift: Forms and Functions of Exchange in Archaic Societies* (New York: W. W. Norton, 1990).

Chapter Seven

1. Hugh Small, "Attorney Hugh Small Urges Government to Be Decisive on Constitutional Changes This Year," interview by Dionne Jackson Miller, *Radio Jamaica News*, March 15, 2022.

2. See, e.g., "Attorney Burns Judicial Wigs, Calls for Removal of Privy Council as Final Court," *Gleaner* (Jamaica), March 12, 2022; Small, "Attorney Hugh Small Urges Government to Be Decisive"; HG Helps, "Sunday Brew," *Jamaica Observer*, March 20, 2022, https://www.jamaicaobserver.com/news/sunday-brew-march-20-2022/.

3. Small, "Attorney Hugh Small Urges Government to Be Decisive."

4. For more detail on that case, see Jones and Ononaiwu, "Smoothing the Way."

5. Jones and Ononaiwu, "Smoothing the Way."

6. Valerie Neita-Robertson, "Concerns That Affect My Confidence in the CCJ," *Jamaica Observer*, April 26, 2022.

7. See Nationwide Newsnet, "QC Valerie Neita Robertson Lobbies for UK Privy Council to Remain Jamaica's Final Appellate Court," April 5, 2022, https://nationwideradiojm.com/qc-valerie-neita-robertson-lobbies-for-uk-privy-council-to-remain-jamaicas-final-appellate-court/.

8. Neita-Robertson, "Concerns That Affect My Confidence."

9. Neita-Robertson, "Concerns That Affect My Confidence."

10. CARICOM, "Statement by the Chair of the Caribbean Community (CARICOM), The Honourable Mia Amor Mottley, Prime Minister of Barbados on the Electoral Crisis Following Guyana's General and Regional Elections 2 March 2020," June 24, 2020, https://caricom.org/statement-by-the-chair-of-the-caribbean-community-caricom-the-honourable-mia-amor-mottley-prime-minister-of-barbados-on-the-electoral-crisis-following-guyanas-general-and-regional-electi/; CARICOM, "Statement by the Chairman of the Caribbean Community (CARICOM) Dr. The Honourable Ralph Gonsalves, Prime Minister of St. Vincent and the Grenadines, on the Ruling by the Caribbean Court of Justice," July 9, 2020, https://caricom.org/statement-by-the-chairman-of-the-caribbean-community-caricom-dr-the-honourable-ralph-gonsalves-prime-minister-of-st-vincent-and-the-grenadines-on-the-ruling-by-the-caribbean-court-of-justice/.

11. See, e.g., *Guyana Times*, "CCJ President Disappointed Some Caricom Countries Still Using Privy Council," April 12, 2022.

12. John L. Comaroff and Jean Comaroff, "Policing Culture, Cultural Policing: Law and Social Order in Postcolonial South Africa," *Law & Social Inquiry* 29, no. 3 (Summer 2004): 539.

13. E.g., Bonilla, *Non-Sovereign Futures*; Bonilla, "Unsettling Sovereignty."

14. Comaroff, "Reflection on the Colonial State," 342. See also Abrams, "Notes on the Difficulty of Studying the State."

15. See, e.g., Anderson, *Imagined Communities*; Hobsbawm, *Nations and Nationalism since 1780*; Gellner, *Nations and Nationalism*.

16. On "state-idea," see Abrams, "Notes on the Difficulty of Studying the State." On "imagined communities," see Anderson, *Imagined Communities*.

References

Books, Journals, and Magazines

Abrams, Philip. "Notes on the Difficulty of Studying the State." *Journal of Historical Sociology* 1 (1988): 58–89.

Agha, Asif. "The Tropes of Branding in Forms of Life." *Signs and Society* 3, no. S1 (2015): S174–194. https://doi.org/10.1086/679004.

Agamben, Giorgio. *Homo Sacer: Sovereign Power and Bare Life.* Stanford, CA: Stanford University Press, 1988.

———. *State of Exception.* Chicago: University of Chicago Press, 2005.

Alexander, Kelly. "Europe in the Balance." *Fieldsights,* October 22, 2019. https://culanth.org/fieldsights/series/europe-in-the-balance.

Althusser, Louis. "Ideology and Ideological State Apparatuses: Notes Towards an Investigation." In *Lenin and Philosophy and Other Essays,* 85–126. Translated by Ben Brewster. 1971. Reprint, New York: Monthly Review Press, 2001.

Anderson, Benedict. *Imagined Communities: Reflections on the Origin and Spread of Nationalism.* 1983. Reprint, New York: Verso, 2006.

Antoine, Patrick. "An Assessment of the Original Jurisdiction." In *The Caribbean Court of Justice, the First 10 Years.* London: Lexis/Nexis, 2016.

Appadurai, Arjun. "Sovereignty without Territoriality." In *The Anthropology of Space and Place: Locating Culture,* edited by S. E. Low and D. Lawrence-Zúñiga, 337–49. 1996. Reprint, Malden, MA: Blackwell.

Arendt, Hannah. "What Is Authority?" In *Between Past and Future,* 91–141. New York: Penguin Books, 1986.

Aretxaga, Begoña. "Maddening States." *Annual Review of Anthropology* 32 (2003): 393–410.

Aronczyk, Melissa. *Branding the Nation: The Global Business of National Identity.* Oxford: Oxford University Press, 2013.

Bauman, Richard, and Charles L. Briggs. *Voices of Modernity: Language Ideologies and the Politics of Modernity.* Cambridge: Cambridge University Press, 2003.

Benjamin, Walter. "Critique of Violence." In *Reflections: Essays, Aphorisms, Autobiographical Writings,* 277–300. Translated by Edmund Jephcott. New York: Harcourt Brace Jovanovich, 1978.

Benton, Lauren. *Law and Colonial Cultures: Legal Regimes in World History, 1400–1900*. Cambridge: Cambridge University Press, 2002.

Ben-Yehoyada, Naor H. *The Mediterranean Incarnate: Transnational Region Formation between Sicily and Tunisia since World War II*. Chicago: University of Chicago Press, 2017.

Bhabha, Homi. *The Location of Culture*. Abingdon, UK: Routledge Classics, 1994.

Bonilla, Yarimar. *Non-Sovereign Futures: French Caribbean Politics in the Wake of Disenchantment*. Chicago: University of Chicago Press, 2015.

———. "Ordinary Sovereignty." *Small Axe: A Caribbean Journal of Criticism* 42 (2013): 152–65.

———. "Unsettling Sovereignty." *Cultural Anthropology* 32, no. 3 (2017): 330–39.

Brereton, Bridget. *An Introduction to the History of Trinidad and Tobago*. Oxford: Heinemann Educational Publishers, 1996.

Briggs, Charles L. "Why Nation-States and Journalists Can't Teach People to Be Healthy: Power and Pragmatic Miscalculation in Public Discourses on Health." *Medical Anthropology Quarterly* 17, no. 3 (2003): 287–321.

Brubaker, Rogers. *Ethnicity without Groups*. Cambridge, MA: Harvard University Press, 2004.

Butler, Judith. *Psychic Life of Power: Theories in Subjection*. Stanford, CA: Stanford University Press, 1997.

Cabatingan, Lee. "Fashioning the Legal Subject: Popular Justice and Courtroom Attire in the Caribbean." *Political and Legal Anthropology Review* 42, no. S1 (2018): 69–84.

———. "Time and Transcendence: Narrating Higher Authority at the Caribbean Court of Justice." *Law and Society Review* 50, no. 3 (2016): 674–702.

———. "'Yes, [We Bow,] But Not a Deep Bow': Qualia and the Thinkability of Caribbean Jurisprudence." *Law, Culture and the Humanities* 18, no. 2 (2022): 462–81.

Cattelino, Jessica. *High Stakes: Florida Seminole Gaming and Sovereignty*. Durham, NC: Duke University Press, 2008.

Chanock, Martin. *Law, Custom, and Social Order: The Colonial Experience in Malawi and Zambia*. New York: Cambridge University Press, 1985.

Clarke, Kamari Maxine. "Assemblages of Experts: The Caribbean Court of Justice and the Modernity of Caribbean Postcoloniality." *Small Axe* 17, no. 2 (July 2013): 88–107.

Clifford, James. *Returns: Becoming Indigenous in the Twenty-First Century*. Cambridge, MA: Harvard University Press, 2013.

Cohen, Colleen Ballerino. "Contestants in a Contested Domain: Staging Identities in the British Virgin Islands." In *Beauty Queens on the Global Stage: Gender, Contests, and Power*, edited by C. B. Cohen, R. Wilk, and B. Stoeltje. New York: Routledge, 1996.

Comaroff, John L. "Colonialism, Culture, and the Law: A Foreword." *Law and Social Inquiry* 26, no. 2 (2001): 305–14.

———. "Reflection on the Colonial State in South Africa and Elsewhere: Factions, Fragments, Facts and Fictions." *Social Identities* 4, no. 3 (1998): 321–61.

———. "Reflections on the Rise of Legal Theology: Law and Religion in the Twenty-First Century." *Social Analysis* 53, no. 1 (2009):193–216.

Comaroff, John L., and Jean Comaroff. *Ethnicity, Inc*. Chicago: University of Chicago Press, 2009.

———. "Policing Culture, Cultural Policing: Law and Social Order in Postcolonial South Africa." *Law & Social Inquiry* 29, no. 3 (Summer 2004): 513–45.

Cormack, Bradin. *A Power to Do Justice: Jurisdiction, English Literature, and the Rise of Common Law, 1509–1625*. Chicago: University of Chicago Press, 2007.

REFERENCES

Dalsgaard, Steffen. "The Time of the State and the Temporality of the *Gavman* in Manus Province, Papua." *Social Analysis* 57, no. 1 (2013): 34–49.

Derrida, Jacques. "Declarations of Independence." *New Political Science* 15 (1986): 7–15.

———. 2002. "The Force of Law: The Mystical Foundation of Authority. In *Acts of Religion*, edited by Gil Anidjar, translated by Mary Quaintance, 230–98. New York: Routledge, 2002.

Eley, Geoff, and Ronald Grigor Suny. "Introduction: From the Moment of Social History to the Work of Cultural Representation." In *Becoming National: A Reader*, edited by Eley and Suny, 3–37. New York: Oxford University Press, 1996.

Eriksen, Thomas Hylland. "Liming in Trinidad: The Art of Doing Nothing." *Folk* 32 (1990): 23–43.

Fanon, Frantz. *The Wretched of the Earth*. New York: Grove Press, 2004.

Ferguson, James. "Declarations of Dependence: Labour, Personhood, and Welfare in Southern Africa." *Journal of the Royal Anthropological Institute* 19 (2013): 223–42.

———. "Of Mimicry and Membership: Africans and the 'New World Society.'" *Cultural Anthropology* 17, no. 4 (2002): 553–54.

Ferguson, James, and Akhil Gupta. "Spatializing States: Toward an Ethnography of Neoliberal Governmentality." *American Ethnologist* 29, no. 4 (2002): 981–1002.

Ford, Robert T. "Law's Territory (A History of Jurisdiction)." *Michigan Law Review* 97, no. 4 (1999): 843–930.

Freeman, Carla. "Designing Women: Corporate Discipline and Barbados's Off-Shore Pink-Collar Sector." *Cultural Anthropology* 8, no. 2 (1993): 169–86.

———. *High Tech and High Heels in the Global Economy: Women, Work, and Pink-Collar Identities in the Caribbean*. Durham, NC: Duke University Press, 2000.

Gal, Susan. "Contradictions of Standard Language in Europe: Implications for the Study of Practices and Publics." *Social Anthropology* 14, no. 2 (2006): 163–81.

———. "Politics of Translation." *Annual Review of Anthropology* 44 (2015): 225–40.

Garth, Hanna. ed. *Food and Identity in the Caribbean*. New York: Bloomsbury Press, 2013.

Gellner, E. *Nations and Nationalism*. Ithaca, NY: Cornell University Press, 1983.

Getachew, Adom. *Worldmaking after Empire: The Rise and Fall of Self-Determination*. Princeton, NJ: Princeton University Press, 2019.

Goodman, Jane E., Matt Tomlinson, and Justin B. Richland. "Citational Practices: Knowledge, Personhood, and Subjectivity." *Annual Review of Anthropology* 43 (2014): 449–63.

Goodrich, Peter. "Specters of Law: Why the History of the Legal Spectacle Has Not Been Written." *UC Irvine Law Review* 1, no. 3 (2011): 773–812.

Graan, Andrew. "Counterfeiting the Nation? Skopje 2014 and the Politics of Nation Branding in Macedonia." *Cultural Anthropology* 28, no. 1 (2013): 161–79.

———. "The Nation Brand Regime: Nation Branding and the Semiotic Regimentation of Public Communication in Contemporary Macedonia." *Signs and Society* 4, no. S1 (2016): S70–S105. https://doi.org/10.1086/684613.

Greenhouse, Carol J. "Just in Time: Temporality and the Cultural Legitimation of Law." *Yale Law Journal* 98, no. 8 (1989): 1631–51.

Hansen, Thomas Blom, and Finn Stepputat. "Sovereignty Revisited." *Annual Review of Anthropology* 35 (2006): 295–315.

Herder, Johann Gottfried von. "Treatise on the Origin of Language." In *Philosophical Writings*, edited and translated by Michael Forster, 65–164. Cambridge: Cambridge University Press, 2002.

Herzfeld, Michael. *Cultural Intimacy: Social Poetics in the Nation-State*. New York: Routledge, 1996.

Hobbes, Thomas. *Leviathan*. Baltimore: Penguin Books, 1968.

Hobsbawm, E. J. *Nations and Nationalism since 1780: Programme, Myth, Reality*. New York: Cambridge University Press, 1990.

Hobsbawm, E. J., and T. O. Ranger. *The Invention of Tradition*. Cambridge: Cambridge University Press, 1983.

Holt, Thomas. *The Problem of Freedom: Race, Labor, and Politics in Jamaica and Britain, 1832–1938*. Baltimore: Johns Hopkins University Press, 1992.

Irvine, Judith, and Susan Gal. "Language Ideology and Linguistic Differentiation." In *Regimes of Language*, edited by P. Kroskrity, 35–84. Santa Fe, NM: School of American Research Press, 2000.

Jones, Oliver, and Chantal Ononaiwu. "Smoothing the Way: The Privy Council and Jamaica's Accession to the Caribbean Court of Appeal." *Caribbean Law Review* 16 (2010): 183–97.

Kahn, Paul W. *The Reign of Law: Marbury v Madison and the Construction of America*. New Haven, CT: Yale University Press, 1997.

Latour, Bruno. *The Making of Law: An Ethnography of the Conseil d'État*. Translated by Marina Brilman and Alain Pottage. Cambridge: Polity Press, 2010.

Lazarus-Black, Mindie. *Everyday Harm: Domestic Violence, Court Rites, and Cultures of Reconciliation*. Urbana: University of Illinois Press, 2007.

———. "The (Heterosexual) Regendering of a Modern State: Criminalizing and Implementing Domestic Violence Law in Trinidad." *Law & Social Inquiry* 28, no. 4 (2003): 979–1008.

Lewis, Linden. "The Dissolution of the Myth of Sovereignty in the Caribbean." In *Caribbean Sovereignty, Development and Democracy in an Age of Globalization*, edited by Linden Lewis, 68–87. New York: Routledge, 2013.

———. "Introduction: Sovereignty, Heterodoxy, and the Last Desperate Shibboleth of Caribbean Nationalism." In *Caribbean Sovereignty, Development and Democracy in an Age of Globalization*, edited by Linden Lewis, 1–16. New York: Routledge, 2013.

Lilla, Michael Anthony. *Promoting the Caribbean Court of Justice as the Final Court of Appeal for States of the Caribbean Community*. Williamsburg, VA: National Center for State Courts, 2008.

Malkki, Liisa. *Purity and Exile: Violence, Memory, and National Cosmology among Hutu Refugees in Tanzania*. Chicago: University of Chicago Press, 1995.

Manning, Paul. "The Semiotics of Brand." *Annual Review of Anthropology* 39 (2010): 33–49.

Maurer, Bill. "Jurisdiction in Dialect: Sovereignty Games in the British Virgin Islands." In *European Integration and Postcolonial Sovereignty Games: The EU Overseas Countries and Territories*, edited by R. Adler-Nissen and U. P. Gad, 130–44. New York: Routledge, 2013.

———. *Recharting the Caribbean: Land, Law, and Citizenship in the British Virgin Islands*. Ann Arbor: University of Michigan Press, 1997.

Mauss, Marcel. *The Gift: Forms and Functions of Exchange in Archaic Societies*. New York: W. W. Norton, 1990.

Merry, Sally. *Colonizing Hawai'i: The Cultural Power of Law*. Princeton, NJ: Princeton University Press, 2000.

McVeigh, Shaun, ed. *Jurisprudence of Jurisdiction*. New York: Routledge Cavendish Press, 2007.

Miller, Daniel. "Absolute Freedom in Trinidad." *Man* 26, no. 2 (1991): 323–41.

Mintz, Sidney W. "The Caribbean as a Socio-Cultural Area." In *Peoples and Cultures of the Caribbean: An Anthropological Reader*, edited by M. M. Horowitz, 17–46. Garden City, NY: American Museum of Natural History Press, 1971.

REFERENCES

———. "The Caribbean Region." *Daedalus* 103, no. 2 (1974): 45–71.
Moore, Sally Falk. *Law as Process: An Anthropological Approach*. London: Routledge and Kegan Paul, 1978.
———. *Social Facts and Fabrications: "Customary" Law on Kilimanjaro, 1880–1980*. London: Cambridge University Press, 1986.
Mueller, Justin. "Temporality, Sovereignty, and Imperialism: When Is Imperialism?" *Politics* 36, no. 4 (2016): 428–40.
Naipaul, V. S. *The Mimic Men*. New York: Vintage International, 2001.
Nakassis, Constantine V. "Brand, Citationality, Performativity." *American Anthropologist* 114, no. 4 (2012): 624–38.
Ng, Kwai Hang. *The Common Law in Two Voices: Language, Law, and the Postcolonial Dilemma in Hong Kong*. Palo Alto, CA: Stanford University Press, 2009.
Palmié, Stephan. "*Ackee and Saltfish* vs. *amalá con quimbombo*? A Note on Sidney Mintz's Contribution to the Historical Anthropology of African American Cultures." *Journal de le société des américanistes* 91–92 (2005): 89–122.
Palmié, Stephan, and Francisco A. Scarano, eds. *The Caribbean: A History of the Region and its Peoples*. Chicago: University of Chicago Press, 2011.
Peebles, Gustav. *The Euro and Its Rivals: Currency and the Construction of a Transnational City*. Bloomington: Indiana University Press, 2011.
Philips, Susan U. "Balancing the Scales of Justice in Tonga." In *Scale: Discourse and Dimensions in Social Life*, edited by E. Summerson Carr and Michael Lempert, 112–32. Berkeley: University of California Press, 2016.
Pollard, Duke E. 2004. *The Caribbean Court of Justice: Closing the Circle of Independence*. Kingston, Jamaica: Caribbean Law Publishing, 2004.
Rawlins, Hugh. *The Caribbean Court of Justice: The History and Analysis of the Debate*. Georgetown, Guyana: CARICOM Secretariat, 2000.
Renan, Ernest. *What Is a Nation?* 1882. Reprint, Toronto: Tapir Press, 1996.
Richland, Justin B. *Cooperation without Submission: Indigenous Jurisdictions in Native Nation–US Engagements*. Chicago: University of Chicago Press, 2021.
———. "Hopi Tradition as Jurisdiction: On the Potentializing Limits of Hopi Sovereignty." *Law & Social Inquiry* 36, no. 1 (2011): 201–34.
———. "Jurisdiction: Grounding Law in Language." *Annual Review of Anthropology* 42 (2013): 209–26.
———. "Pragmatic Paradoxes and Ironies of Indigeneity at the 'Edge' of Hopi Sovereignty." *American Ethnologist* 34, no. 3 (2007): 540–57.
Rose, Jacqueline. *States of Fantasy*. Oxford: Clarendon Press, 1996.
Schmitt, Carl. *Political Theology*. Chicago: University of Chicago Press, 2006.
Schwöbel-Patel, Christine. "The Rule of Law as a Marketing Tool: The International Criminal Court and the Branding of Global Justice." In *Handbook on the Rule of Law*, edited by Christopher May and Adam Winchester, 434–51. Cheltenham, UK: Edward Elgar Publishing, 2018.
Scott, David. *Conscripts of Modernity: The Tragedy of Colonial Enlightenment*. Durham, NC: Duke University Press, 2004.
Shore, Cris. *Building Europe: The Cultural Politics of European Integration*. London: Routledge, 2000.
Simpson, Audra. *Mohawk Interruptus: Political Life Across the Borders of Settler States*. Durham, NC: Duke University Press, 2014.

Stein, Gertrude. *Everybody's Autobiography*. 1937. Reprint, New York: Cooper Square Publishers.
Stoler, Ann Laura. *Duress: Imperial Durabilities in Our Times*. Durham, NC: Duke University Press, 2016.
———, ed. *Imperial Debris: On Ruins and Ruination*. Durham, NC: Duke University Press, 2013.
Thomas, Deborah A. *Exceptional Violence: Embodied Citizenship in Transnational Jamaica*. Durham, NC: Duke University Press, 2011.
———. *Modern Blackness: Nationalism, Globalization, and the Politics of Culture in Jamaica*. Durham, NC: Duke University Press, 2004.
———. *Political Life in the Wake of the Plantation: Sovereignty, Witnessing, Repair*. Durham, NC: Duke University Press, 2019.
———. "Time and the Otherwise: Plantations, Garrisons, and Being Human in the Caribbean." *Anthropological Theory* 16, no. 2–3 (2016): 177–200.
Thompson-Barrow, Cheryl. *Bringing Justice Home: The Road to Final Appellate and Regional Court*. London: Commonwealth Secretariat, 2008.
Tilly, Charles. "The Time of States." *Social Research* 61, no. 2 (1994): 269–95.
Trouillot, Michel Rolph. "The Caribbean Region: An Open Frontier in Anthropological Theory." *Annual Review of Anthropology* 21 (1992): 19–42.
———. "North Atlantic Universals: Analytical Fictions, 1492–1945." *South Atlantic Quarterly* 101, no. 4 (2002): 839–58.
———. *Silencing the Past: Power and the Production of History*. Boston: Beacon Press, 1995.
Valverde, Mariana. *Chronotopes of Law: Jurisdiction, Scale, and Governance*. New York: Routledge, 2015.
———. "'Time Thickens, Takes on Flesh': Spatiotemporal Dynamics in Law." In *The Expanding Spaces of Law: A Timely Legal Geography*. Palo Alto, CA: Stanford University Press, 2014.
van Ham, Peter. "Place Branding: The State of the Art." *Annals of the American Academy of Political and Social Science* 616, no. 1 (March 2008): 126–49.
Venzke, Ingo. "Understanding the Authority of International Courts and Tribunals: On Delegation and Discursive Construction." *Theoretical Inquiries in Law* 14 (November 2013): 381–409.
Warner, Michael. "Publics and Counterpublics." *Public Culture* 14, no. 1 (2002): 49–90.
Weber, Max. *The Protestant Ethic and the Spirit of Capitalism*. New York: Charles Scribner's Sons, 1958.

Newspapers and Blogs

Alexander, Walter B. Letter to the editor. *Stabroek News* (Guyana), May 27, 2013. http://www.stabroeknews.com/2013/opinion/letters/05/27/we-still-have-a-nation-to-build/.
"Attorney Burns Judicial Wigs, Calls for Removal of Privy Council as Final Court," *Gleaner* (Jamaica), March 12, 2022.
Bahamas, Jones. "Privy Council Has Fourth Sitting in The Bahamas." *Bahama Journal*, February 21, 2017. http://jonesbahamas.com/privy-council-has-fourth-sitting-in-the-bahamas/.
Boodram, Kim. "Complaints about Caricom Produce at Macoya Market." *Trinidad Express*, May 7, 2013. http://www.trinidadexpress.com/news/Complaints-about-Caricom-produce-at-Macoya-market-206519781.html.

REFERENCES

"Caribbean Currents—Rhyme and Reason behind Region's Colors." *Philadelphia Tribune*, October 11, 2019.

Daily Express (Trinidad and Tobago). "Caught Red-Handed: Da Costa Handel Marshall v the Queen [2013] CCJ 11 (AJ)." May 30, 2014. https://trinidadexpress.com/news/local/caught-red-handed/article_110d3643-b33f-53ad-8afa-e89c416794e0.html.

———. "Mark: No CCJ Support; Call Us Colonialists if You Want." May 26, 2022. https://trinidadexpress.com/newsextra/mark-no-ccj-support-call-us-colonialists-if-you-want/article_fd285742-dcfc-11ec-ba92-c33d47fedbe3.html.

David. "Caribbean Court of Justice Shanique Myrie Decision." *Barbados Underground* (blog), October 3, 2013. https://barbadosunderground.wordpress.com/2013/10/03/caribbean-court-of-justice-shanique-myrie-decision/.

Evanson, Heather-Lynn. "CCJ Rules in Myrie's Favour." *Nation News* (Barbados), October 5, 2013. http://www.nationnews.com/nationnews/news/16509/ccj-rules-myrie-favour.

Forbes, Marvin. "Letter of the Day: CCJ A Loud Sounding Nothing." *Gleaner* (Jamaica), January 26, 2015. http://jamaica-gleaner.com/gleaner/20150126/letters/letters1.html.

Guyana Times. "CCJ President Disappointed Some Caricom Countries Still Using Privy Council." April 12, 2022. https://guyanatimesgy.com/ccj-president-disappointed-some-caricom-countries-still-using-privy-council/.

Helps, HG. "Sunday Brew." *Jamaica Observer*, March 20, 2022. https://www.jamaicaobserver.com/news/sunday-brew-march-20-2022/.

Lowe, Sue-Ann K. "The CCJ Offers Guidance on Appeals." *Guyana Times*, November 19, 2013. http://www.guyanatimesgy.com/2013/11/19/the-ccj-offers-guidance-on-appeals/.

Maharaj, Parsuram. Letter to the editor. *Indo-Caribbean World*, December 15, 2004. http://www.indocaribbeanworld.com/archives/december15/mainews3.html.

Mason, Ronald. "Kick CARICOM to the Kerb." *Gleaner* (Jamaica), May 5, 2013. http://jamaica-gleaner.com/gleaner/20130505/cleisure/cleisure5.html.

Neita-Robertson, Valerie. "Concerns That Affect My Confidence in the CCJ." *Jamaica Observer*, April 26, 2022.

Nicholas, Derrick. "Not a Caribbean Man?" *Caribarena Antigua*, May 21, 2013. http://www.caribantigua.com/antigua/.

Ramdass, Anna. "No Indian Judges in CCJ." *Trinidad Express*, April 10, 2008. http://caribbeancourtofjustice.blogspot.com/2008/04/race-and-ccj.html.

Sanders, Ronald. "Caribbean Court of Justice Delivers for the Caribbean People." *Sir Ronald Sanders* (blog), October 10, 2013. http://www.sirronaldsanders.com/viewarticle.aspx?ID=400.

———. "Not a Caribbean Man?" *Caribbean 360*, May 16, 2013. http://www.caribbean360.com/.

———. "Not a Caribbean Man?" *Freeport News* (Bahamas), June 3, 2013. http://freeport.nassauguardian.net/.

Seage, Edward. "CCJ Can Still be Manipulated" *Gleaner* (Jamaica), December 14, 2014. http://jamaica-gleaner.com/gleaner/20141214/focus/focus2.html.

Singh, Rickey. "This Amusing Chase After CCJ." *Trinidad Express*, September 25, 2013.

Trinidad Express. "AG: Govts Not in Selection of CCJ Judges." May 5, 2012.

Walker, Karyl. "Stay Out!—13 Jamaicans Turned Away from Trinidad: Action Violates Caricom Treaty." *Jamaica Observer*, November 21, 2013.

Watson, Hillbourne. "Beyond Ronald Mason's Diatribe." *Stabroek News* (Guyana), May 20, 2013. http://www.stabroeknews.com/2013/features/in-the-diaspora/05/20/beyond-ronald-masons-diatribe/.

Legal Cases

Marjorie Knox v. Deane et al. CCJ Civil Appeal No. BBCV2020/002.
Rambarran v. The Queen. CCJ Appeal No. BBC2015/002.
Shanique Myrie and the State of Jamaica v. the State of Barbados [2013] CCJ 3 (OJ).

Treaties and Agreements

Agreement Establishing the Caribbean Court of Justice. Georgetown, Guyana: Caribbean Community (CARICOM) Secretariat, 2001.
Revised Agreement Establishing the Caribbean Court of Justice Trust Fund. Georgetown, Guyana: Caribbean Community (CARICOM) Secretariat, 2004.
Revised Treaty of Chaguaramas Establishing the Caribbean Community Including the CARICOM Single Market and Economy. Georgetown, Guyana: Caribbean Community (CARICOM) Secretariat, 2001.

Other Documents and Websites

Caribbean Court of Justice (CCJ). *Annual Report 2005–2006*. Port of Spain, Trinidad and Tobago: CCJ, 2006. https://ccj.org/wp-content/uploads/2021/03/2005-2006.pdf.
———. *Annual Report 2006–2007*. Port of Spain, Trinidad and Tobago: CCJ. Published March 14, 2007. https://ccj.org/wp-content/uploads/2021/03/2006-2007.pdf.
———. *CCJ Corner*. Port of Spain, Trinidad and Tobago: CCJ, 2013. Brochure.
———. "CCJ Trust Fund." Accessed August 4, 2022. https://ccj.org/about-the-ccj/ccj-trust-fund/.
———. *Court Report 2011/2013*. Port of Spain, Trinidad and Tobago: CCJ, 2013. https://ccj.org/wp-content/uploads/2021/03/2011-2013.pdf.
———. Website. https://ccj.org.
CARICOM. "Our Work." Accessed July 25, 2022. https://caricom.org/our-work/.
———. Website. https://caricom.org.
———. *What It Is, What It Does*. Rev. ed. Georgetown, Guyana: CARICOM Secretariat, 2003.
———. *Your Questions Answered*. Rev. ed. Georgetown, Guyana: CARICOM Secretariat, 2003.
Constitution Commission of Trinidad and Tobago. *Report of the Constitution Commission*. Port of Spain, Trinidad and Tobago, 1974.
Dominions Office, West Indies Department, United Kingdom. *Trinidad & Tobago Independence Constitution: Statement by the Secretary of State for the Colonies*, June 5, 1962.
Foreign and Commonwealth Office, United Kingdom. *Trinidad & Tobago: Annual Review for 1974*, Diplomatic Report No. 56/75.
Government of the Commonwealth of Dominica. "Dominica Accedes to CCJ." Government Information Service news release, March 9, 2015. http://www.news.gov.dm/news/2292-dominica-accedes-to-ccj.
Judicial Committee of the Privy Council. "FAQs: When Was the JCPC Established?" Accessed July 26, 2022. https://www.jcpc.uk/faqs.html#1b.
———. "The Supreme Court." Accessed August 3, 2022. https://www.supremecourt.uk/visiting/accessible-tour.html.

REFERENCES

Nationwide Newsnet. "QC Valerie Neita Robertson Lobbies for UK Privy Council to Remain Jamaica's Final Appellate Court." April 5, 2022. https://nationwideradiojm.com/qc-valerie-neita-robertson-lobbies-for-uk-privy-council-to-remain-jamaicas-final-appellate-court/.

Ramphal, Shridath, and the West Indian Commission. *Report of the West Indian Commission: Time for Action*. 2nd ed. Kingston, Jamaica: The Press—University of the West Indies, 1993.

Schwöbel-Patel, Christine. "The Re-branding of the International Criminal Court (and Why African States Are Not Falling for It)." Opinio Juris. October 28, 2016. https://opiniojuris.org/2016/10/28/the-re-branding-of-the-international-criminal-court-and-why-african-states-are-not-falling-for-it/.

7 News Belize. "What CARICOM Citizenship Means." October 4, 2013. http://www.7newsbelize.com/sstory.php?nid=26712.

Trinidad and Tobago Constitution Reform Commission. *National Consultation on Constitutional Reform: Report*. Port of Spain, Trinidad and Tobago: Ministry of Legal Affairs, December 27, 2013.

United Nations Office on Drugs and Crime (UNODC). "dataUNODC." Accessed May 25, 2020. https://dataunodc.un.org.

Speeches and Interviews

Byron, The Right Honourable Sir Dennis. "The CCJ Developing Caribbean Jurists and Jurisprudence." Speech at Organisation of Eastern Caribbean States (OECS) Bar Association's Eighth Regional Law Fair, Rex Halcyon Hotel, Antigua, September 16, 2011.

———. "Considering Diversity: The Judicial Selection Process for the Caribbean Court of Justice and Beyond." Speech delivered at the International Bar Association Conference, Boston, MA, October 7, 2013.

Girvan, Norman. "Reinventing the CSME." Speech Delivered at the Third Biennial Caribbean Association of Judicial Officers Conference, Accra Breach Hotel, Bridgetown, Barbados, September 27, 2013.

Richland, Justin B. "Perpetuity as (and against) Rule: Law, Tradition, Juris-diction." Paper presented at the American Bar Foundation, Chicago, October 17, 2012.

Small, Hugh. "Attorney Hugh Small Urges Government to Be Decisive on Constitutional Changes This Year." Interview by Dionne Jackson Miller. *Radio Jamaica News*, March 15, 2022.

Trump, President Donald. Speech to United Nations General Assembly, New York, September 19, 2017. https://www.politico.com/story/2017/09/19/trump-un-speech-2017-full-text-transcript-242879.

Index

Page numbers in italics refer to figures.

acolonial, 6, 57, 111. *See also* Caribbeanness
Africa, 1, 38, 124; colonial administrative territories of, 21; "customary laws" in, 29
Afro-Caribbean people, 52, 93
Agamben, Giorgio, 105
Agreement Establishing the Caribbean Court of Justice (2001), 2–4, 43, 52, 53, 100–101, 110
agriculture, 98
Alexander, Walter B., 98
Allen, Epheium, 99–101
Althusser, Louis, 31, 85
Anderson, Benedict, 37
Anderson, the Honourable Mr. Justice Winston, 4, *76*, *149*
Anguilla, 39
Annual Reports, 83–84, 114, *150*, *151*
Antigua and Barbuda, 2, 39, 64, 100, 139, 147
appellate jurisdiction, 1–2, 13–17, 33, 43–49, *44*, 54–57, 91–93, 105, 110, 125, 135, 148, 160, 170n23. *See also* jurisdiction
Association of Southeast Asian Nations (ASEAN), 26

Bahamas, 2, 38, 46, 97, 100, 127, 144
Ballerino Cohen, Colleen, 178n23
Barbados, 2, 31, 39, 43, 52, 60–63, 66–72, 75–86, 92–96, 99–100, 127, 132, 137, 159–61, 175n32; attorneys of, 116–17; courts of, 135; flag of, *79*; Ministry of Justice of, 75, 79; newspapers of, 87; public transportation in, 89; Supreme Court of, 71, 74, *76*, 82. *See also* Bridgetown
Barrow, the Honourable Mr. Justice Denys, 4
Belize, 2, 43, 65, 92, 97, 115–17, 142, 147, 159

Benton, Lauren, 28, 168n69
Ben-Yehoyada, Naor, 26
Bermuda, 97
Bernard, the Honourable Mme. Justice Désirée, 4, *76*, *149*
Bhabha, Homi, 164n7
Bonilla, Yarimar, 15, 20, 22, 25, 103–4, 164n5
branding, 12, 20, 119–43, 177n6; of the Caribbean Court of Justice, 33; of consumer products, 123; of courts, 123–25; in nation-state making, 32–33, 122–25
Brexit, 11
Bridgetown, 77, 82. *See also* Barbados
Britain. *See* United Kingdom
British Colonial Office, 39. *See also* United Kingdom
British Virgin Islands, 39, 97, 171n41, 178n23
British West Indies, 39; governors of the, 54. *See also* West Indies Federation
Burgess, the Honourable Mr. Justice Andrew, 4
Byron, the Right Honourable Sir Justice Dennis, 4–5, *76*, *149*

Canada, 130
Caribbean Association of Judicial Officers (CAJO), 133–34, 142
Caribbean Community and Common Market (CARICOM), 2, 11, 15–16, 26–27, 31, 40–44, 55, 61–62, 66, 92–93, 96–97, 100–101, 110, 139; citizenship in the nation-states of, 62–64, 81; creation of, 91; flag of, 79; general counsel of, 68; regional economic integration of, 82, 97; rights enjoyed by a citizen of a member state of, 59–64, 80–82; three primary languages of,

Caribbean Community and Common Market (CARICOM) (*cont.*) 109; transparency of elections in, 147. *See also* Caribbean region; CARICOM Single Market and Community (CSME)

Caribbean Court of Justice (CCJ): Academy for Law of the, 133; acceptance of the jurisdiction of the, 15–16; as a Caribbean court, 135–40; citation of the nation-state by the, 13; communications of the, 84–90, 92, 103; criticisms of the, 17, 45, 93; development of Caribbean jurisprudence by the, 112–13, 117, 122, 141, 159; as an economic tribunal, 55; flag of the, 74–79; full bench of the, *76*; gift shop of the, 119–21, *120*, *121*; history of the, 11, 30, 43–55, *53*, 102–3, 138; image policing of the, 131–32; Information, Communications, and Technology unit of the, 47; interior of the, *152*; judges of the, 4, 157, 178n21; legitimacy in the eyes of the region's public of the, 33, 45–46, 122, 129, 147; membership of the individual nation-states in the, 10, 110; mirrored facade of the, 17, *18*; as modern, 24, 30, 58, 133–35; myth of creation of the, 30, 50–55, 58, 103, 171n31; Office of the Registry of the, 9, 51, *51*, 67–68, 72–74, 90, 132; "One People. One Region. One Court" in promotional material of the, 108, *108*, *150*; as a people's court, 82–101, 108; president of the, 157–58; Protocol and Information unit of the, 46–47, 50; Public Education and Communication Unit of the, 9, 50, 106, 176n11; public education campaign of the, 105–10; regional authority of the, 77–80; region building of the, 12–19, 23–26, 29–33, 43–49, 55, 66–67, 80–85, 90, 96–99, 102–3, 113–18, 122, 148; seal of the, *151*; seat in Trinidad of the, 1–3, 94, 103; sovereignty of member states acknowledged by the, 13–14; three official languages of the, 109–10, 118, 175n39; Training and Conference Room of the, 67–68, *69*, *70*; Trust Fund of the, 6, 130; videoconference hearings of the, 68, 70–72; Vision statement of the, 167n53. *See also* Annual Reports; Caribbeanness; Caribbean region; communications; interpellation; jurisdiction; language; modernity; non-sovereignty; technology

Caribbean Development Bank (CDB), 6, 96
Caribbean Disaster Emergency Management Agency, 96
Caribbean Examination Council (CXC), 96
Caribbean Festival of Arts (CARIFESTA), 16
Caribbean food, 136–37
Caribbean Free Trade Agreement (CARIFTA), [40]–41
[Pan] HIV&AIDS Alliance, 96
[Caribbean] law schools, 52, 55, 88, 90, 139

Caribbean nation-states: Anglophone, 92; borders of the, 81; and Caribbean region, 12–14, 66–67; citizens of the, 81; independence of the, 10–11, 15, 39, 42, 45, 90–91; "overexpression" of the, 14–17, 23. *See also* Caribbean region; nation-state; state sovereignty

Caribbeanness, 29, 33, 36, 48–55, 125–27, 137, 140–43; mythological, 57; time-transcendent notion of, 55–57. *See also* acolonial; Caribbean region

Caribbean Premier League of Cricket, 96

Caribbean region, 3, 10–11, 50, 59, 66–67, 80–81, 159, 179n31; Anglophone, 90–92, 95–97, 111, 114; biodiversity of the, 119, 140; and Caribbean territory, 65–66; creation of a regional public in the, 82–101, 108; as "crucible of European modernity," 14; democratic traditions in the, 97; economic integration of the, 41–45, 49, 55, 57, 82; folk understandings of the, 96; forms of transportation in the, 90; "hierarchy of nations" in the, 95; law and society in the, 114–17, 122; myth of origin of the, 30, 35–38, 57–58, 125; as non-sovereign, 22–30, 32, 67, 103–5, 117; region-making projects of the, 17, 25–33, 39–50, 55–57, 66–67, 82, 84–85, 91–98, 114, 122, 149; society in the, 34, 125–26; "traditional" values of the, 29; as unfinished project, 33, 49–50, 149; video technology as constitutive of the shared jurisdictional space of the, 72. *See also* Caribbean Community and Common Market (CARICOM); Caribbean Court of Justice (CCJ); Caribbean nation-states; Caribbeanness; regionalism

Caribbean Sea, 3, 65, 79, 90

CARICOM Single Market and Community (CSME), 26, 40–41, 43–44, 48–49, 55. *See also* Caribbean Community and Common Market (CARICOM)

China, 38

colonialism, 11, 21–22, 36, 38–39, 111, 160; inequities of, 162; legacies of, 12, 23, 39, 41–42, 49, 55, 113, 162; projects of, 21, 28, 39, 57; racialized hierarchies of, 39; as a region-making process, 27, 39. *See also* colonization; imperialism

colonization, 21, 38, 57; of Hawaii, 28; violence of, 21. *See also* colonialism

Columbus, Christopher, 38

Committee of the Organisation of Commonwealth Caribbean Bar Associations (OCCBA), 169n19

common-law legal systems, 112; citational practices of, 113. *See also* law

Common Market for Eastern and Southern Africa (COMESA), 26

communications: of the Caribbean Court of Justice, 84–90, 92, 103, 105–10, 128; interpellative, 86; technology of, 70. *See also* media

INDEX

court executive administrator (CEA), 73, 102–3
Cuba, 39, 97
Curaçao, 5, 179n31

de la Bastide, the Right Honourable Mr. Justice Michael, 5
Dominica, 2, 39, 43, 91–92, 147
Dominican Republic, 97

Economic Community of West African States (ECOWAS), 26
Eley, Geoff, 37
Elizabeth II (queen), 5
England, 38; Supreme Court of, 50. *See also* United Kingdom
environment, 18
equal rights, 18
ethnographic, 4, 11, 19, 28, 159; ethnographic reality, 14; ethnographic vision, 158. *See also* ethnography
ethnography, 19, 28–29. *See also* ethnographic
Europe, 38
European Union (EU), 11, 26–27

Facebook, 143
Fanon, Frantz, 164n7
Ferguson, James, 1, 164n7
Forbes, Marvin, 127
France, 123; Caribbean colonies of, 38–39
Freeman, Carla, 132, 178n23
free trade, 41

Gal, Susan, 104, 176n21
gender, 18
geopolitics, 12, 38; hierarchy of, 104
Getachew, Adom, 36, 39–40
Girvan, Norman, 41
globalization, 11, 21, 26, 48
Global North, 115, 124, 161
Global South, 15, 22, 124
Golding, Bruce, 146
governance: alternate forms of, 22; ideal form of modern, 19; models for Caribbean law and, 111; non-sovereign form of, 14–15, 25; sovereign state as the quintessential form of modern, 14, 20–25. *See also* modernity; sovereignty
Graan, Andrew, 123
Grenada, 2, 39, 96, 147
Guadeloupe, 25
Guyana, 2, 43, 65, 68, 70, 81, 92–95, 97, 130; Indo-Caribbean citizens of, 93–94, 147

Haiti, 2, 97, 100–101, 109
Hawaii, 28, 166n37
Hayton, the Honourable Mr. Justice David, 4, 76, 149

Heads of Government Conference (1970), 54
Hobbes, Thomas, 105
Holness, Andrew, 146
human rights, 63, 172n6; violations of, 80
Hutu, 37

ideology: language and, 104; neoliberal, 123; regional, 31; state, 31, 85. *See also* interpellation
imperialism, 21, 38–39. *See also* colonialism
indentured labor, 38–39
India, 38
Indigenous peoples, 28, 38
inequality, 22–23; structures of, 39
International Bar Association Conference (Boston), 94
international capital markets, 6
International Criminal Court (ICC), 124
International Criminal Tribunal for Rwanda (ICTR), 161
international law, 21, 54, 78. *See also* law
international women's movements, 28
interpellation, 31–32; of individuals, 85; interpellative dissonance, 86–87; misfires of, 85–87; of publics, 85–87, 92–93, 99, 101; regional, 32, 84–101. *See also* ideology
Irvine, Judith, 176n21

Jamadar, the Honourable Mr. Justice Peter, 4
Jamaica, 2, 22, 31, 39–41, 46, 54, 59–63, 66–83, 91, 94–96, 99, 127, 130, 145–46, 159–61; court system of, 73–74, 112; flag of, 79, 90; Ministry of Justice of, 75–76, 79; national motto of, 107; newspapers of, 87, 92; Parliament of, 145; Passport, Immigration and Citizenship Agency of, 99; public transportation in, 89, 92; trade and economy of, 93. *See also* Kingston
Jamaica Conference Centre, 73, 75
Jamaica Gleaner, 51, 92, 127
Jamaican Justice Reform Report (2007), 145
Jamaica Observer, 87–88, 146
Judicial Committee of the Privy Council (JCPC), 1–7, 28, 36, 42–46, 50–51, 56, 106–7, 110–14, 117–18, 124–27, 132, 144–46, 160–62, 169n19, 171n33. *See also* United Kingdom
Judicial Reform and Institutional Strengthening (JURIST) Project, 133–34
jurisdiction, 114–15, 135; regional, 159, 169n19. *See also* appellate jurisdiction; juris-diction; law; original jurisdiction
juris-diction, 28, 32, 114, 118. *See also* jurisdiction
justice: access to, 17, 43; brand of global, 124; British, 1, 42, 118, 146; Caribbean, 135, 143, 146; law and, 45; meaning of, 34; miscarriages of, 146. *See also* law

Kingston, 73, 77. *See also* Jamaica

language, 32, 97, 102–18; constitutive power of, 104–5; diversity of Caribbean, 137; legal, 104–5; national creoles and accents of Caribbean, 107–10; shared regional, 107–8; verbal missteps by attorneys at the Caribbean Court of Justice, 115–17

law, 27–30; British, 104, 127; Caribbean, 43, 59, 63, 118, 122, 126–27; commercial, 5; customary, 29, 168n71; as the "cutting edge of colonialism," 166n38; development of modern state, 28; domestic, 63; high standard in the practice of, 135; human rights, 172n6; and justice, 45; legal linguistic scholarship, 103; and modernity, 28–29, 135; of the nation-state, 20; precedent in the, 13; as process, 29; regional, 76–78, 81, 88, 91; rule of, 17–18; and sovereignty, 32; state, 78; state sovereignty and, 27–30. *See also* common-law legal systems; international law; jurisdiction; justice

law and order, 22; British, 168n69
Lazarus-Black, Mindie, 28, 133
Leeward Islands, 39. *See also* British West Indies
Lewis, Linden, 19
Lincoln, Abraham, 58

Macedonia, 123
Malkki, Liisa, 37
Manley, Michael, 146
Manley, Norman, 40
Martinique, 97
Mason, Ronald, 92–93, 95–96, 98–99, 101
Mead, Margaret, 138
media, 61–62; American television shows, 111; "CCJ Corner" in regional newspapers, 87–90, 105, 128; local, 79, 145, 147, 161; major newspapers of the Anglophone Caribbean, 92; regional, 79, 87–90, 147. *See also* communications; social media
Mercado Común del Sur (MERCOSUR), 26
Merry, Sally Engle, 28
#MeToo movement, 176n12
modernity, 17–21, 23–24, 33, 133–35, 140–41; coldness of, 58; construct of colonial, 21; law and, 28–29; liberal, 18; political and economic, 23; and state sovereignty, 20–25, 28–29; vision of Caribbean, 40, 135. *See also* governance; sovereignty
Montserrat, 2, 39
Moore, Sally Falk, 29
Myrie, Shanique, 59–64, 77–78, 80, 82, 94, 100
myth, 34–58; national, 37–38; of the United States, 35, 38. *See also* nation-state

˙ul, V. S., 164n7
˙ Constantine, 13, 127
˙ (Barbados), 87

National Food-crop Farmers Association (Trinidad), 98
nationalism, 11, 37, 123; Caribbean, 36; myths of, 58
Nationnews.com, 95
nation-state: alternatives to the, 39; defining the territory of the, 20; ethnicities and cultures of a, 20; ideological apparatus of the, 20; imperial shaping of the sovereign, 20; law of the, 20; making of the, 12–14, 19, 84–85, 105, 107, 118, 122–23; myths of origin of the, 19; shared "national" language of the, 19–20; sovereign, 59, 118, 165n25; as unfinished project, 149. *See also* Caribbean nation-states; myth; state sovereignty
Neita-Robertson, Valerie, 146–48
Nelson, the Honourable Mr. Justice Rolston, 4, 76, 149
Netherlands, 5, 23; Caribbean colonies of the, 38–39
newspapers. *See* media
New World, 38
Nigeria, 161
non-sovereignty, 15, 20–25, 103–4; regional, 23–25, 30, 32, 103, 117. *See also* sovereignty
North Atlantic universals/universalism, 13, 15, 22, 80, 113

Obama, President Barack, 111
Organization of Eastern Caribbean States (OECS), 95, 172n13, 175n33; Bar Association of the, 141
original jurisdiction, 1–2, 43–44, *44*, 49, 53–54, 56, 82, 101, 110. *See also* jurisdiction

personhood, 112
Philips, Susan, 115
plantation economy, 39
Port of Spain, 3, 8–9, 16, 17, 43, 55, 60, 65, 74, 106, 158–59. *See also* Trinidad and Tobago
postcolonialism, 36, 164n7
precedent, 112–13
Privy Council. *See* Judicial Committee of the Privy Council (JCPC)
public education, 105–11, 128–29, 160, 176n11
Puerto Rico, 39

Radio Jamaica, 145–46
Rajnauth-Lee, the Honourable Mme. Justice Maureen, 4
regionalism, 57–58, 64, 160. *See also* Caribbean region
regionalization, 11–12; in the Anglophone Caribbean, 26; denigration of Caribbean, 14; history of, 55–56; troubles of, 55. *See also* Caribbean region
Regional Judicial and Legal Services Commission (RJLSC), 3–4, 6

INDEX

regional law schools. *See* Caribbean law schools
Renan, Ernest, 37
Revised Agreement Establishing the Caribbean Court of Justice Trust Fund, 6
Revised Treaty of Chaguaramas Establishing the Caribbean Community (RTC), 2, 6, 40–43, 48, 52, 63. *See also* Treaty of Chaguaramas
Richland, Justin, 104, 114

Saint Christopher and Nevis. *See* Saint Kitts and Nevis
Saint Kitts and Nevis, 2, 39, 91
Saint Lucia, 2, 39, 92, 96, 148
Saint Vincent and the Grenadines, 2, 39, 96, 147
Sanders, Ronald, 64
Saunders, the Honourable Mr. Justice Adrian, 4, 76, *149*
Schmitt, Carl, 105
Schwöbel-Patel, Christine, 124
self-determination, 23
sexual identity, 18
Shanique Myrie and the State of Jamaica vs. the State of Barbados, 31, 59–63, 66–68, 71, 73, 79–82, 94, 99, 102, 107, 160, 171n2, 172n6, 173n25
Shore, Cris, 26–27
slavery, 23, 38–39; of Africans, 27
slave trade, 38
Small, Hugh, 144–48
Small, Senior Puisne Judge Ronald, 144
Soca, 107
social media, 144–45, 147. *See also* media
sovereignty: "anticolonial worldmakers" on, 39; British model of law and, 113–14; impossibility of, 22; law and, 32; model of, 23, 30, 32; North Atlantic conceptions of, 23; ordinary desires for, 25; problem of, 22; refusing, 113–17; regional, 32, 117; regionhood and, 148; search for, 22–23; theoretical conceptualization of, 105. *See also* governance; modernity; non-sovereignty; state sovereignty
Spain, 38–39; Caribbean colonies of, 38–39
Spanish-American War, 39
Stabroek News, 98
state sovereignty, 1, 10–14, 19–30, 164n4; idea of, 13, 28; and law, 27–30, 122; making of, 12–14, 19–21, 66–67, 113; model of, 22, 25, 27, 105; modernity and, 20–25, 28–29, 165n24; non-sovereign region and, 23–25, 66–67, 105; "problem" of, 11–12, 14–23; rigidities and proclivities of, 81; signs and symbols of, 17; techniques of, 21, 113; territorially bounded, 67, 165n24. *See also* Caribbean nation-states; modernity; nation-state; sovereignty
Stein, Gertrude, 66
sugar, 38
Suny, Ronald Grigor, 37

Suriname, 2, 16, 65, 97, 100–101, 109

technology, 31, 53, 59, 67–68, 70–75, 133, 173n22; role and risk of, 34
territoriality: regional, 31, 59; state, 31, 59
territory, 59–81
Thomas, Deborah A., 22, 39
Tonga, 115
tourism, 123, 179n31
travel, 31, 59; interregional, 86
Treaty of Chaguaramas, 40, 42–43, 48, 52, *53*. *See also* Revised Treaty of Chaguaramas Establishing the Caribbean Community (RTC)
Treaty of Westphalia (1648), 19
triangle trade, 38
Trinidad and Tobago, 1–3, 8–9, 14–17, 24, 38–45, 52–56, 60, 64–67, 72, 76–81, 91–100, 107, 127–31, 137, 148, 158–62, 175n32; accusations of corruption in, 45, 65, 170n27; Carnival in, 15; Constitution Reform Commission of, 91, 169n19; Court of Appeal of, 34; crime in, 9; cuisine of, 15; Domestic Violence Act of, 28, 133; flag of, 15, 79, 90, 99, 137; history of, 160; Independence Day celebrations of, 8–9, 16, 98–99; Indo-Caribbean citizens of, 93–94; national courts of, 102, 106; newspapers of, 87; public transportation in, 89, 92; pursuit of "modern" laws of, 28; Standards Commission of, 41; Supreme Court of, 47. *See also* Port of Spain; Wooding Commission Report
Trinidad Express, 87, 125–26
Trouillot, Michel-Rolph, 13, 15
Trump, President Donald, 11, 164n4
Tutsi, 37
Twitter, 143

United Kingdom, 5–6, 11, 23, 42, 46, 49–50, 145; attorneys of the, 115–17; Caribbean colonies of the, 38–39; judicial system of the Caribbean territories of the, 42; region-making projects of the, 26, 39; Supreme Court of the, 124. *See also* British Colonial Office; England; Judicial Committee of the Privy Council (JCPC)
United Nations, 73
United States, 23, 94, 130; Caribbean involvement of the, 39; Supreme Court of the, 111, 162; War of Independence of the, 57–58
University of Guyana, 98
University of the West Indies (UWI), 52, 83, 86, 96–98, 159–60
US Virgin Islands, 97

Venezuela, 3
violence: of colonization, 21; and political cronyism in Jamaica, 22

Walcott, Keshorn, 15, 99
Warner, Michael, 85
Washington, George, 38, 57
West Indian Commission, 43; *Time for Action* (report), 43
West Indies cricket team (Windies), 96–97
West Indies Federation, 26, 39–45, 55, 91, 160. *See also* British West Indies
Williams, Eric, 39–40

Windward Islands, 39. *See also* British West Indies
Wit, the Honourable Mr. Jacob, 4, *76*, *149*
Wooding Commission Report, 169n19. *See also* Trinidad and Tobago

YouTube, 143

Zoom, 68